Best Places
to Stay
in the Midwest

THE BEST PLACES TO STAY SERIES

Best Places to Stay in America's Cities
Second Edition/Kenneth Hale-Wehmann, Editor

Best Places to Stay in Asia
Jerome E. Klein

Best Places to Stay in California
Third Edition/Marilyn McFarlane

Best Places to Stay in the Caribbean
Third Edition/Bill Jamison and Cheryl Alters Jamison

Best Places to Stay in Florida
Third Edition/Christine Davidson

Best Places to Stay in Hawaii
Third Edition/Bill Jamison and Cheryl Alters Jamison

Best Places to Stay in the Mid-Atlantic States
Second Edition/Dana Nadel Foley

Best Places to Stay in the Midwest
Second Edition/John Monaghan

Best Places to Stay in New England
Fifth Edition/Christina Tree and Kimberly Grant

Best Places to Stay in the Pacific Northwest
Third Edition/Marilyn McFarlane

Best Places to Stay in the Rockies
Second Edition/Roger Cox

Best Places to Stay in the South
Second Edition/Carol Timblin

Best Places to Stay in the Southwest
Third Edition/Anne E. Wright

Best Places to Stay in the Midwest

SECOND EDITION

John Monaghan

Bruce Shaw, Editorial Director

HOUGHTON MIFFLIN COMPANY
BOSTON • NEW YORK

For information about permission to reproduce selections from
this book, write to Permissions, Houghton Mifflin Company,
215 Park Avenue South, New York, New York 10003.

Second Edition

ISSN: 1060-7749
ISBN: 0-395-66618-X

Printed in the United States of America

Illustrations prepared by Eric Walker
Maps by Charles Bahne
Design by Robert Overholtzer

This book was prepared in conjunction
with Harvard Common Press.

VB 10 9 8 7 6 5 4 3 2 1

Contents

Introduction

I'll know it when I see it. That's the simple answer I gave in the first edition of this guidebook when asked how I choose a best place to stay. The criteria remain the same for this second edition of over 200 unique lodgings in eight Midwestern states.

Of course, there's a risk to recommending places to strangers. Most of these lodgings are as unique as the people who run them. Hopefully the written descriptions will give you a good idea whether or not you want to visit. Still, I'd suggest this: get hold of brochures, talk to friends who have stayed there, and ask lots of questions on the phone before leaving a credit card number or mailing off a deposit check.

You'll find several changes from the first edition. If a lodging is for sale or recently under new management, it may have been deleted. Since much of the appeal of these places revolves around service and the human touch, a new innkeeper or management team can mean an entirely different stay. One of my favorite Midwestern destinations, Hermann, Missouri, is experiencing several changes in inn ownership.

I have attempted to present lodgings in various price ranges, but be aware that some overnights can be expensive. Bed-and-breakfast inns, once an inexpensive alternative to the Ramada down the street, have since gotten pricier, thanks in large part to the traveler's insistence on private bathrooms. Many innkeepers have installed Jacuzzi baths, again at guests' requests. Another dramatic (and welcome) change I noticed during this update is the number of inns that have enacted no-smoking policies. Likewise, more and more non-smoking rooms and floors are surfacing in big-city hotels.

None of the lodgings listed in this book paid to be included. I have visited almost all of them myself. A handful of others were seen by scouts, fellow writers, or travel industry professionals. This second edition lists inns by states, often breaking up the larger ones into northern and southern regions. There are specific "Best" recommendations in the following categories: Bed-and-Breakfast Inns; Full-Service Country Inns;

Hotels; Lodges, Spas, and Resorts; and Budget Stays. Full-Service Country Inns usually have a restaurant on the premises, Bed-and-Breakfast Inns do not.

There are bound to be great places I missed in the estimated 16,000 miles of auto travel that went into this book. Up to the day before I finished this manuscript, innkeepers were sending materials about their places. I'm still interested in those unique ma-and-pa motels that I know exist in the Midwest but have not yet been able to locate. If you have a favorite place to stay, please use the recommendation form in the back of this book. You'll be doing me (and the lodging) a great favor.

There are a number of people without whom this book would never have been realized: Cindy LaFerle, my former editor at *Innsider* magazine and a loyal friend; the various regional and state tourism bureaus, especially Michigan's; Jan Kerr and others at the Michigan Lake-to-Lake Bed and Breakfast Association, where I proudly serve as an inn reviewer; Bruce Shaw and Dan Rosenberg of Harvard Common Press, who have guided this and other Best Places books from the planning stages to reality; and my parents, who gave me an early appreciation for Midwest travel.

And, of course, I want to thank all the folks who run those inns, hotels, motels, resorts, even yurts. They make vacation dreams come true. I hope you enjoy your visits with them as much as I did.

John Monaghan

September 1994

Illinois

Best Bed-and-Breakfast Inns

Galena
Captain Gear Guest House
Park Avenue Guest House
Spring Street Guest House
Gurnee
Sweet Basil Hill Farm
Wheaton
The Wheaton Inn

Best Full-Service Country Inn

Galena
The Inn at Irish Hollow

Best Hotels

Chicago
The Drake
Four Seasons Hotel
Hotel Inter-Continental
Hotel Nikko Chicago
The Ritz-Carlton Chicago
Galena
DeSoto House Hotel

Best Lodges and Resorts

Galena
Eagle Ridge Inn and Resort
Grafton
Pere Marquette Lodge and Conference Center
Utica
Starved Rock Lodge and Conference Center

Best Budget Stays

Chicago
Ohio House Hotel
Nauvoo
Hotel Nauvoo

Chicago lies at the heart of Illinois tourism. Populated by friendly residents and boasting a transit system that makes most parts of the city easily accessible, Chicago guarantees an unforgettable stay. The famous Magnificent Mile follows Michigan Avenue and includes shopping at Water Tower Place and Bloomingdale's. Visit the "Here's Chicago" exhibition in the old Water Tower Pumping Station. It recounts the city's history, including the great Chicago fire, through a battalion of slide projectors and 70mm film.

Countless Chicago restaurants claim bragging rights for the best Chicago-style deep dish pizza, but Pizzeria Uno is where it all began. If the lines are too long at the Ohio Street location, walk two blocks to Pizzeria Due, its sister establishment. Come to think of it, the lines will probably be long there too. Ed Debevic's, a popular tourist spot, finds a gum-snapping wait staff serving good stick-to-your-ribs food in an atmosphere of '50s kitsch.

You'd need a month to tour all the museums here, but some remain must-sees. The Art Institute of Chicago houses an incredible collection of French impressionist paintings. The Field Museum of Natural History thrills children of all ages with its Egyptian mummy and dinosaur displays. The Museum of Science and Industry, a substantial bus ride from town, includes a replica of a coal mine, a submarine, and a 16-foot human heart among its permanent exhibitions.

Chicago is brimming with jazz and blues clubs, especially on the North Side. Comedy clubs also thrive here. The Second City troupe, which launched John Belushi, among others, still performs in simple digs in trendy Lincoln Park. The Chicago Symphony Orchestra, which recently celebrated its centennial, performs at Orchestra Hall. Theatergoers can purchase half-price tickets at Hot Tix booths downtown.

Galena, another great Illinois destination, lies in the northwestern corner of the state, about a 3-hour drive from the Windy City. Galena's early success came from lead mining, but the city fell on hard times because of bad planning and a channel full of silt. Its current popularity supports the largest concentration of B&B inns in the Midwest. Riverboat gambling on the Illinois side of the Mississippi River, about 10 minutes away, will only increase the area's popularity.

For history, check out the Galena/Joe Daviess County Museum. The Galena Wax Museum has 32 figures of historic characters and contemporary celebrities, including Ulysses S. Grant and Abraham Lincoln. President Grant lived here for a time, and his home, a stately Italianate structure, is open for tours. W. Paul LeGreco, a local actor and historian, dons Civil War clothing and offers tours in the personage of Grant.

When you're through visiting the countless antiques shops in Galena, take the half-hour drive south on Highways 20 and 84 to Savanna. This small town has little to offer in the way of tourist attractions. It does, however, house a pair of large antiques malls with better values than you'll find in Galena.

CHICAGO

The Drake

Lake Shore Drive and Michigan
 Avenue
Chicago, IL 60611
312-787-2200
800-55-DRAKE
Fax: 312-787-1431
Reservations: 800-HILTONS

> *Visiting celebrities still choose this historic hotel*

General manager: Martin Lawrence. **Accommodations:** 535 rooms and suites. **Rates:** $195–$255 single, $205–$265 double. **Included:** Newspaper. **Minimum stay:** No. **Added:** 14.9% tax. **Payment:** Major credit cards. **Children:** Yes. **Pets:** No. **Smoking:** Nonsmoking rooms available. **Open:** Year-round.

Sunday morning. Police officers and hotel employees rope off a path from the elevators to the lobby entrance. The curious gather to watch Mary Robinson, the president of Ireland, casually sweep through and enter the motorcade that will whisk her to the airport. In a moment, the ropes are down and the lobby is back to business as usual.

This scene is not uncommon at the bustling Drake Hotel. After all, it is the favorite spot of Britain's royal family and other celebrities when they visit the Windy City.

> **You can't get much closer to Chicago's center than this Gold Coast hotel overlooking Lake Michigan.**

The Drake opened on New Year's Eve, 1920, and except for a few shaky years during the Depression and its occupation by the military during World War II, it has remained open ever since.

Set off spacious wainscoted hallways, the guest rooms are attractively decorated with floral print draperies and overstuffed couches. All the rooms have telephones, clock radios, remote-control televisions, mini-bars, magnifying mirrors, and bathrobes. Nightly turndown service with bedside chocolates is a nice touch. The keys to the 30 executive-floor rooms allow access to the Panorama Lounge.

The hotel is famous for the Cape Cod Room, whose mounted stuffed sailfish, red-checked tablecloths, and copper pots suspended from beamed ceilings evoke the New England coast. Diners often start with the Bookbinder Red Snapper soup, followed by lobster, scallops, and shrimp entrées. When the restaurant considered replacing its oyster bar a few years back, loyal diners threw a fit. In the course of 60 years, visitors such as Marilyn Monroe, Jack Benny, and Joe DiMaggio carved their names into the rough wood countertop. Needless to say, the bar is still there.

The Oak Terrace dining room is another restaurant possibility, with popular prime rib carved tableside, while the Palm Court continues the tradition of midafternoon high tea with scones, pastries, and a harpist.

The guest shops include florists, a drugstore, men's and women's apparel stores, a barber shop, confectionary, airline ticket office, jewelry store, and art gallery. You are within steps of the Magnificent Mile and Water Tower Plaza and just minutes away from River North jazz and Rush Street blues.

Four Seasons Hotel

120 East Delaware Place
   at 900 North Michigan
Chicago, IL 60611
312-280-8800
Fax: 312-280-1748
Telex: 00-214923
Reservations: 800-332-3442

*This luxury hotel
towers over
the competition*

General manager: Hans Williman. **Accommodations:** 313 rooms, 31 suites. **Rates:** Rooms $230–$275 single, $260–$305 double; suites $325–$725 single, $355–$725 double; packages available. **Included:** All meals available. **Minimum stay:** No. **Added:** 14.9% tax. **Payment:** Major credit cards. **Children:** Yes. **Pets:** By arrangement. **Smoking:** Nonsmoking rooms available. **Open:** Year-round.

Late Sunday morning at the Four Seasons. What has been called the best brunch in Chicago attracts everyone from overwhelmed out-of-towners to three rich Chicago widows, who try to talk a fourth into picking up the $14,000 necklace she has been eyeing in a Michigan Avenue shop window.

Both groups agree that brunch in the 124-seat Seasons Restaurant lives up to its reputation. Men in tall chefs' hats prepare waffles and omelettes while you wait. Another cuts slices of rare roast beef. Buffet tables present a complete variety of oysters, clams, smoked salmon, whitefish, ham, chicken, and lamb, along with pasta, vegetable, and seafood salads. A glass of fresh orange juice doesn't stay empty for long before the wait staff has it filled again. For dessert, there are peaches topped with Grand Marnier or a creamy chocolate mousse. A pianist offers soothing renditions of George Gershwin and Cole Porter.

Brunch is usually the cap to an unforgettable weekend at the Four Seasons, which rivals its sister hotel across the street, the Ritz-Carlton, as the city's most luxurious. Part of a 66-story, mixed-use skyscraper that also houses Bloomingdale's department store, the hotel blends English antiques and reproductions, fine woods and marbles, and an extensive art collection.

Guests enter from Delaware Place, where a small elevator whisks them to the large 7th-floor lobby. Crystal chandeliers and Georgian furnishings set the tone here, with opulent touches that include 18th-century marble fireplace mantels, a 15-foot marble fountain, and tapestry fabrics. The Seasons Restaurant is here, along with an adjacent bar and café.

The guest rooms, on floors 30–46, offer spectacular views of Chicago's lakefront and skyline. The large rooms combine a bedroom and sitting room; the one- and two-bedroom suites and a Presidential Suite ($2,500 per night) mix antiques, chintzes, and porcelains. Every room has three two-line telephones, maid service twice a day, remote-control televisions and radios, fully stocked mini-bars, and 24-hour room service. Ask for a room ending with 01 if you want more space. And you may prefer a city to a lake view, since you can't see much of the water after dark.

> While many hotels try to tap into current design fads, the Four Seasons succeeds in creating a luxury hotel whose classic accents and attention to service make it truly timeless.

The room rate at the Four Seasons includes access to the Spa, a fitness center complete with Roman columns as well as saunas, whirlpool, massage and steam rooms, exercise equipment, and a pool beneath a skylight.

Hotel Inter-Continental

505 North Michigan Ave.
Chicago, IL 60611
312-944-4100
800-628-2468
Fax: 312-944-3050
Telex: 62654670
Reservations:
Inter-Continental Hotels
800-332-4246

> *Historic detail has returned to a former athletic club*

General manager: Rex Rice. **Accommodations:** 338 rooms, with 19 suites. **Rates:** Rooms $169–$239 single, $189–$269 double; suites $250–$500 single or double; packages available. **Minimum stay:** No. **Added:** 14.9% tax. **Payment:** Major credit cards. **Children:** Yes. **Pets:** No. **Smoking:** Nonsmoking rooms available. **Open:** Year-round.

This 41-story tower, with its Indiana limestone facade crowned by a Moorish-styled dome, was built as the Medinah Athletic Club just six months before the stock market crash in 1929. Bankrupt by 1934, it spent the following years as a Sheraton and Raddison before the Inter-Continental Hotels Corporation added it to their growing list of restored hotels. Lido Lippi, a world-renowned fine art conservator and a key figure in the restoration of the Sistine Chapel, assisted in the project.

> **The Boulevard Restaurant overlooks the lobby rotunda at the head of a graceful stairway. Two sides of the horseshoe-shaped restaurant offer views up and down Michigan Avenue.**

Now returned are the painted ceilings, winding balustrade staircases, arched entryways, marble inlays, detailed bronze and brass highlighting, and murals and friezes. The restorers relied on old blueprints and photographs along with the cherished memories of former guests. The imposing Hall of Lions is an extension of the main lobby, with two Assyrian lions carved in marble guarding each side of a staircase.

The lion motif carries into the guest rooms, which are decorated in the classic Biedermeier style of the 19th century, with simple lines and designs in light-colored fruitwoods. Dark-colored inlays of ebony and maple along with Axminster carpets and bold patterned wallpapers create striking contrasts. Griffins remain a key ornamental motif for guest-room furniture, while some chairs have Egyptian female figures carved into the arms. From some windows you can see the stone-cut details of mythological creatures on the exterior walls of the hotel. The spacious rooms are equipped with mini-bars, dual-line telephones, and bathrooms with separate tubs and showers.

While the Hotel Inter-Continental shows off its stunning restoration in virtually every corner, its mosaic-tiled junior Olympic-size swimming pool remains the showstopper. Shimmering beneath a two-and-a-half-story atrium, it was used often by Olympic gold medalist Johnny Weismuller. This is all that's left of the old Athletic Club facilities, which once boasted a running track, gymnasium, bowling alley, and boxing ring. There are now state-of-the-art exercise machines, massage facilities, and an aerobics room available for guests.

The Inter-Continental has executive floors, providing such extras as a Butler's Service and access to an Executive Lounge on the 32nd floor. Here you'll find coffee, tea, and pastries served throughout the day. Limousine service shuttles guests to and from the airport.

The hotel contains some 20,000 square feet of meeting and banquet space, including a 600-seat grand ballroom whose ornate marble balcony and decor recaptures the hotel's Egyptian-inspired elegance.

The hotel is conveniently located near Water Tower shopping and the Magnificent Mile. The $130 million renovation and restoration project also includes an adjoining tower, built in 1961. It houses the Forum Hotel Chicago, which caters to a large business clientele.

Hotel Nikko Chicago

320 North Dearborn
Chicago, IL 60610
312-744-1900
800-NIKKO-US
Fax: 312-527-26664

> *Oriental flair in decor and service*

General manager: Peter Dangerfield. **Accommodations:** 403 rooms, 18 suites. **Rates:** Rooms $205–$315 single, $225–$315 double; suites $300–$2,500; packages available. **Included:** All meals available. **Minimum stay:** No. **Added:** 14.9% tax. **Payment:** Major credit cards. **Children:** Yes. **Pets:** By prior arrangement. **Smoking:** Nonsmoking rooms available. **Open:** Year-round.

From a distance, the Nikko looks like any other high-rise glass tower in Chicago. Up close, it's another picture entirely. Elegant landscaping with boulders and flowers decorate the area around the circular driveway. The lobby's polished granite walls and floors are accented by Japanese ash and African mahogany furnishings. Bamboo rods crisscross the ceilings, while a paneled Oriental screen decorates a wall. Opened in 1987, the Nikko exemplifies Japanese efficiency and attention to detail, both in room decor and guest services.

The standard guest rooms also feature the plain lines and flat black surfaces found downstairs. The spacious rooms feature large bay windows, marble baths, custom-made cabinetry, three telephones, and televisions enclosed in armoires. The bathrooms are modern, with terry robes. Even the toiletries are elegant, with the black and white packaging a work of art in itself. In the morning, tea, coffee, and the newspaper are provided.

> **There are plenty of pluses for the business traveler. An executive fitness area offers sauna and massage facilities, while the hotel's business center offers computers, fax machines, dictating equipment, and secretarial services.**

Guests entering the Japanese suites are kindly asked to slip out of their shoes and into slippers supplied by the hotel. Traditional mats serve as seating around a low dining room table. At bedtime, the table is set aside and a futon is removed from the closet and spread on the floor. Deep soaking tubs with separate showers and Japanese rock gardens are part of the bathroom decor.

There are six conference rooms on the lower floors of the Nikko as well as Benkay, a 150-seat restaurant that offers traditional Japanese cuisine, including sushi, sashimi, tempura, and teriyaki. The restaurant features a main dining area, a sushi bar, and private tatami rooms, where diners enjoy a traditional Japanese experience on low tables in addition to lovely views of the Chicago River. If you're not in the mood for sushi, the Celebrity Cafe offers contemporary American cuisine.

Ohio House Motel

600 North La Salle Street
Chicago, IL 60610
312-943-6000

> *A wise budget alternative in the Windy City*

Manager: Tina Angorone. **Accommodations:** 50 rooms. **Rates:** $53 single, $60 double. **Minimum stay:** No. **Added:** 12% tax. **Payment:** Major credit cards. **Children:** Yes. **Pets:** Yes. **Smoking:** No. **Open:** Year-round.

How the Ohio House Motel found its way to Chicago is something of a mystery. Could it be that some tornado long ago lifted this low-slung aqua-colored motor hotel from a Kansas interstate and dropped it between skyscrapers and high-rise hotels in downtown Chicago?

However it got here, the Ohio House has become known as a clean, comfortable (but far from fancy) choice for visitors to Chicago. The exterior is highlighted by audacious shades of blue and red, with stardust patterns on diamond-shaped detailing. Free parking, wake-up calls, and a 24-hour switchboard are just a few of the niceties found here.

> **The Ohio House's central location puts you within five blocks of Michigan Avenue and the famed Magnificent Mile.**
> **For more '50s fun, try the wacky decor and short-order meals served by the gum-snapping staff at Ed Debevic's, just around the corner. The Chicago version of Planet Hollywood is also across the street.**

Your response to the guest rooms will depend on your capacity for kitsch. Some of the furnishings, especially the light fixtures and the combination radio/bedside table, haven't been updated since the place was built in 1960. The bathrooms have groovy multicolored tiles. Plastic protects the lampshades, and the color televisions are strictly 1970s no-brand standard motel issue. There have only been two sets of owners since the motel's construction, and some of the staff, including a friendly housekeeper named Hattie, have also been working here since the beginning.

The Ohio House has its own coffee shop, where five booths and ten counter seats are filled daily with resident greasy spoon aficionados and overnight guests. Try the Deuces Wild breakfast, which has two of everything, for a little more than three bucks.

The Ritz-Carlton, Chicago

At Water Tower Place
160 East Pearson Street
Chicago, IL 60611
312-266-1000
800-621-6906 outside Chicago
Reservations: 800-332-4222

> *The Ritz still
> defines luxury
> lodging in Chicago*

General manager: Nicholas Mutton. **Accommodations:** 346 rooms, 85 suites. **Rates:** Rooms $230–$275 single, $260–$350 double; suites $325–$725 single or double; packages available. **Included:** All meals available. **Minimum stay:** No. **Added:** 12.4% tax. **Payment:** Major credit cards. **Children:** Yes. **Pets:** By arrangement. **Smoking:** Nonsmoking rooms available. **Open:** Year-round.

For the past two decades, the Ritz-Carlton Chicago has more or less defined luxury lodging in the Windy City. Now, after a $16 million renovation, the 22 floors at the top of Water Tower Place offer even more spectacular accommodations. Rich mahogany or cherry headboards and armoires and Bavarian diamond-cut crystal lamps have been added to the Georgian-style bedchambers. Many rooms also feature VCRs and CD players. More than 277 tons of rich Verde marble have been laid in the bathrooms.

> **Complimentary beverages are set up in the morning, and newspapers are delivered on request. The concierge staff claims to speak nine languages, including Japanese, while staff members always number more than one person for each guest.**

The attention to detail is evident the minute you enter the lobby. Inserts of imported Scottish carpet are tucked between squares of Italian marble. A seating area near the elevators features baroque wing chairs, exquisite brass and glass end tables, and plush damask sofas. The reception desk has even more creamy Italian marble, enhanced by floral displays and oil paintings.

Next to the lobby, the Café recalls an English dining room, though the atmosphere remains casual. You can enjoy all three meals and even a late snack since the restaurant stays open until 1:30 A.M. It now serves chicken and pasta dishes along with standard club sandwich fare. The acclaimed Dining Room offers a more luxurious setting and French cuisine. A piano player provides music beneath crystal chandeliers. The Greenhouse serves a light luncheon, afternoon tea, then cocktails in an atrium with a striking view of the lakefront. Evening piano entertainment is also offered here while the Bar provides dancing and live entertainment nightly.

Business guests and lavish weddings fill six major banquet and meeting facilities. The 9,000-square-foot Grand Ballroom accommodates up to 1,200 beneath its dramatic crystal chandelier. Corporate guests will appreciate the convenience of portable fax machines, which can be provided in their rooms.

You will have to pay extra (about $6 per day) to use the 11th-floor Carlton Club, with its skylighted swimming pool, whirlpool, and separate men's and women's athletic departments with exercise equipment, steam rooms, saunas, and massage facilities.

GALENA

Captain Gear Guest House

1000 South Bench Street
Galena, IL 61036
815-777-0222

Innkeeper: Alyce Green. **Accommodations:** 2 rooms; 1 suite, all with private bath. **Rates:** $75–$100 single, $80–$105 double. **Included:** Continental breakfast. **Minimum stay:** 2 nights on peak weekends. **Added:** 9% tax. **Payment:** Major credit cards.

> *A secluded location and a gracious innkeeper*

Children: No. **Pets:** No. **Smoking:** Downstairs only. **Open:** Year-round.

You may think you missed it. The paved road leading to this inn turns to dirt surrounded by fields before it reaches the Federal brick mansion. The secluded location, a good block from the nearest neighbor and almost a mile from Galena's congested main street, is one reason that guests find the Captain Gear so appealing.

> **The inviting double parlor is welcoming, with its Victorian furnishings and a piano. Continental breakfast, served in the kitchen or dining room, includes fruit, homemade pear bread or muffins, coffee, and juice.**

Another reason is innkeeper Alyce Green, a grandmotherly woman who opened the Captain Gear in 1989 after retiring from a Chicago hospital. Built in 1855, the house was the last home of Captain Hezekiah Gear, who made his fortune in Galena's once-lucrative lead mining industry and later served as a state senator.

High ceilings are found on both floors of the home. The country-style Mary's Room has throw rugs on wide-planked floors and a king-size white iron bed that can also be broken down into twins. Clarissa's Room has red and white wallpaper, a walnut bedstead from the 1860s, and a brick fireplace just for show. The two dressers here came from Alyce's great-grandparents. The double whirlpool bath makes this one of the inn's most popular rooms. The recently remodeled Hamilton's Suite has a maple queen-size bed dressed in a country quilt, a pine armoire, and a nonworking fireplace. The private sitting room is done in white wicker.

DeSoto House Hotel

230 South Main Street
Galena, IL 61036
815-777-0090
Fax: 815-777-9529

A renovated hotel that once welcomed Grant, Lincoln, and Twain.

Manager: Daniel Kelley. **Accommodations:** 51 rooms, 4 suites. **Rates:** Rooms $79–$109 single or double; suites $109–$149 single or double; packages available. **Included:** All meals available. **Minimum stay:** 2 nights on weekends. **Added:** 9% tax. **Payment:** Major credit cards. **Children:** Yes. **Pets:** No. **Smoking:** Nonsmoking rooms available. **Open:** Year-round.

Abraham Lincoln, Ulysses S. Grant, Mark Twain, Susan B. Anthony, Theodore Roosevelt, and Ralph Waldo Emerson are just a few of the prominent names you will join when you add yours to the guest register of the DeSoto House Hotel. Advertised as the largest hotel in the Midwest when it opened in 1855, the Italianate structure enjoyed its glory days when Galena rivaled Chicago as a mining, trade, and transportation center. Times changed, and so did DeSoto House, as this

Good restaurants can now be found in Galena, such as the Kingston Inn, where meals are served by a singing wait staff, and Café Italia, for superb no-nonsense pasta dishes.

grand hotel became a boardinghouse and eventually a white elephant. After a multimillion-dollar renovation, the DeSoto again welcomes visitors to this charming town.

The imposing lobby retains its original pressed-tin ceilings along with stained glass windows and a brass Victorian chandelier. The sweeping staircase leads to the guest rooms, decorated in attractive blues and beiges and overlooking Galena's main street or the hotel's atrium. All the rooms have cable television, a telephone, and either king-size or double beds.

The Courtyard offers breakfast and lunch daily in the four-story atrium. The Green Street Tavern offers lighter meals and drinks. Casual attire is permitted in the dining room, Generals', which is famous for steaks and seafood.

Eagle Ridge Inn and Resort

U.S. Route 20, Box 777
Galena, IL 61036
815-777-2444
800-892-2269
Fax: 815-777-0445

*Family activities
thrive at this
popular resort*

General manager: John Osmanski.
Accommodations: 80 rooms, 260 1–5-bedroom homes. **Rates:**
Rooms $125–$250 double; homes $140–$420 double. **Included:** Morning coffee; all meals available. **Minimum stay:** 2
nights on weekends may be required. **Added:** 9% tax. **Payment:** Major credit cards. **Children:** Yes. **Pets:** No. **Smoking:**
Nonsmoking rooms available. **Open:** Year-round.

A major fire early in 1992 kept much of Eagle Ridge out of
commission for most of that year. Now they're back with a
new main lodge, 20,000 square feet larger than the original
facility, with specialty shops and an art gallery, along with
more guest rooms.

Six Superior rooms have fireplaces, Jacuzzis, and king-size
four-poster beds. All the rooms have VCRs, mini-bars, terrycloth robes, hair dryers, and makeup mirrors. Guests can
also stay in condominium resort homes deep in the woods, by
the golf course, or overlooking the lake. These units all have
kitchens, and as they are decorated individually, you may be
able to request one with a pool table, antiques, or a Jacuzzi.
The reservationist will have detailed information about each
one.

The staff at Eagle Ridge Inn and Resort is especially clever
when it comes to children's activities. A youth program, offered daily during the summer, includes swimming on Lake

Galena, games, and arts and crafts. Kids' Night Out happens on weekends year-round. Come here around Christmas, for instance, and the children can dine with Santa and even see his reindeer (actually the property's herd of 600 extremely friendly deer). Around Halloween, children are given a bag for trick-or-treating at various spots around the resort. Teenagers are also accommodated here with skiing, bowling, golf, tennis, and horseback riding. Cookies and milk are served to all guests during evening turndown.

> **Of course, one of the best features of the resort is its proximity to historic Galena, about eight miles away. But with all the services offered here (even its own general store), you may never want to set foot off the property.**

The resort offers 45 holes of golf, three fully staffed pro shops, and a large practice fairway and green. A winter golf center has an indoor driving range, putting challenge games, and computerized and video club swing analysis. An indoor pool has a retractable ceiling and a large sunning deck. A massage therapist is available daily in the complete fitness center. In winter, there is an ice-skating rink, tobogganing and sledding, and 60 kilometers of cross-country ski trails on the resort's 6,800 acres. Horse-drawn hay and sleigh rides can also be arranged.

Woodlands Restaurant provides a formal setting for dinner. Specialties include prime aged steaks, seafood, pastas, and the pastry chef's creations. Families often head to the Granary for reasonably priced barbecued ribs or seafood pasta. A seafood buffet is served here on Friday nights. Bar and grill service is also offered at the Shooters Sports Bar on the east golf course during the winter months.

The Inn at Irish Hollow

2800 South Irish Hollow Road
Galena, IL 61036
815-777-2010

> *An old general store and post office is now a romantic B&B*

Innkeepers: Tony Kemp and Bill Barrick. **Accommodations:** 4 rooms and 1 suite, all with private bath, 1 cottage. **Rates:** Rooms $85–$105 single or double, suites $105, cottage $155–$175. **Included:** Full breakfast. **Minimum stay:** 2 nights on weekends; 3 nights in fall. **Added:** 9% tax. **Payment:** Discover, MasterCard, Visa. **Children:** 10 years and older. **Pets:** No. **Smoking:** Front porch only. **Open:** Year-round.

Tony Kemp and Bill Barrick worked for the Ritz and Hilton hotel chains before returning to the area where Bill's parents reside. Their quest for the perfect spot to open a bed-and-breakfast inn led to an old general store and post office that once served the farming communities surrounding Rodden, about eight miles outside Galena. Closed for some 40 years, the circa 1880 building was a virtual time capsule, with its original signs, scales, and wooden display counters still intact.

Breakfast, served in this turn-of-the-century atmosphere, is unforgettable. Vintage tins, bottles, and soapboxes line the back shelves, while a sign tacked to the front counter proudly states, "Pleasing you keeps us in business." Pineapple–blueberry muffins begin the meal, followed by grapefruit halves and French toast topped with cream cheese and peach syrup. Rashers of crisp bacon grace the side.

The inn's vegetable garden provides the raw ingredients for dinner. The menu changes seasonally, so in fall you might enjoy Bill's pork tenderloin roast with plum *au jus*. Tony and Bill also stage traditional Thanksgiving and Christmas dinners. Ask about the intriguing weekend packages.

> Bargain hunters can visit the massive antiques mall at Savanna, about 30 miles away. Chestnut Mountain Ski Resort and Mississippi Palisades Park are also nearby.

The guest rooms are places for relaxed, romantic solitude, with fireplaces, queen-size beds, and private balconies. In the parlor, guests enjoy leafing through a book of antique wedding photos. A small cottage is part of ongoing room additions.

Guests arriving in daylight enjoy an enchanting approach to the inn, across rolling farmland and past grazing cattle and charming farmhouses. The inn is close to Galena's shops and restaurants.

Spring Street Guest House

414 Spring Street
Galena, IL 61036
815-777-0354

> *A sculptor's touches highlight spacious guest suites*

Innkeepers: Sandra and Charles Fach. **Accommodations:** 2 suites, both with private bath. **Rates:** $65.35 single; $87.15 double. **Included:** Full breakfast (may change to Continental). **Minimum stay:** 2 nights on weekends. **Added:** Tax included. **Payment:** Major credit cards. **Children:** 10 years and older. **Pets:** No. **Smoking:** No. **Open:** Year-round.

The old stone and brick icehouse for a Galena brewery now houses two of the town's warmest overnight suites. Spring Street Guest House is the brain child of Sandra and Charles Fach, who run the City Brewery Museum next door. Charles is a sculptor, painter, and potter whose welded steel king-size beds dominate the suites. Hand-cast bronze statues sit on the posts while mattresses require a small handmade platform to climb on board.

The unromantically named Back Unit is most impressive; its hunt theme is seen in bedposts crowned with statues of Diana the huntress. Bas-relief faces of dogs line the walls and floor around a wood-burning stove. The vaulted brick bathroom, once the icehouse refrigerator, is painted bright white. Black-painted bronze canine heads flank the entrance to the open shower area while smaller heads grasp long towel rails in their jaws. There is also a spacious kitchen area, but guests may use only the refrigerator and sink. Breakfast here is enjoyed in the innkeepers' quarters.

> **The bed in the Front Unit has bronze figures representing the phases of life on its bedposts.**

Park Avenue Guest House

208 Park Avenue
Galena, IL 61036
815-777-1075
800-359-0743

> *Products
> of yesteryear
> in a collectors'
> paradise*

Innkeepers: John and Sharon Fallbacher. **Accommodations:** 3 rooms, all with private bath, 1 suite. **Rates:** Rooms $75–$80 double; suite $95 single or double. **Included:**

Continental breakfast. **Minimum stay:** 2 nights on weekends. **Added:** 9% tax. **Payment:** Discover, MasterCard, Visa. **Children:** 12 years and older. **Pets:** No. **Smoking:** Downstairs only. **Open:** Year-round.

Guests can't help but gravitate toward the Park Avenue's kitchen, which Sharon Fallbacher has decorated with the entire contents of a turn-of-the-century general store. Old advertising signs line the walls, and boxes of everything from pancake flour to pop bottles perch on shelves above the breakfast table. In the laundry room you'll find old boxes of RIT dye and Rinso detergent.

> **History buffs will appreciate that the home was built for Admiral Bias Sampson, the commander of the *U.S.S. Maine* ("Remember the *Maine*") during the Spanish-American War.**

The Fallbachers entered the competitive world of Galena bed-and-breakfasting in 1989, and they have found their niche. Their 1893 Queen Anne inn is just two blocks from downtown, yet it's delightfully out of the way in a picturesque neighborhood.

Original woodwork is found in the parlors, formal dining room, and guest rooms. Anna, named after Sampson's daughter, has pink and blue decor and an iron and brass bed. All the rooms have Laura Ashley sheets on queen-size beds. The Fallbachers keep adding to their exquisite flower gardens, which bloom with some two thousand bulbs in spring.

GRAFTON

Pere Marquette Lodge and Conference Center

Route 100
Grafton, IL 62037
618-786-2331
Fax: 618-786-3498

*A rustic
state park lodge*

General manager: Steve Waack.
Accommodations: 50 lodge rooms, 22 cottage rooms. **Rates:** $65 double. **Minimum stay:** No. **Added:** 11% tax. **Payment:** Major credit cards. **Children:** Yes. **Pets:** No. **Smoking:** Non-smoking rooms available. **Open:** Year-round.

Pere Marquette State Park was named for Father Jacques Marquette, the French Jesuit missionary who in 1673 was among the first Europeans to enter what is now Illinois. His namesake lodge, made of native stone and rustic timbers, is set on rolling bluffs overlooking the Illinois River. It was built in the 1930s, then restored in 1988 to let the lodge provide convenience without disturbing its historic character.

> While the Pere Marquette State Park is beautiful in all seasons, it really shines in the fall, when you can often spy deer, wild turkeys, even foxes and coyotes, among the colorful leaves. In winter, bald eagles are known to congregate here.

While many state park lodges ditch their original furniture, Pere Marquette has refurbished the 1930s utilitarian oak couches and chairs in the Great Room Lobby. A corner has been attractively outfitted with wicker. A 700-ton stone fireplace, with an inset portrait of Marquette in a canoe, reaches above exposed beams to form the lobby's centerpiece.

The hotel-style rooms in the bustling main lodge are sparsely decorated but comfortable. Choose a room in one of the 22 cottages, some with homey touches like shutters and exposed wood or stone walls. All the rooms have splendid views of the river or the surrounding park.

The dining room serves family-style meals featuring Continental dishes as well as regional American fare. Choices include catfish, prime rib, fried chicken, scallops, fettuccine, grilled chicken breast, and broiled orange roughy. Try the Amaretto cheesecake. Sunday brunch is especially popular.

Indoor recreation includes a swimming pool, exercise room, whirlpool, and saunas. Children will enjoy the small video game room. There is also a conference room with stone walls, which can be partitioned into four separate areas.

The 15 miles of hiking trails offer stunning views of the Illinois River and the Mississippi just beyond. You can board your own horse here or rent one from the stable for exploring 12 more miles of trails. There are also launching ramps for boating and excellent fishing.

The efficient staff help make the lodge popular. Weekends in all seasons are booked almost a year in advance.

GURNEE

Sweet Basil Hill Farm

15937 West Washington Street
Gurnee, IL 60031
708-244-3333
800-228-HERB

> *Farm atmosphere in the shadow of a theme park*

Innkeepers: Bob and Teri Jones. **Accommodations:** 1 room with private bath, 2 suites, 1 cottage. **Rates:** $85 single or double;

cottage $100. **Included:** Full breakfast. **Minimum stay:** No. **Added:** 6% tax. **Payment:** MasterCard, Visa, Discover. **Children:** Yes. **Pets:** Not encouraged. **Smoking:** No. **Open:** Year-round.

Sheep and llamas graze on the seven acres of Sweet Basil Hill Farm, a Cape Cod–style farmhouse 40 miles and worlds away from both Chicago and Milwaukee. Paths trace the perimeter, offering the perfect setting for summer hikes or winter cross-country skiing. Fragrant herb gardens adorn the backyard, along with a hammock in the shade.

> **Many guests head for Six Flags Great America Park, just a few blocks away. Others go to White Sox games or spend the day shopping near Gurnee or historic Long Grove.**

The guest rooms are quite comfortably outfitted with feather pillows and comforters on four-poster canopy beds. The Basil Room is a favorite, with its green and white handmade quilt and snowflake stenciling that continues right into the closets. All the rooms feature potpourri, fresh pine furnishings and floors, English antiques, and Crabtree & Evelyn soaps and shampoos. Televisions, VCRs, and telephones are available upon request. Breakfast is served in the knotty pine breakfast room and always includes fresh fruit, breads, muffins, and coffee cake. Coffee and tea are always brewing.

Bob and Teri Jones live next door. He's a freelance actor, writer, and musician who worked as a drummer for Al Jarreau in the 1960s. She's a photographer. They have a flair for the dramatic and whimsical, especially when it comes to their pair of llamas, Fernando and Dali. The Joneses say that llamas make excellent, friendly pets who gladly "schnuzzle" with anyone who comes up to the fence.

The recently opened Lamb's Cottage still needs some tweaking, but it has many of the whimsical touches found in the main house. It's especially popular with honeymoon couples.

Summer brings a Renaissance Faire and Tempel Farm's Lippizaner horse show. It is also possible to stay and enjoy the rural simplicity of the farm or curl up in front of the downstairs fireplace to browse through the innkeepers' fascinating collection of books.

NAUVOO

Hotel Nauvoo

Route 96
P.O. Box 398
Nauvoo, IL 62354
217-453-2211

> *A popular inn
> and restaurant
> with a
> Mormon history*

General manager: The Kraus Family. **Accommodations:** 6 rooms, all with private bath, 2 suites. **Rates:** Rooms $45 single or double, suites $55 single or double. **Included:** All meals available. **Minimum stay:** No. **Added:** 9% tax. **Payment:** Personal checks, cash. **Children:** Yes. **Pets:** No. **Smoking:** Nonsmoking rooms; designated smoking areas. **Open:** Mid-March through mid-November.

The Hotel Nauvoo is in a historic Mississippi River town that was the center of Mormon culture in the 1800s. Though the actual Mormon community lasted less than a decade, its influence is still felt. The hotel, built in 1840, was purchased by the Kraus family in 1946.

The guest rooms here are simple and sparsely decorated but also quite cozy. All have phones, desks, and tub-showers. Room 5 is a favorite, with a fireplace and four-poster bed.

Guests flock here for the famous buffet served in one of seven dining rooms. The generous spread includes bread selections, vegetables, three kinds of potatoes, and a wild rice dressing that the restaurant has been serving since the 1940s. Main courses include barbecued ribs, steaks, chicken, fish, catfish, ocean fish, and even some unusual items like pickled herring. The restaurant is not open for breakfast, but guests can head to Grandpa John's café across the street, which the Krauses also own.

The decor of each dining room is as varied as the food selection. One has a bicentennial theme. The Heritage Room has created a street scene in one corner, using the facades of brick and wood homes surrounded by a white picket fence. This large room is a popular spot for wedding receptions. Another room is dedicated to the artist Lane K. Newberry, whose work is displayed throughout.

Nauvoo has year-round events that celebrate its unusual history. A colorful pageant called *City of Joseph* is held several evenings in mid-August, and the annual grape festival occurs the weekend before Labor Day. Restored homes and historic sites are open for tours, including the old jail where the founder of the Mormons, Joseph Smith, met his maker at the hands of an angry mob.

UTICA

Starved Rock Lodge and Conference Center

Starved Rock State Park
P.O. Box 471
Utica, IL 61373
815-667-4211
Fax: 815-667-4455

A state park lodge offers newly remodeled rooms

Director of Sales: Linda Meagher.
Accommodations: 72 rooms, 18 cabins. **Rates:** Rooms $56.95–$75 single, $63.95–$75 double; cabins $39.95–$75 sin-

gle, $46.95–$75 double; packages available. **Included:** All meals available. **Minimum stay:** No. **Added:** 6% tax. **Payment:** Major credit cards. **Children:** Yes. **Pets:** No. **Smoking:** Nonsmoking rooms available. **Open:** Year-round.

Local legend states that Starved Rock Park derived its name from a 1760s incident in which a band of Illiniwek Indians took refuge on top of a towering 125-foot sandstone butte and were surrounded by warring Ottawa and Potawatomi tribes. After being trapped for several days, they died of starvation.

Guests looking for relaxation and great outdoor facilities will now find both at Starved Rock. Built in part by the Civilian Conservation Corps in the 1930s, Starved Rock Lodge and Conference Center underwent extensive renovations in 1989, updating many of the rooms and adding an Olympic-size pool. A new hotel wing was also added.

> **Common rooms are highlighted by the great room, where guests meet for cards or conversation beneath the native stone and rustic timbers. They also have the choice of several outdoor verandahs.**

While the original lodge rooms and new hotel rooms now look very similar, differences are a bit more distinct in the cabins. While the deluxe cabins offer wood trim and decorator touches, the pioneer versions desperately need new paneled walls and carpeting. The exterior wood is scarred where guests have carved their names over the years, and some might say this adds to the charm. Look for these to be remodeled slowly over the next few years.

There's a popular Sunday brunch at the Starved Rock restaurant, which serves all three meals daily. The Starved Rock Cafe, right off the lobby, offers snacks, gifts, candy, and homemade fudge. Some of the conference rooms and banquet facilities can accommodate up to 250.

Outdoor activities include hiking trails around and atop the 18 bluffs and canyons on almost 2,700 acres of state park land. Old stumps on the property have been turned into whimsical wood carvings of eagles and bears. A felt wall hanging commissioned from a local artist brightens up the lobby area.

WHEATON

The Wheaton Inn

301 West Roosevelt Road
Wheaton, IL 60187
708-690-2600
800-447-4667
Fax: 708-690-2623

> *A Williamsburg-
> style inn just
> 25 miles from
> Chicago*

Innkeepers: Linda Matzen. **Accommodations:** 16 rooms, all with private bath. **Rates:** $99–$195 single or double. **Included:** Full breakfast. **Minimum stay:** No. **Added:** 11% tax. **Payment:** Major credit cards. **Children:** Yes. **Pets:** No. **Smoking:** Yes. **Open:** Year-round.

The Williamsburg-style Wheaton Inn, built in 1987, lies just 21 miles west of Chicago. The pair of conference facilities includes one with beamed ceilings and chandeliers that can hold up to 50 people. A smaller room with paneled walls and leather chairs provides a clubby atmosphere for groups of 10 or 12.

> **Tour the nearby McCormick Mansion and Cantigny War Museum. The inn is just three blocks from downtown and Wheaton College. The inn has its own croquet course and gardens.**

Buffet-style breakfast is served in the cheerful breakfast room or out on the brick patio. The meal may include bacon and eggs with scalloped apples or baked pineapple. Breads and coffee cakes are all baked on the premises. Complimentary afternoon wine and cheese are served in the parlor.

The Williamsburg theme carries over to the spacious guest rooms, all named for famous Wheaton citizens. Some have whirlpools and fireplaces. The Woodward Room, named for a judge and the father of the newspaperman Bob Woodward, has a Jacuzzi in front of a bay window. A modern look is found in the Ottoson Room, with its distinctive cathedral ceiling and skylight. All rooms have telephones both by the bed and in the bathroom. European towel warmers add a nice touch.

Indiana

Northern
Indiana

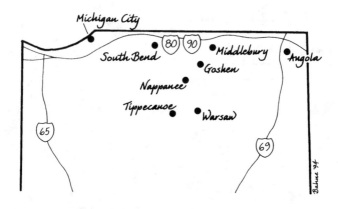

Angola
Potawatomi Inn, 36
Goshen
The Checkerberry Inn, 37
Michigan City
Creekwood Inn, 39
Middlebury
Essenhaus Country Inn, 40
The Patchwork Quilt Country Inn, 42
Nappanee
The Victorian Guest House, 43
South Bend
The Book Inn, 44
Tippecanoe
Bessinger's Wildlife Refuge, 45
Warsaw
White Hill Manor, 46

Best Bed-and-Breakfast Inns

Michigan City
  Creekwood Inn
Nappanee
  The Victorian Guest House
South Bend
  The Book Inn
Tippecanoe
  Bessinger's Wildlife Refuge
Warsaw
  White Hill Manor

Best Full-Service Country Inns

Goshen
  The Checkerberry Inn
Middlebury
  Essenhaus Country Inn
  The Patchwork Quilt Country Inn

Best Lodge

Angola
  Potawatomi Inn

Northern Indiana is known as Amish country, especially at the top of the state in Elkhart County. Amish Acres in **Nappanee** is an authentic 80-acre restoration of a century-old farming community, with men plowing the fields, women dipping candles, and a plethora of flat-topped black buggies on the roads. The Midwest Museum of American Art, in Elkhart, has an extensive collection of Norman Rockwell lithographs and Ansel Adams photographs.

In the northeast corner of Indiana is the small town of Shipshewana, with one of the Midwest's liveliest auction and flea markets. Tuesday and Wednesday bring out antiques and junk for sale. On weekends, Amish draft horses go on the auction block.

Movie fans might want to cruise through James Dean's former stomping grounds. He was born in Marion but grew up in nearby Fairmount, where the downtown James Dean/Fairmount Historical Museum displays some of the actor's possessions from a family collection. Mourners still make the pilgrimage in late September, when Dean died in an auto accident, to visit his grave in the Fairmount Cemetery.

To most Americans, **South Bend** means Notre Dame. You can tour the 1,250-acre campus and, with a lot of advanced planning, catch a football game in fall. The campus boasts century-old murals inside the Gold Dome, outstanding churches, and the Snite Museum of Art. While in town, consider dining at Tippecanoe Place, the circa 1888 home of Clement Studebaker now open as a restaurant.

ANGOLA

Potawatomi Inn

Pokagon State Park
6 Lane 100 A, Lake James
Angola, IN 46703
219-833-1077
Fax: 219-833-4087

*State park lodging
on the shores of
Lake James*

General manager: Alfred "Bud" Starling. **Accommodations:** 83 rooms in lodge, motel, and cabins. **Rates:** Rooms $36.38–$60.99 midweek per room, $55.64–$66.34 weekends; cabins $50.29 midweek, $55.64 weekend. **Minimum stay:** No. **Included:** Tax. **Payment:** Major credit cards. **Children:** Yes. **Pets:** No. **Smoking:** Nonsmoking rooms available. **Open:** Year-round.

The blond brick Potawatomi Inn originally housed dormitories in 1926. Today, three different types of guest accommodations are offered. The main lodge rooms are down hallways papered with Canadian goose borders. They are decorated similarly, with double beds and paneled walls, though the rooms closer to the lobby risk a greater level of noise. All have air conditioning, telephones, and televisions.

The comfortable motel rooms, with double beds and decorated in pastel peaches and greens, offer writing desks and TVs tucked into armoires. An advertised suite is actually one big room with a comfortable stuffed couch and four chairs around a game table. The cabins, in groupings about 100 yards from the main building, are surrounded by trees and offer decor similar to the standard rooms.

An expansive lawn behind the inn continues to the shore of Lake James, the second-largest natural lake in Indiana. The stables are also popular in summer.

> **The lodge is active in winter: the enclosed pool area has a Jacuzzi, sauna, and exercise room.**
> **A toboggan run is open on weekends.**

The lodge's restaurant, with exposed brick walls and country blue accents, serves a popular buffet. The health-conscious menu also features substitute egg dishes. Be warned that rooms sometimes fill a year in advance for holiday weekends, as at most state park lodges.

GOSHEN

The Checkerberry Inn

62644 C.R. 37
Goshen, IN 46526
219-642-4445
Fax: 219-642-4445

> *An elegant inn*
> *in Amish country*

Innkeepers: John and Susan Graff.
Accommodations: 12 rooms, all with private bath, 2 suites.
Rates: Rooms $75–$100 single, $104–$130 double; suites $190–$300 double. **Included:** Continental breakfast. **Minimum stay:** 2 nights on special weekends. **Added:** 5% tax. **Payment:** Visa, MasterCard, Discover. **Children:** Yes. **Pets:** No. **Smoking:** Permitted only in designated areas. **Open:** Closed in January.

The Checkerberry Inn is a French country oasis in the heart of Indiana's Amish country. While guests still flock here to purchase Amish crafts, the inn keeps itself purposely removed from its neighbors. After all, the atmosphere here is anything but plain and utilitarian, with meticulously decorated guest rooms and elegant dining surrounded by 100 acres of well-groomed farmland. The dining room is open to the public for lunch and dinner.

John and Susan Graff, who also operate a resort in the West Indies, are well traveled and sophisticated, as are many of their guests. John's photographs of the French countryside, enlarged to poster size, decorate the walls

The rooms, named after flowers like trillium and Queen Anne's lace, mix contemporary flair with French country antiques. The most popular is Foxglove, a large suite with a king-size bed, a fireplace in a spacious living room, and a Jacuzzi and shower in the bath. The 1,500-square-foot Checkerberry Suite has Palladian windows and its own kitchen. Some have regional touches like Amish quilts and even an occasional straw hat on a bed. The third-floor rooms have skylights and dormers.

> **Outdoor facilities include a swimming pool, a tennis court, and a croquet court, the latter also serving as a chipping and putting green. For evening entertainment, you can't beat the simple pleasure of lazing on the front porch's wicker furniture while Amish buggies trot past.**

Four-course dinners are offered in the tasteful blue and white dining room on tables set with embroidered linens. Salad and palate-cleansing sorbet are followed by an ever-changing list of enticing entrées. The grilled rack of lamb is served over spinach fettuccine and garnished with pesto aioli. One specialty, paired breast of duckling, comes sautéed with Marsala and julienned vegetables. Desserts can include pumpkin ice cream with cranberry or raspberry sauce, or white chocolate mousse in dark chocolate cups. A light Continental breakfast for guests is also served here.

MICHIGAN CITY

Creekwood Inn

Route 20-35 at I–94
Michigan City, IN 46360
219-872-8357
Fax: 219-872-8357

> *A country oasis
> a stone's throw
> from the
> interstate*

Owner: Mary Lou Linnen. **Managers:** Peggie Wall and Mary Hatton. **Accommodations:** 12 rooms, all with private bath, 1 suite. **Rates:** Rooms $95–$118 single, $102–$125 double; suite $150 double. **Included:** Continental breakfast. **Minimum stay:** 2 nights during peak season weekends. **Added:** 5% tax. **Payment:** Major credit cards. **Children:** Yes. **Pets:** No. **Smoking:** Nonsmoking rooms available. **Open:** Closed for 10 days in March.

Though advertised as a bed-and-breakfast, this inn is really more like a small hotel. The guest rooms, off long corridors, start to look alike, even though all are decorated with Schumacher wallpapers and quality reproduction furniture. Original paintings in some rooms add special flourishes. The Willow Creek Suite is popular with business travelers, since small meetings of up to twelve people can be held here. French doors separate the conference room from a bedroom/bath area with its own sun porch.

The Creekwood Inn is just a few blocks from I-94. It seems a world away, however, as you approach it along a beautiful tree-lined drive. Each year, strategically planted trees and shrubs obscure the view of traffic even more.

The former garage of this Cotswold-style manor house is

now the reception room. Small conference rooms and the parlor can comfortably accommodate groups up to 25. The Continental breakfast is served in one of two dining rooms, one with white wicker, the other in dark woods. While the meal includes fruit, juice, coffee, and homemade breads and muffins, many guests pay the extra $6 to upgrade to a full breakfast. Five-course dinners are served here on weekends.

Ideal for short walks, trails cut through the inn's 30 acres and lead to a small lake on the property. Bicycles can also be rented here. The magnificent Indiana Dunes National Lakeshore is just a short drive away.

MIDDLEBURY

Essenhaus Country Inn

240 U.S. 20
Middlebury, IN 46540
219-825-9447
Fax: 219-825-9447, ext. 233

Amish culture reflected in restaurants, shops, and lodging

Owners: Bob and Sue Miller. **General manager:** John A. Sauder. **Accommodations:** 29 rooms, 4 suites, all with private bath. **Rates:** Rooms $55 single, $73 double; suites $85–$115 single or double. **Included:** Continental breakfast on Sundays; all meals available. **Minimum stay:** No. **Added:** 7% tax. **Payment:** Major credit cards. **Children:** Yes. **Pets:** No. **Smoking:** Nonsmoking rooms available. **Open:** Year-round.

The buildings that make up Essenhaus may be the Midwest's most enterprising link with Amish culture. This charming collection of shops, restaurants, and overnight lodging gives guests a feel for the simple life packaged with all the amenities enjoyed at fine hotels and restaurants today.

The charming atrium is the hub of the Essenhaus Country Inn, which was built in 1986 as an adaptation of an Amish farmhouse. A silver-bellied woodstove is at the heart of the house, flanked by high-backed sofas and rockers created by crafts-

> **Essenhaus has sold up to 6,000 pies in a single day from its restaurant and adjacent Dutch bakery, Die Bock Kich.**

people from a nearby Amish settlement in Nappanee. Amish quilts line the walls, and old tractor seats top stools. Guests can relax or read here, or enjoy complimentary coffee and cookies in the evening. On the balcony, surrounded by a white picket fence, lies a white clapboard one-room schoolhouse, where small meetings are held. There's a 19th-century nickelodeon on the first floor, and in the third-floor game room, antique arcade games join their video counterparts.

The guest rooms, off the atrium, are decorated with Amish pine furnishings, including four-poster beds. All the Heritage Suites have kitchenettes and dining areas. Most have steam baths. Much of the Amish-inspired artwork in the rooms was created by the South Bend artist Howard Scott.

Famous long before lodgings were offered here, Das Dutchman Essenhaus restaurant serves traditional beef, chicken, fish, and ham entrées, all for less than $10. The Amish influence is everywhere, from the simplicity of the food preparation to the white batiste prayer caps worn by the wait staff. The pies are popular here, especially rhubarb, cherry, peanut butter, and raspberry cream.

Sue Miller and her family have also created unusual retail spaces in the property's outbuildings. Two antique log cabins have been combined to form the Cabin Café, which serves light meals quickly. The Knot 'N' Grain sells fine furniture and fixtures, while the Country Cupboard carries country clothing and accessories. Corn Crib Crafts offers Amish quilts, wood carvings, rag rugs, and hand-stitched dolls against a backdrop of dried corn behind chicken wire. There is also a book section detailing Amish and Mennonite life and history. An old silo now has a circular staircase that leads first to a card shop on the second level, then even higher for a spectacular view of the surrounding fields.

The Patchwork Quilt Country Inn

11748 County Road 2
Middlebury, IN 46540
219-825-2417

An Amish-country inn with excellent meals

Innkeepers: Maxine Zook, Susan Thomas. **Accommodations:** 8 rooms, 1 suite, most with private bath. **Rates:** Rooms $40–$60 single, $50–$70 double; suites $95. **Included:** Full breakfast; dinner available. **Minimum stay:** No. **Added:** 5% tax. **Payment:** MasterCard, Visa. **Children:** 5 years and older. **Pets:** No. **Smoking:** No. **Open:** Year-round.

The Patchwork Quilt began welcoming guests more than 25 years ago, first with farm vacations, then with the restaurant, and finally with B&B lodgings. Despite redecoration and the addition of rooms, it retains much of its country feel.

The inn offers popular Amish Backroad Tours. The four-hour excursion takes you along the narrow dirt roads of the Crystal Valley Amish settlement, where more than 30 homes and businesses are open.

The three original upstairs rooms, which share a bath, have the most character. The brick walls in Meadow, the fireplace in Treetop, and the handmade basket quilts in Orchard all evoke an era long past. The 1991 addition attempts a similar feeling and sometimes succeeds. Named for the deer that come up to the window, the Deer Field represents the animal in its quilted bedspread and Bradbury and Bradbury wallpaper border. The Loft Suite has its own kitchenette and whirlpool tub and uses a fabric-swagged shower curtain as part of its decor. Gone, however, is the unifying theme of showcasing fancy quilts in each room.

The inn continues to offer excellent meals in its walnut-paneled dining room, which seats 80 comfortably. Award-winning buttermilk pecan chicken and roast beef highlight the evening menu. A trip to the salad bar is included with family-style meals. For dessert, try the cherry walnut torte, cho-mocha silk pie, or a hot fudge sundae. At breakfast, fresh fruit and muffins always precede a hearty hot dish of diced potato egg soufflé, buttermilk pancakes, or biscuits and gravy.

The inn also has a country gift shed, with Amish arts and crafts for sale.

NAPPANEE

The Victorian Guest House

302 East Market Street
Nappanee, IN 46550
219-773-4383

> *Victorian charm in the heart of Amish country*

Innkeepers: Bruce and Vickie Hunsberger. **Accommodations:** 5 rooms, 3 with private bath. **Rates:** $39–$75 single or double. **Included:** Full breakfast. **Minimum stay:** No. **Added:** 5% tax. **Payment:** Visa, MasterCard. **Children:** Yes. **Pets:** Yes. **Smoking:** No. **Open:** Year-round.

The Victorian Guest House recently celebrated its centennial year. It can also celebrate the arrival of its new innkeepers, who have improved upon its special amenities. Vickie, a former computer operator, delights guests celebrating an anniversary by printing out a rundown of events, movies, and songs in the news on the date they were married.

Frank Coppes lived here in 1893, followed by three generations of his family. The Coppes Suite

> **The inn lies at the edge of downtown Nappannee and is just a few miles away from Amish Acres, a restaurant and working farm open for tours.**

features a queen-size bed and a fancy-tiled bathroom with a 100-year-old soaking tub. Vickie's favorite is the Maid's Room, with its crosscut oak woodwork. The innkeepers plan to have the inn spend its second hundred years as a fancy Victorian painted lady.

Breakfast is served on Depression glass and crystal on the home's original dining table. The meal may include cantaloupe, homemade bread, and a casserole or French toast. Hot chocolate, tea, and cookies are set out in the afternoon.

SOUTH BEND

The Book Inn

508 West Washington
South Bend, IN 46601
219-288-1990

*A mix of literature
and lodging*

Innkeepers: Peggy and John Livingston. **Accommodations:** 3 rooms, all with private bath, 2 suites. **Rates:** $75 single or double. **Included:** Continental breakfast. **Minimum stay:** No. **Added:** 10% tax. **Payment:** American Express, MasterCard, Visa. **Children:** Limited. **Pets:** No. **Smoking:** No. **Open:** Year-round.

Peggy Livingston combined her love of old books with lodging in this cleverly decorated bed-and-breakfast that stands amid other restored Victorians in downtown South Bend. With its mansard roof and arched dormer, the home is a prime example of Second Empire architecture. It was built in 1872 by Albert and Martha Cushing, who once owned a drug and book store on Michigan Street. The tiny grounds out front overflow with Victorian-style flowers, while roses climb up black wrought iron.

> **The Book Inn bookstore, which takes up most of the basement, is heavy on nonfiction, but also includes classics, detective fiction, cookbooks, and children's favorites on old wooden shelves. Book-loving guests have been known to browse the stacks into the wee hours of the morning.**

Inside you'll find 12-foot ceilings, hand-hewn, butternut woodwork, and oodles of fresh-cut flowers. The Book Inn was part of a designer showcase for the South Bend Symphony in 1991, so some of the radiator covers or wardrobes have been painted like bookshelves. A mural on the way down the back staircase depicts a pastoral scene. Downstairs, there's a piano, two cabbage rose chintz couches, and an elegant buffet.

Five spacious sleeping rooms, named after writers, have their own unique touches. The luxurious Cushing Suite has a bay window, handpainted walls with roses, a four-poster king-size bed, and a red velvet Victorian couch. The Louisa May Alcott Room employs soft greens and chintz and features a Victorian walnut chest and writing desk. A lace-draped plaster angel perches above the king-size headboard. The Jane Austen Room has rose-colored wallpaper and silk drapes with fancy fringe.

Breakfast can be quite elaborate, with five different kinds of fruit, fresh-squeezed orange juice, and a large morning glory muffin. They are served on Waterford crystal and Haviland or Limoges china. For dinner, you can walk next door to the famous Tippecanoe Restaurant.

TIPPECANOE

Bessinger's Hillfarm Wildlife Refuge

4588 State Road 110
Tippecanoe, IN 46570
219-223-3288

> *Simple comforts and a knockout view*

Innkeepers: Wayne and Betty Bessinger. **Accommodations:** 3 rooms. **Rates:** $50–$60 single; $55–$65 double. **Included:** Full breakfast. **Minimum stay:** No. **Added:** 6% tax. **Payment:** Cash, check, credit cards. **Children:** Over 10 years old or by arrangement. **Pets:** No. **Smoking:** No. **Open:** Year-round.

The view from the back porch alone is worth a night's stay at this well-kept Indiana secret. Hummingbirds whoosh by while ducks, Canadian geese, and herons paddle across the marsh and lake, which spreads out as far as the eye can see. The innkeepers, veteran grain and livestock farmers, sometimes let cattle graze behind the house, offering more than one guest the glimpse of a calf birth.

The guest rooms in this recently built log home aren't fancy — a couple have shag carpeting under woodbeamed ceilings — but they are impeccably clean and homey. Breakfast includes French toast or scrambled eggs and bacon, always with fruit cup and blueberry muffins. You can enjoy lunch on a glassed-in porch when the mosquitoes are biting.

> **So comfortable is Bessinger's that innkeepers in towns up to an hour away send their workers here for a day of rest and recuperation.**

Dinner can be shared with the Bessingers for an additional cost and often includes the day's catch from the lake.

Guests enjoy the hiking trails with scenic overlooks along the edge of the lake, stretching out some five miles and dotted with 33 small islands.

Favorite spots include Goose Marsh, Woodchuck Pond, and Sunrise-Sunset Overlook. On summer evenings, guests can join Wayne on his fish-feeding ritual. Canoeing is available here, while skiing and sledding dominate in the winter.

WARSAW

White Hill Manor

2513 East Center Street
Warsaw, IN 46580
219-269-6933

> *A Tudor mansion well equipped for business guests*

Manager: Gladys Deloe. **Accommodations:** 7 rooms, all with private bath, 1 suite. **Rates:** Rooms $68–$101 double; suites $112 double; corporate rates available. **Included:** Full breakfast; tax. **Minimum stay:** No. **Payment:** Major credit cards. **Children:** Yes. **Pets:** No. **Smoking:** Limited. **Open:** Year-round.

This impressive Tudor mansion, surrounded by 60-year-old evergreens, is tucked behind a wall of shrubs off a busy US 30 intersection in Warsaw, "the orthopedic capital of the world." Justin O. Zimmer, an innovator in orthopedics, built the 4,500-square-foot home in 1934, at the height of the Depression. Its proximity to manufacturing companies makes it a natural for business stops.

> The inn is close to the Wagon Wheel Playhouse, a popular year-round theater. The county's 100 recreation lakes are also a good drawing card.

While retaining the crown molding, arched entryways, and mullioned windows, the mansion has contemporary chintzes and walls painted in a palette of rose, pale peach, and ebony. The inn remains classic, austere, and extremely tasteful, and you can easily picture a guest surveying the *Wall Street Journal* in one of the burgundy leather sofas in the parlor.

The guest rooms continue the aesthetic. The downstairs Buttery, once lined with kitchen cupboards, now has a queen-size bed with eyelet coverings, an antique clawfoot tub, and a stained glass window. The Library is heavily decorated with wooden beams and built-in bookcases stocked with vintage Shakespeare, Wells, and Conan Doyle. The Garret, formerly the garage, is a mauve hideaway with a queen-size brass bed and a large bathroom. Anniversary and honeymoon couples usually request the Windsor Suite, with its classic English decor, king-size bed with floor-to-ceiling headboard, and spacious sitting area overlooking a courtyard.

There are telephones and desks in each room, and typing, copying, fax, and express mail services can be arranged by the helpful manager on duty. Conference facilities suit eight comfortably for daytime or evening meetings, with lunches catered upon request. Afternoon tea can be taken among the white wicker and glass tabletops of the garden room. Breakfast includes fruit and muffins followed by French toast, a quiche, or a casserole, juice, and coffee. A small refrigerator is also available for guests.

Southern
Indiana

Best Bed-and-Breakfast Inns

Austin
  Morgan's Farm
Nashville
  Allison House Inn
Hagerstown
  Teetor House
Greencastle
  Seminary Place

Best Full-Service Country Inns

Columbus
  The Columbus Inn
Greencastle
  Walden Inn
Nashville
  Brown County Inn
New Harmony
  The New Harmony Inn
Story
  Story Inn

Best Hotels

Indianapolis
  The Canterbury Hotel
  Holiday Inn at Union Station

Best Lodges and Resorts

Marshall
  Turkey Run Inn
Mitchell
  Spring Mill Inn
Nashville
  Abe Martin Lodge

Best Budget Stays

Terre Haute
Larry Bird's Boston Connection

Indianapolis is sometimes called the Circle City because the city planners designed its downtown streets like a wheel, with four major avenues radiating from its center. This is definitely a sports town, with the popular NFL Colts and NBA Pacers teams along with the Indianapolis Motor Speedway. A Hall of Fame Museum inside the track is worth a look.

The Indianapolis Museum of Art houses Oriental art and the world's premier collection of paintings and watercolors by J. M. W. Turner. The Indianapolis Zoo features not only the standard elephants and zebras but also an impressive whale and dolphin pavilion. It is part of the White River State Park's 267 acres. Eagle Creek Park is the home of the Museum of Indian Heritage. For other children's activities, Indianapolis has the world's largest Children's Museum, with plenty of hands-on exhibitions.

History is relived at the home once occupied by James Whitcomb Riley, which is open for tours. The Union Station, built in 1853, has been refurbished to hold specialty shops, restaurants, and nightclubs.

Follow 135 south into Brown County, a collection of towns with names like Bean Blossom, Slippery Elm Chute Road, and Booger Holler. Nashville is the county seat and the hub of activity here. The main street is lined with some 250 shops, museums, and restaurants, all with dark brown shingled storefronts. The John Dillinger Historical Wax Museum has the bandit's original Indianapolis tombstone, bank robbery plans, and a wooden pistol used during a jailbreak. The Brown County Playhouse attracts performers from Indiana University in Bloomington who perform on summer and fall weekends.

Brown County is the home of Indiana's largest state park, with some 15,000 acres for boating, fishing, and swimming. It's especially spectacular in the fall. For a less populated commune with nature, try Yellowwood State Park, in the western portion of the county.

New Harmony, near Evansville in the southwestern corner of the state, originally attracted scientists, artists, writers, and other intellectuals who began a communal life here. Though they disbanded in a short while, their ideas had a lasting impact. You'll receive an excellent overview from the video presentation at the New Harmony Visitors Center. The Roofless Church here has a number of sculptures by Jacques Lipchitz. The entire town has a spiritual, relaxed atmosphere.

AUSTIN

Morgan's Farm

R.R. 2
Austin, IN 47102
812-794-2536

> *A gentleman's farm offers unpretentious accommodations*

Innkeeper: Norma Bebout. **Accommodations:** 4 rooms, all with private bath. **Rates:** $55 single, $80 double. **Included:** Continental breakfast. **Minimum stay:** No. **Added:** 5% tax. **Payment:** MasterCard, Visa. **Children:** Yes. **Pets:** Kennel on property. **Smoking:** Allowed in some common areas. **Open:** Year-round.

This Williamsburg-style home was built in 1939 by Elsinore and Jack Morgan, whose family founded Morgan Foods in 1901. The business still thrives. The homestead has also remained in the family but is now a bed-and-breakfast inn. Though not a grand home, it offers spacious rooms with comfortable furnishings. You may feel as if you're visiting a prosperous but unpretentious relative some 40 years ago.

The masculine Cherry Room has a down comforter on an antique brass bed, leather reading chairs, and vintage photos of the Morgans. The original owners' presence is also felt through the large M in the smoky glass of the shower stall. With its original porcelain sinks and black and beige tile, the bathroom has an understated art deco quality. The Rose Room, with hardwood floors and rose-patterned wallpaper, has a view of the garden and pool, which is available to guests.

The Evergreen Room is named for its view of the beautiful trees that surround the property. This was the Morgan girls' room, with long rows of closets and an obscenely large dressing room. The Maple Room, where the boys once slept, has maple paneling, twin beds, and framed newspaper clippings about the World Series.

Guests can enjoy the common rooms and kitchen, where soft drinks and a jar of homemade cookies are always set out. Guests have only limited access to the 100-acre gentleman's farm but can walk the fence line for a glimpse of the buffalo, peacocks, swans, and horses that roam the property.

COLUMBUS

The Columbus Inn

445 Fifth Street
Columbus, IN 47201
812-378-4289
Fax: 812-378-3299

This stately inn begins your architectural tour of Columbus

Innkeeper: Paul Staublin. **Accommodations:** 29 rooms, 5 suites, all with private bath. **Rates:** Rooms $83 single, $93 double; suites $115–$225 single, $125–$225 double. **Included:** Full breakfast. **Minimum stay:** No. **Added:** 10% tax. **Payment:** Major credit cards. **Children:** Yes. **Pets:** No. **Smoking:** Yes. **Open:** Year-round.

Built in 1895, this stately Romanesque Revival building on the corner of Fifth and Franklin was once the hub of activity in Columbus. In addition to public offices, over the years it housed a dance hall, a market house, and an auditorium that staged everything from basketball games to poultry shows.

It is now the Columbus Inn, which has been so meticulously restored that, from the outside, it looks virtually the same as it did a century ago. It's one of many historic sites in the Indiana town that proclaims itself "the architectural showplace of America."

A monumental reception area and ten guest rooms with high ceilings occupy the first floor. The lobby features engraved tin ceilings, hand-carved oak woodwork, terra cotta flooring, brass chandeliers, clawfoot mahogany banquet tables, and a pair of Eastlake Victorian love seats.

The former Grand Hall, with 22-foot ceilings and tall arched windows, has

> **Accessibility from Cincinnati, Louisville, and Indianapolis makes the inn a natural stop for business travelers. It has a variety of meeting rooms, and the guest rooms offer such niceties as leather-topped writing desks and telephones.**

made way for two levels of guest rooms upstairs, but the windows remain. As a result, the second-floor rooms enjoy windows that reach to the ceiling, and rooms on the third-floor have windows beginning at floor level and grandly scaled tin ceilings. The rooms are decorated comfortably and attractively, with cherry sleigh beds from France.

Most spectacular is the Charles Sparrell Suite, named for the building's architect. The 1,200-foot duplex has two and a half baths and a loft bedroom, as well as a first-level bedroom entered through mirrored French doors off a Victorian parlor.

An informal atmosphere pervades the lower level, where breakfast is served in a dining area papered in a William Morris print. The meal begins with fresh fruit and juice and includes a variety of breads, pastries, bread pudding, and scrambled egg casseroles with meat, cheese, or vegetables. At the elegant high tea, served daily at 4:00 P.M., Paul Staublin serves tea flown in fresh from Sri Lanka.

The architecture of Columbus ranges from gingerbread Victorian to midcentury modern. After World War II, the town commissioned public buildings and sculptures by famous people such as Eliel Saarinen and Henry Moore. You can get a taste of the neighborhood via the horse-drawn carriage that pulls right up to the inn's front door, or arrange for a more detailed tour at the visitors' center across the street.

GREENCASTLE

Seminary Place

210 East Seminary Street
Greencastle, IN 46135
317-653-3177
317-653-9277

> *An elegant stay on the edge of DePauw University*

Proprietor: Mary Tesmer. **Accommodations:** 4 rooms, all with private bath. **Rates:** $65–$115 single, $75–$115 double. **Included:** Continental breakfast. **Minimum stay:** Two nights on graduation weekend. **Added:** 5% tax. **Payment:** MasterCard, Visa. **Children:** Yes. **Pets:** No. **Smoking:** No. **Open:** Year-round.

At first the rates may appear a bit steep for this tiny Victorian bed-and-breakfast on the edge of the DePauw University campus. But when you see Seminary Place and the passion that Mary Tesmer has poured into it, a visit will seem quite a bargain.

> **Elegant Victorian antiques, original oil paintings, and prints decorate the guest rooms. Mary has put up reams of Mario Buatta wallpaper with elaborate bird and flower designs, and added marble to many of the bathrooms.**

Mary opened the 1887 Queen Anne home to guests in 1991. Her decoration begins downstairs in the formal parlor, virtually overflowing with a vast museum-quality collection of antique musical instruments. There are Swiss music boxes, Edison phonographs, an accordion, a grand piano, and a rare Cobb organ, so called because it plays metal cylinders resembling corncobs. Persian rugs complement the quarter-sawn oak flooring with oak parquet borders.

Breakfast, served in the adjoining dining room, includes homemade breads, muffins, coffee cakes, and heaping bowls of fresh fruit in season.

The suite boasts an antique crystal chandelier, a Duncan Phyfe sofa, a hand-carved writing desk, and a pewter and brass bed dating from the 1860s. The Pine Room has a more masculine theme, with twin brass beds, a whirlpool bath, and an exquisite black marble bathroom.

On the third floor, the Gables is the most requested and romantic room. It has a whirlpool for two set in marble beneath a dormer window, a massive Queen Victoria Mansion bed from the 1880s, intricately hand-carved mahogany settees, and a roseback rocker. A television is tucked into the armoire, along with a VCR and dozens of classic films on tape.

What is most impressive about Seminary Place are the personal touches. Against the advice of her accountant, Mary turned a potential guest room upstairs into a wicker-filled common area so that guests wouldn't feel confined to their rooms. She also created a kitchen area here, with complimentary coffee, tea, and popcorn always available. In each room, a tiny ironing board pulls down from the wall. All these and other details are bringing Mary a well-deserved following.

Walden Inn

2 Seminary Square
P.O. Box 490
Greencastle, IN 46135
317-653-2761
Fax: 317-653-4833

Small-hotel amenities and a cultured New England feel

Innkeeper: Matthew O'Neill. **Accommodations:** 50 rooms, 5 suites. **Rates:** Rooms $70 single, $80 double; suites $118–$125; packages available. **Included:** All meals available. **Minimum stay:** 2 nights on special weekends. **Added:** 5% tax. **Payment:** Major credit cards. **Children:** Yes. **Pets:** No. **Smoking:** Yes. **Open:** Year-round.

The Walden Inn, with its simple brick construction and wraparound verandah, was built in 1986 but looks much older. It seeks to combine the charm of a New England country inn with the amenities of a European hotel, and for the most part it succeeds.

A friendly desk and turndown and room service are provided primarily by university students, though the nattily dressed innkeeper, Matt O'Neill, also makes his presence felt. The inn is named for Henry David Thoreau's most famous book, though many rooms commemorate the lives of Hoosier natives, from James Whitcomb Riley and Cole Porter to Eli Lilly, who opened Greencastle's first pharmacy.

> **The guest rooms offer niceties you won't find in a big hotel. Much of the furniture was made by Amish craftsmen from Ohio, in cherry, golden pine, and light oak. Some rooms have fireplaces. Local craftspeople created the quilts, dolls, and baskets for sale in the common areas.**

O'Neill, who was born in Dublin, also serves as the chef, offering American regional cuisine in the Different Drummer Restaurant. Using locally grown ingredients, his menu may include loin of lamb grilled with herbs and topped with a lingonberry, black currant, and orange sauce. Fresh banana nut, strawberry, peach, or cherry breads are also served.

A friendly lounge frequented by guests and residents alike is called the Fluttering Duck. Photos here and in the hallways depict vintage Greencastle and DePauw scenes.

Because the inn sits on the edge of the university, guests can enjoy the cultural events and athletic facilities on campus. Golf is also available at the nearby Windy Hill Country Club. Don't expect to find much going on in downtown Greencastle, however. It closes up tight by early evening.

HAGERSTOWN

Teetor House

300 West Main Street
Hagerstown, IN 47346
317-489-4422
800-824-4319

*A mix of history
and understated
elegance*

Innkeepers: Jack and Joanne War-
mouth. **Accommodations:** 4 rooms,
all with private bath. **Rates:** $70–$85 single, $75–$90 double.
Included: Full breakfast. **Minimum stay:** No. **Added:** 10% tax.
Payment: Visa, MasterCard. **Children:** Yes. **Pets:** No. **Smoking:** No. **Open:** Year-round.

Ralph Teetor may not be a household name, but many of the
items he patented certainly qualify. The Indiana inventor is
responsible for the folding fishing rod, the common door
latch, the motorized lawnmower, and automobile cruise control. Add to this the fact that Teetor was blind from the age of
five, and you have a true American success story.

He's also responsible for building a home that now ranks
among the state's most pleasant stays. The home belongs to
the inventor's niece, who has passed the day-to-day operations to innkeepers who have worked for the family for most
of their lives.

The four guest rooms are extremely well-equipped. There
are king-size beds in three of them. Another has two twin
beds. All bathrooms are tiled, but the one in room 1 is the
biggest and best, with a sea of yellow and white. One of several nice touches here is a glass of cold water left at the turndown service.

This will be welcome after a night at Welliver's Smorgasbord, a buffet-style feast famous for shrimp, in downtown Hagerstown. Lines regularly stretch down the block on weekends. Antiques stores on either side of the restaurant keep late hours, while Abbott's Candies offers gooey caramels. Ask the innkeepers to tell you the story of Tedco, the educational game and toy company that the Teetor family still oversees. Sample toys (like the always-popular gyroscope) can be enjoyed in one of the drawing rooms.

> **The home itself has changed little since Teetor and his wife passed away in the early 1980s.**
> **The grandfather clock still chimes on the hour, and the Steinway grand player piano still beckons in the parlor.**

Breakfast, ordered from a menu, is enjoyed on white-clothed tables in the dining room downstairs. The room overlooks the sweeping grounds, where you might see deer passing through.

Don't miss the tour of the downstairs work room, accessed by a secret door off of the reception area. Here is the workshop where Ralph Teetor created his inventions. You'll see prototypes of cruise control (which he patented as "the Speed-o-Stat") and others that didn't quite work out. You'll see pictures of the inventor with Henry Ford, Lowell Thomas, and Wendell Wilkie, all former guests at the Teetor house.

INDIANAPOLIS

The Canterbury Hotel

123 South Illinois
Indianapolis, IN 46225
317-634-3000
800-538-8186
Fax: 317-685-2519
Reservations: 800-323-7500

> *A small luxury hotel carrying on English traditions*

General manager: Letitia Moscrip. **Accommodations:** 84 rooms, 15 suites. **Rates:** Rooms $105–$175 single, $145–$200 double; suites $175–$250 single or double; packages available. **Included:** Continental breakfast; all meals available. **Minimum stay:** No. **Added:** 10% tax. **Payment:** Major credit cards. **Children:** Yes. **Pets:** With prior approval. **Smoking:** Nonsmoking rooms available. **Open:** Year-round.

Opened as the Lockerbie in 1928, this grand old hotel was refurbished in 1984, with the duke of Canterbury himself attending the opening. The English tradition of high tea is still practiced here from four to six in the afternoon, with scones, finger sandwiches, and elegant desserts served.

Small and luxurious, the hotel offers limousine, concierge, and 24-hour room service, weekday dry cleaning, and valet parking. There are no health facilities or pool on the property, but guests have access to two nearby clubs. Four conference rooms can serve up to 80 people.

Beaulieu, the hotel's restaurant, features salmon and lamb among the nightly specials. A newspaper accompanies the Continental breakfast each morning.

The spacious rooms have Chippendale furnishings and king- and queen-size beds. Two of the elegant Parlor Suites have whirlpool baths and marble-lined sinks. The downstairs lobby has dark green carpeting and is accented by brass fixtures and hunting prints.

The usually splendid city views are currently obscured by noisy construction on a shopping center next door. But when the work is complete in 1994, the hotel will be linked directly to its excellent restaurants and shops.

Holiday Inn at Union Station

P.O. Box 2186
123 West Louisiana Street
Indianapolis, IN 46206
317-631-2221
Fax: 317-236-7474
Reservations: 800-HOLIDAY

*Spend the night
on board a
vintage train*

Managing director: Bill Townsend. **Accommodations:** 243 rooms, 33 suites. **Rates:** Rooms $95–$98 single (add $10 per additional person); suites $154–$184 per room; train rooms $124 single, $134 double; packages available. **Included:** All meals available. **Minimum stay:** No. **Added:** 10% tax. **Pay-**

ment: Major credit cards. **Children:** Yes. **Pets:** No. **Smoking:** Nonsmoking rooms available. **Open:** Year-round.

It's quite a surprise to find yourself sleeping in an authentic, beautifully decorated Pullman car in a historic railroad station. But to realize that the fantasy has been pulled off by Holiday Inn, king of the cookie-cutter chain hotel — that's astounding.

> **Thomas Edison was once employed at Union Station as a telegraph operator, and Abraham Lincoln was known to travel these rails frequently.**

During the renovation of Union Station in 1989, 13 original 1920s Pullman sleepers were acquired to create 26 special guest accommodations. Brass, cherrywood, and marble were added to the rooms, which were named after personalities from the early part of the century. Sexy Jean Harlow mixes pink and green foil wallpaper with zebra-skin accents. Amelia Earhart gives the feeling of an early airplane cabin, with exposed mahogany and forest green touches. Paraphernalia relating to the celebrities include a *New York Times* article announcing Earhart's disappearance, a framed Louis Armstrong recording, and a showcard advertising a new film with Rudolph Valentino.

Cozy sitting areas resemble old-fashioned parlors, blending sofas and chairs with antique tables, lighting fixtures, wooden blinds, elaborate draperies, and lace curtains. Some say the rooms are so well decorated that they no longer have the utilitarian feeling of the old sleepers. But with the long, thin layout and the muffled rumblings of the active train station overhead, the illusion comes across loud and clear.

Another novelty room, the blue and white Indianapolis Colts Suite, has big-screen television, football helmet–shaped chairs, and a transparent table marked with yard lines. Although it can accommodate up to 30 fans, it's pretty tacky and only helps you appreciate the care that has gone into decorating the rooms.

The hotel also has standard guest rooms and suites. The modern glass elevator, plant-filled atriums, and indoor pool and sauna blend attractively with the exposed steel girders of the old station.

The rest of the renovated station is worth exploring. Built in 1853, this was the first Union Station in the country. In

1888, the original structure was replaced by a brick Romanesque Revival headhouse, where 200 passenger trains steamed through daily. Today, the station is a shopping, dining, and entertainment facility. Most weekend packages feature a carriage ride, which takes you on a scenic tour of downtown Indianapolis.

MARSHALL

Turkey Run Inn

Rural Route 1, Box 444
Marshall, IN 47859
317-597-2211
Fax: 317-597-2660

> *Modern amenities in a state park setting*

Manager: Phyllis Snodgrass. **Accommodations:** 52 lodge rooms, 9 suites, 21 cabins, 1 family cabin. **Rates:** Lodge/cabin rooms $47.30–$51.70 weekdays, $50.60–$57.20 weekends; suites and family cabin $59.85 weekdays, $65.10 Friday and Saturday. **Minimum stay:** No. **Included:** Tax. **Payment:** Major credit cards. **Children:** Yes. **Pets:** No. **Smoking:** Nonsmoking rooms available. **Open:** Year-round.

Turkey Run State Park was established in 1916 and today preserves virgin stands of sycamore, tulip poplar, and black walnut trees on 2,182 acres. Its name came from the early residents, who remembered thousands of wild turkeys congregating in great flocks under the natural protection of the area's overhanging cliffs.

The latest renovation of the Turkey Run Inn includes the addition of an indoor pool, an elevator, and nine suites on the third floor. Most of the rustic charm has been decorated out of the standard lodge rooms, but the pastel-papered suites offer queen-size beds and refrigerators tucked under sinks in modern bathrooms. One even boasts a whirlpool tub. The cabin rooms have paneling instead of wallpaper but offer the same amenities as the main lodge rooms.

The 150-seat dining room has brick-lined walls and pegged wood floors. The Sunday buffet includes hefty portions of ham, roast beef, chicken, and fish. With mashed potatoes, gravy, stewed tomatoes, and dessert included in the $8 tariff, dinner here is a steal.

More than 14 miles of extraordinary hiking trails reveal ancient sandstone gorges, canyons, and stream beds. The Turkey Run nature center puts it all in perspective, offering a wildlife observation room, a children's corner, and hikes led by naturalists on the property.

MITCHELL

Spring Mill Inn

P.O. Box 68
Mitchell, IN 47446
812-849-4081
Fax: 812-849-4647

> *This updated state park lodge also caters to business travelers*

General manager: Wilhelmina Robison. **Accommodations:** 75 rooms. **Rates:** $39–$45. **Included:** All meals available. **Minimum stay:** No. **Added:** 6% tax. **Payment:** Major credit cards. **Children:** Yes. **Pets:** No. **Smoking:** Nonsmoking rooms available. **Open:** Year-round.

Spring Mill State Park, established in 1927 in the heart of Indiana's limestone country, doesn't just attract families. With 4,000 feet of meeting space, including the Lake View Room with vaulted ceilings and glass panels, it also caters to business travelers.

The main lodge rooms, opened in 1934, are comfortable and clean, with small desks and televisions tucked into armoires. Wildlife prints by William Zimmerman lend an artistic touch. Children enjoy the well-equipped game room downstairs, with a jukebox, pinball machines, air hockey, and even a popcorn popper. There is also an indoor pool.

A variety of activities and historic sites are on the property. A massive gristmill, powered by water from the nearby Hamer cave, is the focal point of the reconstructed pioneer village. Also here is a memorial to astronaut and Mitchell native Virgil I. "Gus" Grissom, with his space suit, capsule, and a montage of photographs on display.

The Spring Mill Inn restaurant is especially popular, with a simple country menu of fish, chicken, and steak. On the side, try cornmeal pie, with ingredients ground in the pioneer village. The persimmon pudding is created by a resident who harvests fruit from the persimmon trees native to the area.

> **A naturalist is on duty year-round to lead tours through caves and along trails.**

The park has two major cave systems, and the waters from both drain into the 30-acre Spring Mill Lake. A nature center has live snake and turtle displays and a bird-feeding area.

NASHVILLE

Abe Martin Lodge

P.O. Box 547
Nashville, IN 47448
812-988-4418
812-988-7316
Fax: 812-988-7334

> *Native stone and timbers create a country feel*

General manager: Andy Rogers.
Accommodations: 84 lodge rooms, 76 cabin rooms. **Rates:** Lodge rooms $42–$45, cabin rooms $36–$67. **Minimum stay:** 2 nights on weekends. **Added:** 7% tax. **Payment:** Major credit cards. **Children:** Yes. **Pets:** No. **Smoking:** Nonsmoking rooms available. **Open:** Year-round.

In 1905, comic strip character Abe Martin announced, "I'm goin' ter move ter Brown County temerrew." For more than two decades, loyal readers across the country followed the exploits of this earthy folk hero and his family. When it came time to unveil the Brown County State Park's lodge in 1932, the name seemed a shoo-in.

A portrait of Martin's creator, Kin Hubbard, hangs over the fireplace in the gathering room, and the 56 family cabins on Skunk Ridge bear names like Gabe Craw, Stew Nugent, and Emma Moots after characters from the comic strip. These units are open from April through November, while 20 newer housekeeping cabins, with arched ceilings, wood floors, and full kitchens, welcome guests year-round. Fireplaces serve as the centerpieces of the main rooms, and decks overlook the woods.

Constructed of hand-hewn native stone and oak timbers cut in the park, the main lodge has a sitting room with a cathedral ceiling on the second floor. The dining room is broken up into smaller rooms, one with a fireplace. The dinner buffet is especially popular, serving meat and fish entrées and a variety of vegetables. Thirty exceptionally clean guest accommodations are here, decorated in motel style with carpeting, air conditioning, televisions, and modern bathrooms.

> **This is Indiana's largest state park, more than 15,000 acres, with 49 miles of bridle trails (horses are available for rent) and more than 12 miles of hiking paths through the steep, forested hills.**

The park offers a swimming pool, playground equipment, fishing on two lakes, and a country store for picnic supplies and souvenirs. Nature programs are held daily, perhaps including a Scrutinizing the Spiders talk or a Ferns and Their Allies walk. From a pair of lookout towers, you can survey the hills and valleys of Brown County.

The Allison House Inn

90 South Jefferson Street
P.O. Box 1625
Nashville, IN 47448
812-988-0814

> *Antique-hunters
> will love Tammy
> Galm's stories*

Innkeeper: Tammy Galm. **Accommodations:** 5 rooms, all with private bath. **Rates:** $85 single or double. **Included:** Continental breakfast. **Minimum stay:** 2 nights. **Added:** 10% tax. **Payment:** No credit cards. **Children:** Over 12 years. **Pets:** No. **Smoking:** No. **Open:** Year-round.

Tammy Galm loves to tell stories over breakfast, especially success stories about guests who come to Nashville for the antiques and crafts hunting, the main attraction in the tiny town. One guest's station wagon was so full, she remembers, that the passengers couldn't wave good-bye. They actually held dining chairs upside down on their laps and strapped a table to the roof.

Tammy understands the appeal. The brown cedar-paneled storefronts of Nashville attracted her in 1985, when she and Bob, a real estate agent, gutted the 1883 yellow frame house and renovated it as a bed-and-breakfast inn. Today, the Allison House looks no different from the other homes on the quiet, tree-lined street, just two blocks from the shops, restaurants, and community theater. Inside, a professional check-in counter blends comfortably with the warm glow of the adjoining sitting room's fireplace.

The guest rooms upstairs are small and brightly decorated

with country accents. Bird prints by the artist Bill Zimmerman, a family friend, inspired the decor. The Eagle features a pair of iron-rail beds, a handmade quilt, and local country crafts. The Cardinal, with its treetop view, plays off the red and blue hues in the Oriental rug. And while the Moor Hen has an authentic World War I field desk, the decoration focuses on clean reproduction furniture instead of antiques.

> **Tammy knows bargain hunters who check prices at all the shops, chalk-marking the sidewalk in front of good ones so that later they can remember where to return.**

Sitting at a round oak table beneath a bay window, you'll soon realize that Tammy serves more than just stories for breakfast. She starts by pouring a cup of coffee. Next come local strawberries and fresh baked goods. Her sticky caramel-nut rolls, a house specialty, almost always leave sweet tooths asking for seconds.

Brown County Inn

Highways 46 and 135
Box 128
Nashville, IN 47448
812-988-2291
800-772-5249

> *A rustic family inn in the country*

General manager: Marilyn Fulton. **Accommodations:** 97 rooms, 2 suites. **Rates:** Rooms $48–$97 single or double; suites $58–$122; packages available. **Included:** All meals available. **Minimum stay:** 2 nights on weekends April–November. **Added:** 10% tax. **Payment:** Major credit cards. **Children:** Free in parent's room. **Pets:** No. **Smoking:** Nonsmoking rooms available. **Open:** Year-round.

The rustic wood exterior of the Brown County Inn fits seamlessly with the surrounding southern Indiana countryside. Adults enjoy staying here because of its proximity to the arts and crafts community of Nashville, with more than 300 shops and galleries.

Children can also have a good time here. A miniature golf

course and a large, enclosed swimming pool are for their enjoyment, along with tennis, basketball, and volleyball courts and a playground for small fry. There is a video room at the inn and a video arcade across the street. Brown County State Park is also nearby.

> **A shuttle train called the Little National Express stops in front of the inn and takes guests on a 20-minute tour of the area.**

The motel-style guest rooms have country touches, like rough wood walls and old-fashioned rocking chairs, and modern amenities like free in-room movies, direct-dial telephones, and king- or queen-size beds. All the second-floor rooms have private balconies. The Red Cedar Suite caters to small meetings, and downstairs facilities hold groups of up to 350.

The Harvest restaurant, decorated with antique farm implements, serves a varied menu of roast pork, catfish, barbecued beef ribs, and country fried chicken. Saturdays from June through August, an all-you-can-eat pig roast is held on the poolside patio, complete with live bluegrass music. Children can swim or play miniature golf while the food is prepared. Live music is also featured in the Corn Crib Lounge on weekends.

NEW HARMONY

The New Harmony Inn

504 North Street
New Harmony, IN 47631
812-682-4491
800-782-8605
Fax: 812-682-4491, ext. 329

> *Spiritual-minded
> guests flock to
> New Harmony*

Manager: Nancy McIntire. **Accommodations:** 90 rooms, 4 houses. **Rates:** $50 single, $60 double in winter; $65 single, $75 double in summer; houses $100–$150. **Included:** All meals available. **Minimum stay:** No. **Added:** 5% tax. **Payment:** Major credit cards. **Children:** Yes. **Pets:** No. **Smoking:** Yes. **Open:** Year-round.

New Harmony was founded by the Harmonist followers of George Rapp in 1843 as an experimental Utopian colony. Though the idea failed, the town remains an enclave for the spiritual-minded. For more than 30 years, diners have been making a pilgrimage to the Red Geranium Restaurant for its regional and Continental fare, and its success led to the opening of the New Harmony Inn in 1974.

The Red Geranium, open Tuesdays through Sundays for lunch and dinner, offers distinctive dining rooms. One has a wall of windows, while the Garden Room boasts colorful painted ceilings. The Shaker lemon pie is a favorite dessert. The bounty of the wine cellar can be enjoyed with your meal or at the Grapevine Bar. The newer Bayou Grill has its own flavor. It offers an appropriately spicy Bayou chicken and a number of vegetarian dishes on its health-conscious menu.

The inn's main building has a check-in desk and common rooms connected to a small chapel. Wood chairs sit comfortably on the poplar floors. The property includes a glass-enclosed swimming pool with a private pond beyond.

> **The understated luxury found at New Harmony Inn sometimes defies explanation, but it can be easily said that this should top any list of places to visit in the Midwest.**

Except for a few antiques shops and a bookstore, the inn and its restaurant dominate the small town. There are historic home tours and presentations that give you a sense of the old New Harmony. One of the main attractions is the Roofless Church, whose builders believed that only one roof — the sky — could embrace all of worshiping humanity.

From the outside, the lodgings look like dormitories, but plain does not mean uncomfortable. A standard room has Shaker furniture, a television, a small desk, and a firm mattress with cotton sheets. Scatter rugs cover wood floors in the older rooms; newer models offer carpeting. Eighteen rooms boast fireplaces, three have kitchenettes, and four have sleeping lofts. Many have lovely views of the surrounding grounds. The lofts have spiral staircases that wind to spacious sitting rooms. Original prints and paintings can be found throughout the complex. Even the ice bucket looks like a bird feeder.

A handful of nearby houses furnished with antiques are also available, including one from 1840 that has a living room with a fireplace and a spacious backyard. A small brick shed in the back has been converted into a cozy sitting area.

Flower beds filled with perennials, annuals, and vegetables can be found throughout the property, with much of the flora labeled for guests. You may also see Jane Owen, who founded the inn and restaurant, zip by in a golf cart. Her eyes shaded by a floppy sun hat, she makes it her business to tend the gardens and artwork.

The inn welcomes corporate seminars in its 300-seat conference center, where art pieces combine religious imagery with war protest. Most unusual is a light sculpture, with shadow images depicting a figure with outstretched arms.

STORY

Story Inn

State Road 135 South
P.O. Box 64
Story, IN 47448
812-988-2273

> *Elegant cuisine
> in an old
> general store*

Innkeepers: Cyndi and Benjamin Schultz. **Accommodations:** Five rooms, 3 cottages with 2 units each. **Rates:** Rooms $55–$65 single, $65–$75 double; cottages $75 single, $85 double. **Included:** Full breakfast; dinner available. **Minimum stay:** 2 nights on weekends September 15–November 15. **Added:** 8% tax. **Payment:** Discover, MasterCard, Visa. **Children:** Only in cottages. **Pets:** Only in cottages. **Smoking:** Only on porches. **Open:** Year-round.

Talk about the Story Inn begins with the food, which diners from Indianapolis regularly drive an hour to sample. Pasta sauce Raphael. Rum cherry pork. Poulet printemps. Five-spice sea treasure. Swordfish pepperonata. Pretty fancy dishes for a place at which most people hesitate to even stop.

In an old general store, the inn is one of the few occupied buildings in this virtual ghost town. The exterior blends with the rugged surroundings. The tin roof has been left to rust, and old porcelain stoves and gasoline pumps squat on the front porch. According to Cyndi Schultz, Studebaker buggy chassis were once assembled on the second floor. Look hard and you may find some lurking about the property.

Another Story waits inside, however, where the rustic decor both contrasts and blends perfectly with elegant cuisine in the 75-seat restaurant. Stained glass church windows cast an inviting glow from the front door onto small wood tables with crisp white linens and bark-backed chairs. The old store shelves are loaded with lunchboxes, mason jars, farm implements, metal advertising signs, old radios, and even a bottle of worm syrup made by Dr. Story, the town's 19th-century namesake. A pot-bellied stove serves as a centerpiece. You can also eat on the screened porch that seats 20 overlooking the gardens and brook.

> **The Schultzes own the entire town of Story (pop. 8), which primarily consists of the inn, a rundown hammer mill, a doctor's office, and a schoolhouse. Cyndi has no aspirations to be mayor, but she sometimes wishes she could hand out speeding tickets.**

For dinner, try one of the fresh fish or pasta dishes, or enjoy both in Cyndi's seafood lasagna. She often uses herbs, vegetables, and fruit from the inn's extensive gardens. Nearby farmers supply additional produce and fresh eggs. Turtle cheesecake is a popular dessert. Entrées range from $15 to $20 and include soup or salad, two vegetables, and homemade bread.

The rooms upstairs and in the cottages also feature antique furnishings. The Olive Room, decorated in olive green accents, has a cherry four-poster, art nouveau wing chairs, and silk-shaded lamps. The Poplar Room has poplar wainscoting, floral wallpaper, and an etching of a medieval wedding scene. All the rooms have air conditioning, original artwork, and fresh flowers.

A full breakfast here can be ordered from the menu, which includes griddle cakes with maple syrup, biscuits and gravy, fresh fruit platters, and granola.

Monthly mystery weekends are popular here. Cyndi chuckles at one of the mystery titles: "Where There's a Will, There's Relatives."

After exploring Story, take the winding 14-mile drive to Nashville, Indiana, with its antiques and crafts shops. The inn is on the edge of the Brown County State Park, so deer, blue herons, quail, wild turkeys, and gray and red foxes are commonly spotted on the property.

TERRE HAUTE

Larry Bird's Boston Connection

555 South Third Street
P.O. Box 8386
Terre Haute, IN 47808
812-235-3333
800-255-3399 in Indiana
800-262-0033 elsewhere
Fax: 812-232-9563

> *A family hotel
> packed with
> basketball
> memorabilia*

General manager: Rick Lundstorm. **Accommodations:** 92 rooms, 3 suites. **Rates:** Rooms $55–$65 single, $60–$70 double; suites $105–$150 per room. **Included:** Continental breakfast on weekdays; all meals available. **Minimum stay:** No. **Added:** 7% tax. **Payment:** Major credit cards. **Children:** Under 19, free in room with parent. **Pets:** No. **Smoking:** Nonsmoking rooms available. **Open:** Year-round.

In parts of Indiana, Larry Bird commands the same adoration that Elvis does in Memphis. It's not surprising, then, that Terre Haute should have a hotel called Larry Bird's Boston Connection, owned by Bird and packed with memorabilia from his college and professional basketball career.

A life-size standing picture of Bird greets you in the lobby, where an attentive and friendly staff waits to check you in. This former Sheraton Hotel was purchased in 1987 by the NBA great, who has added his own personal touches. Photographs and magazine covers now line the walls. Some are pretty wild, such as a shot of Bird and Dr. J. with their hands wrapped around each other's throats. There are autographed pictures of other celebrities — Bill Murray, Ricky Skaggs, Orville Reddenbacher — who have stayed here.

The four floors of the hotel are decorated in different color schemes, all representing colleges or basketball teams. Green and white highlight the Boston Celtics floor. Others pay tribute to Indiana State University, Rose-Hulman Institute of Technology, and Saint Mary-of-the-Woods.

In comfortable, clean guest rooms, the beds have extra-long mattresses and remote control cable television. As an added touch, some nicer rooms even offer recliner chairs so you can pretend you're at home and fall asleep in front of the television. In others, images of Bird are emblazoned on the shower curtains.

Celtic championship banners, trophies, and uniforms decorate the Boston Garden Family Restaurant, which serves salads, sandwiches, and entrées such as New York strip steaks and filet mignon. The placemats are printed with huge handprints and invite you to "compare your hands with Larry's . . . the best in the NBA."

While they wait for dinner, children can shoot hoops in a glassed-in room. If they sink three in a row, they can claim a certificate with Bird's Xeroxed signature.

The Bird's Nest Sports Lounge has big-screen televisions, modern decor, and a staff dressed like cheerleaders or referees. Tapes of Larry Bird's greatest games are available, and there's live music most weekends. You can watch every Celtics game here in an atmosphere highly conducive to talking sports with other guests. A private MVP lounge and two conference rooms are also available.

Larry Bird's Boston Connection is especially attractive to families. The outdoor pool hops in the summer, with hamburgers and hot dogs served by the pool at lunch.

Iowa

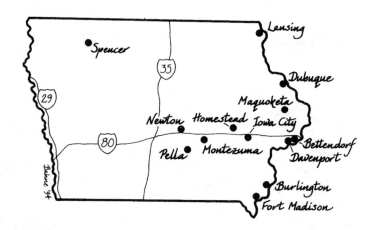

Best Bed and Breakfast Inns

Bettendorf
  The Abbey Hotel
Burlington
  The Mississippi Manor
Davenport
  Bishop's House Inn
  River Oaks Bed and Breakfast
Dubuque
  The Hancock House
  Juniper Hill Farm
  The Redstone Inn
  The Stout House
Iowa City
  Haverkamp's Linn Street Homestay
Lansing
  FitzGerald's Inn
Maquoketa
  Squiers Manor
Montezuma
  English Valley Bed and Breakfast
Spencer
  Hannah Marie Country Inn

Best Full-Service Country Inns

Fort Madison
  Kingsley Inn
Newton
  La Corsette Maison Inn
Pella
  Strawtown Inn

Best Hotel

Bettendorf
  Jumer's Castle Lodge

Best Budget Stay

Homestead
  Die Heimat Country Inn

The advent of Mississippi River gambling has brought new tourism to Iowa. And with it has come an awakening for those who thought the state was all cornfields and flat terrain.

Dubuque, on the eastern side of Iowa, is a great place to begin your tour of the state. The territory opened to white settlement in 1833 and thrived with lead-mining through the turn of the century. The downtown is dramatic, with mansions perched high on bluffs. Visitors can get the bluff's eye-view by taking the Fenelon Place Elevator, the world's shortest, steepest scenic railway. It offers magnificent views of Iowa, Illinois, and Wisconsin.

There are also fine restaurants here, including the Ryan House, an 1873 Victorian home on Locust Street. A special progressive dinner and house tour in the summer allows access to some of the city's most beautiful homes, including the high Victorian Redstone and Stout House inns. Riverboat gambling is a popular pastime year-round, while the Sundown Ski Area attracts winter business.

Just five miles south of Dubuque, on Highway 52, you'll find Crystal Lake Cave. East of Dubuque, a few miles off Highway 20 on 136, Dyersville has a pair of farms used during the filming of *Field of Dreams.* They have become an amazingly popular tourist attraction.

The Quad Cities are five Iowa and Illinois towns that come together on the Mississippi River. **Davenport** is perhaps the most interesting, sporting such attractions as the art deco-style Adler Theatre. The restored Village of East Davenport is a historic retail area dating back to 1851, with 60 shops.

The President dominates the river gambling trade here, offering 27,000-square-feet of gaming tables and slots. More boats are on the way, both for gambling and nongambling cruises. The Arsenal Island tours, which show you how soldiers and prisoners lived during the Civil War, are especially fascinating. Factories established here in 1862 still manufacture defense products. The homesteads of both Buffalo Bill Cody and John Deere are nearby and open for tours.

Due west from the Quad Cities off I-80 lie the Amana Colonies. Started by German settlers seeking religious freedom, the Colonies practiced communal living until 1932. Visitors arrive here today to shop at the German furniture and woolen mills, as well as to enjoy Old World cuisine. Dinner at Bill Zuber's Restaurant is a special treat, offering authentic German dishes and walls lined with baseball memorabilia relating to Zuber's days in the big leagues. There are also nature and biking trails and a golf course nearby.

Iowa City is the home of the thriving University of Iowa and diverse cultural activities. Aside from sports, there is also an art museum on campus with an impressive collection of European and African works. The Riverside and University theatres present live productions year-round while a writers' workshop draws national literary talent for public readings. You'll also see the state's original capitol building, lovingly restored to its Greek Revival glory.

BETTENDORF

The Abbey Hotel

1401 Central Avenue
Bettendorf, IA 52722
319-355-0291
800-438-7535

Once a monastery,
now a B&B

Innkeepers: Joe and Joan Lemon.
Accommodations: 19 rooms, all with private bath. **Rates:** $75–$125 single or double. **Included:** Continental breakfast. **Minimum stay:** No. **Added:** 12% tax. **Payment:** Major credit cards. **Children:** Yes. **Pets:** No. **Smoking:** No. **Open:** Year-round.

With its rooftop crosses and courtyard statuary, the old Romanesque monastery high above the Mississippi River hardly looks like a hotel. Inside, however, the feeling is entirely different. The current owners gutted the inside and, after a million-dollar renovation, opened the Abbey as a small hotel in 1992.

> The preserved Gothic chapel, with its marble altar and stained glass windows, is the site of mass on Sunday morning and of weddings virtually every weekend. The chapel connects to a banquet room that can hold up to 100 guests. A larger banquet facility can handle 225.

The buff-colored brick structure was built between 1914 and 1917 as a cloistered Carmelite monastery known as "Queen of Heaven." Once a young woman entered, she was never supposed to leave or even look at the face of an outsider, except through a metal screen covered by a black cloth. When the Sisters moved in 1975, Franciscan brothers arrived shortly after, turning it into a retreat house and opening its doors for banquets and tours. One local woman, who used to visit during Christmas, remembers the decor was dark and oppressive.

The reception area is now bright and sunny, with white painted walls and classy striped chairs and couches. The original nuns' cells have been joined to create the spacious rooms, which feature queen- or king-size beds, Italian marble baths, and wool carpeting, along with the best of modern hotel furnishings. Most rooms feature a view of the Mississippi River and are decorated in peach, mauve, and blue. If you want a taste of the old days, you'll have to venture to the third floor's museum room, which displays original furnishings supplied by the Carmelites.

Guests enjoy the outdoor pool and the grounds. You are also within just a short drive of the other Quad Cities, the Adler Theater and River Center, and the President Riverboat Casino.

Jumer's Castle Lodge

I-74 at Spruce Hills Drive
Bettendorf, IA 52722-1698
319-359-7141
800-285-8637
Fax: 319-359-7141

*Bavarian touches
grace a
Quad City classic*

General manager: James P. Rix.
Accommodations: 149 rooms, 61 suites. **Rates:** Rooms $75–
$85 single, $82–$92 double; suites $85–$130 single, $92–$137
double; packages available. **Included:** All meals available.
Minimum stay: No. **Added:** 12% tax. **Payment:** Major credit
cards. **Children:** Yes. **Pets:** Yes. **Smoking:** Nonsmoking rooms
available. **Open:** Year-round.

The midwestern chain of five Jumer's Hotels mixes 20th-cen-
tury comfort with a Bavarian-style setting. Its only Iowa location, in Bettendorf, carries this off beautifully with tapestries,
dark woods, porcelains, oil paintings, and European antiques.
Classical music is piped
into the reception area,
next to a sitting room
with exposed brick walls,
deep-toned carpeting, and
carved wood chairs.

**Jumer's offers a number of
appealing packages that
include trips to the gaming
tables on its riverboat,
the *Rock Island Casino*.**

The guest rooms offer
varied accommodations.
Fireplace Rooms are fur-
nished with four-poster
beds and gas fireplaces beneath ornate, carved mantels. Some
give you the feeling of sleeping in a private library, with anti-
quarian books lining a full wall. In a two-level Tower Loft, a
spiral staircase leads to a king-size bed and half bath. Downstairs is a formal living room with a table and chairs, a queen-
size pullout sofa, and a gas fireplace. There are also rooms
with waterbeds.

Jumer's Restaurant serves hearty German dishes, including
wienerschnitzel, braised lamb shank, and Nürnberger pork
roast. White walls are decorated with mounted animal heads.
The Bavarian theme, which could easily grow tacky, works
wonderfully here.

There is also an indoor pool, along with a sauna and
whirlpool.

BURLINGTON

The Mississippi Manor

809 North Fourth
Burlington, IA 52601
319-753-2218

> *A charming inn near the riverboat casinos*

Manager: Florence Taperow. **Accommodations:** 4 rooms, all with private bath. **Rates:** $60–$85 single, $70–$95 double. **Included:** Full breakfast. **Minimum stay:** No. **Added:** 9% tax. **Payment:** Major credit cards. **Children:** Limited. **Pets:** No. **Smoking:** No. **Open:** Year-round.

The Mississippi Manor is one of several bed-and-breakfast inns appearing in the wake of Iowa's highly successful riverboat gambling. It's also one of the most charming. A yellow brick walk winds in front, complementing the creamy butterscotch exterior of the Italianate home. Originally known as the Simon Wadleigh House, the 1876 mansion has been meticulously renovated, from the elaborate ceiling medallions to the parquet floors in the dining room.

> **The Manor is on a hilly street just a few short blocks from downtown, where you can shop or gamble on the casino cruise ship.**

The Mark Twain is the grandest room, furnished with a soapstone fireplace, four-poster bed, and bold floral wallpaper.

The Becky Thatcher Room has a pickled wood floor, a river view, and a huge bathroom with a clawfoot tub. Huck Finn is the least impressive, with its white linoleum floor and utilitarian handmade bed.

Beneath the sprayed copper, pressed tin ceiling in the kitchen, Florence prepares a full breakfast — "Too full," she says, laughing — that begins with fresh blueberry muffins. An egg dish may be a frittata, quiche, or casserole. It can be enjoyed in the dining room, on the porch in warmer weather, or in the guest rooms. Florence's breakfast recipes have been passed down for several generations.

The inn provides free transportation from the train station or the airport, just five miles away.

DAVENPORT

Bishop's House Inn

1527 Brady Street
Davenport, IA 52803
319-324-2454

A meticulous restoration of a Bishop's mansion

Innkeeper: Kurt Stevens. **Host:** Mike Naab. **Accommodations:** 4 rooms, 2 suites, all with private bath. **Rates:** Rooms $59–$99 single or double; suites $109–$139 single or double. **Included:** Full breakfast. **Minimum stay:** 2 nights during holiday weekends. **Added:** 10% tax. **Payment:** MasterCard, Visa. **Children:** Yes. **Pets:** No. **Smoking:** Limited. **Open:** Year-round.

The extensive restoration of the Bishop's House Inn has renewed the splendor first enjoyed by the Roman Catholic bishop John Davis, who selected this Italianate mansion as his residence at the turn of the century. The inn's unusual features include decorative ceiling medallions, Italian marble mantelpieces, oak and walnut parquet floors with "starburst" insets, hand-painted and stenciled walls, and a sensual curved staircase.

Upstairs, the Rohlman Chamber is named for the second bishop to occupy the house. It has an Eastlake-style walnut bedroom set, beveled and stained glass windows, and an oak fireplace. The bathroom has an unusual marble shower stall that dates from the 1920s. Highlighted by the deep, rich tones of the Bradbury and Bradbury wallpapers, the Davis Suite boasts a massive oak bedroom set and an 1890 fireplace mantelpiece with decorative spindlework. Despite all the finery, this is a comfortable place, where the feather beds are puffed up to almost a foot high.

> **The Bishop's House Inn is on a busy corner in Davenport, the largest Mississippi River port of call in Iowa. It offers easy access to shops and galleries, riverfront festivals, and nearby colleges.**

A second-floor common room provides a television, a telephone, and a small refrigerator stocked with complimentary soft drinks and ice. Many rooms are accented by a collection of bird prints created by John James Audubon and his contemporaries. The early wall coverings have been retained, some of which give the illusion of masonry.

Breakfast is served on fine china in the dining room. To start, bite-size muffins surround a bowl filled with apple and granola, with yogurt on top. Kurt Stevens's favorite egg entrée uses three different cheeses and is topped with raspberries or blueberries. The water has a twist of lemon. Kurt can also cater luncheons or dinners for business, wedding, and bus tour groups of up to 125 people.

River Oaks Inn Bed and Breakfast

1234 East River Drive
Davenport, IA 52803
319-326-2629
800-352-6016
Fax: 319-324-6920

*Davenport's first
B&B inn*

Innkeepers: Mary Jo and Ron Pohl. **Accommodations:** 5 rooms, all with private bath; 3 carriage house rooms sharing two baths. **Rates:** $55–$95 single or double; carriage house rooms $125–$175. **Included:** Full breakfast. **Minimum stay:** 2 nights some weekends. **Added:** 9% tax. **Payment:** Master-Card, Visa. **Children:** Yes. **Pets:** No. **Smoking:** Restricted. **Open:** Year-round.

Perched on a hill overlooking the Mississippi, River Oaks was the first bed-and-breakfast inn in the Davenport area. The Pohls are only the third owners of the 1850s home, which combines bits of Italianate, Victorian, and Prairie architecture in a satisfying mélange. The tricolored exterior paint, which earned the inn a historic preservation award, also extends to the ornate gazebo on the front lawn.

The Victorian touches are found mostly in the Abner Davison Room, named for the original owner, which has twin beds and a bay window view. The River View Suite has a king-size bed, sun porch, and dressing room. The Fulton Room has rosy pink wallpaper and a brass and iron bed.

Downstairs, the huge Greek columns in the living room evoke a more formal feel. The Pohls defuse this by offering guests hot or iced tea, coffee, or lemonade upon arrival.

There's also a second-floor refrigerator stocked with soda.

The Pohls have recently opened their three-bedroom carriage house to overnight guests. The great room is actually a glass-enclosed sun porch with a splendid view of the Mississippi River. The guest rooms are decorated in simple country style, with plenty of oak and maple details. The largest of two bathrooms has a clawfoot tub and a marble shower; a hot tub is available only to carriage house occupants. There is a full kitchen here, and guests usually opt to have their breakfast left in the refrigerator the night before.

> You won't go away hungry from Mary Jo's generous breakfast, with eggs, bacon or sausage, potatoes, and a basket of toast with jam.

DUBUQUE

The Hancock House

1105 Grove Terrace
Dubuque, IA 52001
319-557-8989

> *A homey inn on millionaire's row*

Owners/innkeepers: Jim and Julie Gross. **Accommodations:** 5 rooms, 2 suites, all with private bath. **Rates:** Rooms $75 single or double; suites $125–$150. **Included:** Full breakfast. **Minimum**

stay: 2 nights April–October. **Added:** 9% tax. **Payment:** Discover, MasterCard, Visa. **Children:** Yes. **Pets:** No. **Smoking:** No. **Open:** Year-round.

Weekday breakfast at the Hancock House can seem like a family affair, for the regular clientele, mostly company men on business in Dubuque, are comfortable here. It's easy to feel at home.

Unlike the Redstone Inn and Stout House just down the hill, which are owned by a corporation, the Hancock House offers a true bed-and-breakfast experience amid an unusual assemblage of artifacts collected by the innkeepers, Jim and Julie Gross.

> From downtown Dubuque, you may wonder how on earth you're going to get up to the cliffs where Hancock House sits among other elegant Victorians.

With its combination of service, decor, and location on bluffs overlooking the city, this may well be Iowa's most outstanding contribution to bed-and-breakfast.

Not that long ago, these mansions served as low-income apartment buildings, and, according to Jim, a motorcycle gang regularly roared through the downstairs on their bikes. Miraculously, many of the original features are intact, such as the gingerbread-trimmed carved cherry fireplace mantel, which won a blue ribbon at the 1893 World's Fair. The dining room has a charming mural of a city scene, painted on oatmeal paper.

Jim and Julie seek out the unusual when they decorate. They love to demonstrate the railroad car washstand in the Train Room, which also features antique Lionels on shelves near the ceilings. Jim, a realtor, also owns an impressive collection of antique stained glass. Unfortunately, only a fraction of his pieces fit the home's 89 windows, so some pieces are suspended in front of clear glass.

In one of the inn's most decadent touches, the Doll's Room has a Jacuzzi tucked into the third-floor tower. Even the smallest room has a queen-size bed. Telescopes or binoculars have been placed in the rooms on the front of the house to enhance the spectacular views. There is no television here, though many rooms have cathedral-shaped radios.

Guests feel equally comfortable downstairs, where the player piano has a collection of much-used rolls. There is also a kitchen area off the dining room with popcorn, cookies, and a refrigerator stocked with soft drinks. Ask Jim or Julie to point you to the stairs in front of the house that lead downtown. You are just a few blocks from shops and restaurants.

Juniper Hill Farm

15325 Budd Road
Dubuque, IA 52002
319-582-4405
800-572-1449

Hike or ski right out the door of this country B&B

Innkeepers: Ruth and Bill McEllhiney. **Accommodations:** 3 rooms, all with private bath. **Rates:** $70–$140 single or double. **Included:** Full breakfast. **Minimum stay:** 2 nights on weekends. **Added:** 6% tax. **Payment:** Discover, MasterCard, Visa. **Children:** Yes. **Pets:** No. **Smoking:** In TV room only. **Open:** Year-round.

Overlooking a 28-mile valley and surrounded by hills, woods, and nature trails, Juniper Hill Farm is breathtaking in any season. Guests come in winter, however, to test the slopes of the Sundown Ski Area, which is owned in part by Ruth and Bill McEllhiney. The inn's 40 sloping acres are perfect for hikers and cross-country skiers.

> **Skiers especially enjoy the new eight-person hot tub on the deck, with its own knockout view of the valley.**

The guest suites are furnished and decorated in a modern country style, with handmade quilts and crafts. The Valley View Suite, the largest, has two double beds, a sitting area, and a bathroom skylight. The romantic Garden Suite features white wicker furniture, Mennonite crafts, and a spacious bathroom with a double whirlpool and shower. The king-size bed in the Jonquil Suite can be made into two twin beds if desired.

To add to the country theme, Bill has created a silhouetted farm scene against one wall. Skis are propped in the area between the addition and original house, which was built in 1940. The hearty breakfast is cooked on an old cast-iron stove. Although this was never a working farm, there are plenty of animals, including deer, raccoons, possum, and turkeys, spotted regularly on the property.

Since Juniper Hill is only eight miles northwest of Dubuque, guests can enjoy dinner in the city or test their luck at riverboat gambling. Ask Bill for dinner suggestions.

The Redstone Inn

504 Bluff Street
Dubuque, IA 52001
319-582-1894

> *Showy pillars and conical chimneys say High Victorian*

General manager: Paula Lange. **Accommodations:** 9 rooms, 6 suites, all with private bath. **Rates:** Rooms $75–$98; suites $135–$175; corporate rates available. **Included:** Continental breakfast. **Minimum stay:** No. **Added:** 12% tax. **Payment:** MasterCard, Visa, American Express. **Children:** Yes. **Pets:** No. **Smoking:** Limited. **Open:** Year-round.

A. A. Cooper built this mansion in 1894 as a wedding gift for his daughter Elizabeth. Legend says the wealthy wagon manufacturer was approached by Henry Ford to produce horseless carriages, but Cooper thought the automobile had no future.

A group of Dubuque investors showed better business sense when they purchased the historic mansion and turned it into a small hotel. The red brick exterior, with showy turrets and conical chimneys, definitely says High Victorian. Inside, the first floor has deep oak paneling, and the parlor ceiling features a plaster frieze of frolicking gold leaf cherubs.

Don't expect Victorian luxury throughout, however. The guest rooms comfortably blend modern amenities with Victorian furnishings such as massive carved beds and armoires. Hotel-style televisions, telephones, luggage racks, and rumbling air conditioners intrude somewhat on the atmosphere.

Junior and deluxe suites include whirlpool baths and come with cheese and sausage trays and champagne. Breakfast is served in the sunny dining room downstairs.

The Stout House

1105 Locust Street
Dubuque, IA 52001
319-582-1894

Ornate interiors highlight this distinctive B&B

Innkeeper: Paula Lange. **Accommodations:** 4 rooms, 2 with private bath. **Rates:** Rooms: $69–$148 single or double; corporate rates available. **Included:** Continental breakfast. **Minimum stay:** No. **Added:** 12% tax. **Payment:** MasterCard, Visa, American Express. **Children:** Yes. **Pets:** No. **Smoking:** Limited. **Open:** Year-round.

The same investors who opened the Redstone Inn also renovated this 1890 red sandstone mansion as a bed-and-breakfast inn. Guests check in at the rosewood-paneled reception hall, highlighted by stained glass and a stately grandfather clock. The common rooms downstairs include a library with a gorgeous fireplace flanked by onyx pillars. An ornately carved staircase twists and turns toward the upstairs guest rooms and parlor.

The French Room is the most ornate, with a brass and iron bed, a marble-topped dresser with long mirror, and a framed French tapestry. The somewhat less splendid but private Burgundy Room was added in 1940, during the 75 years when the building was owned by the Archdiocese of Dubuque. Oil paintings of religious scenes still line the halls. Some bathrooms feature mosaic tile floors and stained glass windows.

From the Stout House front door you are within easy walking distance of Dubuque's shops and restaurants and a quick drive from Mississippi riverboat gambling. Be sure to take the scenic railcar ride that climbs the city's bluffs for a breathtaking view of three states.

FORT MADISON

Kingsley Inn

707 Avenue H
Fort Madison, IA 52627
319-372-7074
800-441-2327

An old newspaper building is now Fort Madison's premier B&B

Manager: Myrna M. Reinhard. **Accommodations:** 14 rooms, all with private bath. **Rates:** $65–$105 single or double. **Included:** Continental breakfast. **Minimum stay:** 2 nights on holiday weekends and first weekend after Labor Day. **Added:** 10% tax. **Payment:** Major credit cards. **Children:** 12 years and older. **Pets:** No. **Smoking:** No. **Open:** Year-round.

Countless yards of red anaglypta cover the hallways of the impressive Kingsley Inn on the shores of the Mississippi River. The circa 1859 Italianate structure served as a newspaper office and commercial laundry before a group of investors renovated it as a hotel in 1990 to attract weekday business travelers.

Great care has been taken to retain the Victorian feel of the exterior. Inside, however, the inn looks much like a commercial hotel, with an elevator shooting up the center of an atrium. The ambitious project joins three historic buildings with the newly renovated restaurant, Alpha's on the Riverfront.

> **Near Fort Madison are riverboat gambling and the Nauvoo, Illinois, historic restoration.**

The guest rooms are decorated with exquisite vintage furnishings. The owners used only cherry, mahogany, and walnut pieces made no later than 1890. Matching three-piece sets in Rooms 205 and 207 make these rooms popular with history and antiques buffs. Three rooms have whirlpool baths.

Breakfast is served in the Morning Room and includes homemade granola and pastries, fresh fruits, juice, and coffee. In the evening, guests relax here and in the neighboring parlor in overstuffed chairs.

Amtrak runs right by the inn and stops at the depot in town. But don't worry about noise. Extra-thick glass in the inn's windows reduces train clatter to a nostalgic whisper.

HOMESTEAD

Die Heimat Country Inn

Main Street, Amana Colonies
Homestead, IA 52236
319-622-3937

> *A simple inn welcomes guests to the Amana Colonies*

Innkeepers: Warren and Jacki Lock. **Accommodations:** 19 rooms, all with private bath. **Rates:** $36–$66 single or double. **Included:** Full breakfast. **Minimum stay:** No. **Added:** 10% tax. **Payment:** Discover, MasterCard, Visa. **Children:** Yes. **Pets:** Yes. **Smoking:** Nonsmoking rooms available. **Open:** Year-round.

The Amana Colonies were settled in the 1840s by German immigrants seeking religious freedom. Today, traditional furniture makers and craftspeople still populate the seven colonies, offering their wares to travelers. Originally a communal kitchen and later a boardinghouse, the simple blue-gray building continues to welcome visitors as Die Heimat Country Inn.

Country-style rooms at Die Heimat (pronounced *dee HY-mat*, "the home place") are far from fancy, though many have four-poster Amana walnut and cherry beds with handmade quilts. All have been updated with modern baths, individual air conditioners, desks, and televisions.

> **In the summer, lawn furniture and a glider encourage guests to relax outside and survey the flat, open farm fields.**

A breakfast buffet is set out in the lounge, which is also decorated with Amana furniture and art. The meal typically includes eggs, toast, and a special breakfast dessert.

You'll undoubtedly want to explore the colonies' historic villages, antiques shops, furniture shops, and woolen mills. For dinner, head down the street to Bill Zuber's Restaurant, named for the New York Yankees pitcher.

IOWA CITY

Haverkamp's Linn Street Homestay

619 North Linn Street
Iowa City, IA 52245
319-337-4363

A family home near the University of Iowa

Innkeepers: Clarence and Dorothy Haverkamp. **Accommodations:** 3 rooms with shared bath. **Rates:** $25–$35 single; $35–$40 double. **Included:** Continental breakfast weekdays; full on weekends. **Minimum stay:** No. **Added:** 12% tax. **Payment:** Personal checks, cash. **Children:** Yes. **Pets:** No. **Smoking:** No. **Open:** Year-round.

The shady porch of Haverkamp's is the gathering spot of choice at this Edwardian homestay near the University of Iowa campus. From the oak swing, guests watch life pass by on the brick-lined street.

Of the guest rooms, the North Room is the largest and most romantic, decorated with bird's-eye maple furniture and a brass bed. Turn-of-the-century lovers line the walls in framed magazine covers and illustrations. What looks like a wardrobe is actually a Murphy bed in the East Room, which has Clarence's baby quilt from 1933.

Guests enjoy access to the living room, dining room, and den here; you may find students working on dissertations or preparing for job interviews. Clarence and Dorothy are both teachers, so on weekdays they set out pastries, fruit, and cereal for breakfast. On weekends, the full country breakfast may include pancakes and bacon with cooked apples and a slice of pie. Conversation gets so lively on occasion that the morning meal has stretched into the afternoon.

LANSING

FitzGerald's Inn

160 North Third Street
P.O. Box 157
Lansing, IA 52151
319-538-4872

*Climb the hill
for a perfect view
at this
small-town find*

Innkeepers: Jeff and Marie FitzGerald. **Accommodations:** 4 rooms, some with private bath; 1 suite.
Rates: Rooms $60 double, suite $75 double. **Included:** Full

breakfast. **Minimum stay:** No. **Added:** 4% tax. **Payment:** MasterCard, Visa. **Children:** Yes. **Pets:** No. **Smoking:** Yes. **Open:** Year-round.

The FitzGeralds once received a nice compliment. Fred Boeckh, who lived in the white two-story house from 1902 through 1928, returned to the homestead for the first time in 60 years. He liked what he saw. With its beautifully restored parquet floors, tin ceilings, and pretty white picket fence, the home does indeed retain its original turn-of-the-century charm.

> A screened-in gazebo can be reached by climbing the steep stone steps off the back of the inn. It's worth the trip for the stunning view of the Mississippi River and Blackhawk Bridge.

On a terraced hillside overlooking the Mississippi, FitzGerald's Inn offers a tasteful blend of modern and antique furnishings. The Starlight guest room is a favorite, decorated in soft blues and offering a view of the stars through a skylight directly over the queen-size bed. The Oak Suite, shaded by a century-old oak tree, has a private bath and is furnished with English antiques. Breakfast here includes fruit, juice, an egg and meat main course, and fresh baked goods.

The FitzGeralds live down the street but can be counted on for excellent dinner and day trip suggestions. (They brag that you can drive in any direction for 30 miles without hitting a fast-food restaurant.) Life moves slowly in this river town, where hunting, fishing, canoeing, and sightseeing draw guests regularly from Minneapolis. The FitzGerald family also offers accommodations in two nearby lodgings: the Center Street Lodging and Lansing House.

MAQUOKETA

Squiers Manor

418 West Pleasant
Maquoketa, IA 52060
319-652-6961

*An antique-
lover's dream*

Innkeepers: Virl and Kathy Banowetz, Ben Banowetz. **Accommodations:** 5 rooms, 1 suite, all with private bath. **Rates:** Rooms $65–$95 double, suites $125. **Included:** Full breakfast. **Minimum stay:** No. **Added:** 5% tax. **Payment:** MasterCard, Visa. **Children:** Yes. **Pets:** No. **Smoking:** Yes. **Open:** Year-round.

Squiers Manor is run by Virl and Kathy Banowetz, who own a pair of nationally respected antiques stores in Maquoketa and Galena, Illinois. Not surprisingly, the inn is a showcase for museum-quality furnishings, most from the Victorian era.

The Banowetzes, who opened their doors to guests in 1991, admit they had an incredible home to work with. Built in 1882 for James and Harriet Squiers, the Queen Anne brick mansion features walnut, cherry, oak, and butternut wood throughout. The fireplace mantel and dynamic colored tiles depict mythological gods and goddesses, the four seasons, and the four elements. This was the first home in Maquoketa to have running water and power, and many of the original lighting fixtures remain.

The guest rooms have antique beds, especially made for queen-size mattresses, some covered with antique crocheted bedspreads. In the Beulah E. Stephens Room, the mahogany bed with intricately carved birds and flowers was original to the home, then sold at auction in 1946; the new owners brought it back home. This is one of four guest rooms with a whirlpool bath.

The J. E. Squiers Room, a handsome blend of iris wallpaper and dark green carpeting, has a three-piece marble-top butternut bedroom set. The elegant bath has a corner whirlpool for two above the Verde marble floor. Shades of blue, white, and pink highlight the Harriet W. Squiers Room, which has an 1820s Federal four-poster mahogany bed with acanthus leaf carving and a pineapple motif. This room has a standard shower.

Breakfast, served family-style in the cherrywood dining room, may include Kathy's specialty of a seafood omelette or quiche, along with homemade cinnamon rolls and breads.

Unusual details abound. A mirror above the pedestal bathroom sink is an authentic piece of hobo or tramp art, an American folk art form in which wooden crates and cigar boxes were made into decorative items. The double vanity in Opal's Parlor was eventually refitted with standard bowls and faucets. The same room has a Swiss shower with a regular showerhead plus six side jets.

> **The solid walnut Victorian dining table, with 11 leaves, can seat up to 18 people comfortably. The chairs, circa 1880, came from a Philadelphia lodge. A stately Regulator clock keeps time in a corner.**

You can ooh and aah over lots more antiques at the Banowetzes' store just outside town.

MONTEZUMA

English Valley Bed and Breakfast

R.R. 2
Montezuma, IA 50171
515-623-3663

> *Life on the farm in a century-old clapboard inn*

Innkeepers: Jim and Sue Eichhorn. **Accommodations:** 3 rooms sharing 2 baths. **Rates:** $40–$45 single, $45–$50 double. **Included:** Full breakfast; dinner available. **Minimum stay:** No. **Added:** 5% tax. **Payment:** MasterCard, Visa. **Children:** Yes. **Pets:** Yes. **Smoking:** Downstairs only. **Open:** Year-round.

Turkeys, sheep, horses, cows, hogs, dogs, cats, and quail are among the permanent residents of this bed-and-breakfast, a 500-acre corn and soybean farm nestled in the English River valley of central Iowa.

The century-old white clapboard farmhouse offers guest rooms filled with antiques. The Victorian Rose Room has floral and striped wallpapers and wicker furnishings. A grapevine wreath with dried flowers serves as a king-size headboard. A study in blue, lavender, and pink, the Blue Room has heirloom quilts, oodles of lace, and a white iron bed. Upstairs is a fancy Jacuzzi for two and a small refrigerator that holds complimentary juices and soft drinks.

> **Families often stay for a full week at this inviting farm. Guests can spend relaxing hours with a book in front of the gathering room fireplace. They can help the innkeepers with chores, such as collecting eggs, feeding lambs, or riding out to check cattle. They can fish in the property's large stocked pond.**

Breakfast is served on the screened porch or in the country kitchen. In addition to fresh homemade breads, the morning meal includes German apple pancakes or omelettes with sides of bacon or ham.

The Eichhorns have jobs off the farm during the day, so guests have the place pretty much to themselves, with full access to the kitchen, gathering room, and piano room. Guests usually pay the small additional fee to gather around the kitchen table for a family-style dinner with the innkeepers. Bonfires and wiener roasts on the banks of the nearby pond are popular events with children.

Five-course formal dinners (at $17) can be held for more than 50 people in the Victorian dining room. Served on authentic Depression glass and crystal, the fixed menu may include prime rib or stuffed beef tenderloin. Entertainment is included, which usually means singing old tunes around the player piano. On nights when dinner isn't served, guests usually head to nearby Grinnell.

NEVADA

Queen Anne Bed and Breakfast

1110 Ninth Street
Nevada, IA 50201
515-382-6444

*Historic lodgings
10 minutes from
the university*

Innkeepers: Paula and Phil Page. **Accommodations:** 2 rooms with shared bath. **Rates:** $50–$70 single, $55–$75 double. **Included:** Full breakfast. **Minimum stay:** No. **Added:** 5% tax. **Payment:** Personal checks, cash. **Children:** Yes. **Pets:** No. **Smoking:** No. **Open:** Year-round.

You could go a little nutty looking for historic lodgings near the Iowa State campus in Ames. So many folks drive the extra few minutes to Nevada to stay at the Queen Anne Bed and Breakfast. The restoration of this 1878 Victorian home has happened gradually since 1967, when Phil and Paula Page moved in with their family. At that time, a wall at the top of the grand staircase had been added to divide the home into separate apartments. The Pages have not only restored that original

More than just a great story of historic preservation, the Queen Anne is also a comfortable, hospitable place to spend the night.

staircase but saved the foyer's stained glass as well, releading it and protecting it from the weather with permanent storm windows. Most intriguing are the miraculously preserved downstairs ceilings, fashioned of embossed papier-mâché with an egg carton texture. The exterior trim will soon be finished in Victorian painted lady style.

Paula is especially proud of her breakfasts, served in the formal dining room. They may include eggs Benedict with smoked turkey, a ham and cheese quiche, or French toast with an ice cream and sautéed apple topping. Meals always begin with fresh fruit and homemade muffins and bread.

The bedrooms offer Renaissance Revival furnishings with Eastlake influences. The spacious Queen Anne's Chamber has a three-piece matching set, a slate fireplace, a marble-topped table in front of the bay window, and a spacious dressing room. Sir Aaron's Room has a more masculine look, with paisley wallpaper and a queen-size bed. The wallcovering and fabrics are all top quality — not surprising since the innkeepers operate Page Decorating and Design in Nevada.

NEWTON

La Corsette Maison Inn

629 First Avenue East
Newton, IA 50208
515-792-6833

Kay Owen serves unforgettable meals and hospitality

Innkeeper: Kay Owen. **Accommodations:** 3 rooms, 2 with private bath; 2 suites. **Rates:** Rooms $60–$80, suites $75–$125. **Included:** Full breakfast; dinner available. **Minimum stay:** No. **Added:** 10% tax. **Payment:** MasterCard, Visa, American Express. **Children:** By prior arrangement. **Pets:** By prior arrangement. **Smoking:** No. **Open:** Year-round.

The first course of a La Corsette Maison dinner is a tour of the house, led by Kay Owen. The Mission-style mansion, she explains, was built in 1909 by an Iowa state senator, August Bergman, and still contains original Arts and Crafts touches. Especially outstanding is the three-piece dining set, a classic and valuable example of the utilitarian Mission oak style. The stained glass ceiling in the atrium is the downstairs centerpiece.

Despite the elegant architectural touches, ever-hospitable Kay cultivates an unpretentious atmosphere at La Corsette. This is especially true in the guest rooms, which are cleverly decorated but not luxurious. The Penthouse is a favorite, with a private balcony and beveled glass windows on all sides. There is a caveat: you have to walk downstairs and through the common rooms to reach the bathroom.

After the tour, guests take their seats in the dining room or at romantic tables for two in adjoining downstairs rooms. The meal, served by a waiter wearing a tuxedo, may officially begin with a Swiss chard and goat cheese timbale with tomato vinaigrette. Hungarian cream of green soup and salad is followed by the main course — tips of tenderloin in tarragon butter, with potatoes in heavy cream on the side. All meals are served with a small loaf of fresh French bread. The lemon crêpe dessert soufflé is light and perfect. A pianist plays easy-listening favorites on the parlor's baby grand while Kay pops over to inquire about your meal.

> The lower level, with a mosaic tile floor, once held a pool table. In its new life as a spacious honeymoon room, it features an antique sleigh and a fireplace.

Breakfast is also generous, beginning with a fruit bowl and choice of juices. It may be followed by frittata with two cheeses, bacon, and onions. The molasses bread can be topped with hot apple cider.

Kay began serving these special meals on an Iowa farm. Word spread fast and her business grew, eventually giving her the confidence to move closer to the city. She chuckles at the irony of her new location — at a busy intersection with three fast-food restaurants.

PELLA

Strawtown Inn

1111 Washington Street
Pella, IA 50219
515-628-9636
Dining: 515-628-2681

> *Dutch heritage
> in decor and food*

Owner/innkeeper: Eunice Kuyper.
Accommodations: 12 rooms, 5 suites, all with private bath.

Rates: Rooms $67.50–$77.50 single, $75–$85 double; suites $97.50 single, $110 double. **Included:** Full breakfast. **Minimum stay:** No. **Added:** 5% tax. **Payment:** Major credit cards. **Children:** Yes. **Pets:** No. **Smoking:** No. **Open:** Year-round.

The Strawtown Inn derives its name from the early Dutch settlers who fashioned cold-weather shelters out of sod. The roofs were woven like thatch, so the strawtown name stuck. The inn retains its Dutch heritage in both its decoration and food.

> **The Dutch menu features** *Hollandse rollade,* **Dutch spiced beef served in its own juice.** *Gevulde karbonade,* **a stuffed pork chop, is accompanied by apple dressing and a mushroom wine sauce. Pheasant under glass makes an elegant dinner for two.**

The dining rooms include an informal café that is decorated in Delft blue, the Garden Room on the second level, and the Rembrandt Room, with a roaring fire. All dinners are served with traditional Dutch barbecued meatballs and Tuch apple bread. Dutch chocolate ice cream follows for dessert.

The rooms are named after prominent guests and decorated with antiques and Dutch detailing. The Juliana Kamer honors Queen Juliana of the Netherlands, who visited Pella in 1942. It has sloped ceilings, striped and floral wallpaper, a king-size bed, and a Jacuzzi behind a screen. Bedstee Kamer has Dutch bunk beds built into the wall. The Marken Suite is the favorite, with white walls, a spacious living room, and a complete kitchen. At the end of a hall is a glassed-in hot tub for guests.

SPENCER

Hannah Marie Country Inn

Route 1
Spencer, IA 51301
712-262-1286

> *Theme teas in northwestern Iowa*

Innkeeper: Mary Nichols. **Accommodations:** 4 rooms, all with private bath. **Rates:** $50–$80 single, $55–$85 double. **Included:** Full breakfast. **Minimum stay:** No. **Added:** 5% tax. **Payment:** Major credit cards. **Children:** Yes. **Pets:** Allowed outside or in the barn. **Smoking:** No. **Open:** April through mid-December.

Mary Nichols is having a tea party, and everyone is invited. That's the word from Hannah Marie Country Inn, where theme teas lure travelers to this cozy farm stay in northwestern Iowa. During the Hats off to You Tea, for instance, participants don chapeaus. The British Cockney Tea is delivered by costumed servers offering fruit tartlets. Guests can celebrate their "unbirthdays" at Queen Victoria's Chocolate Tea, where dessert is topped with a lighted candle.

Guests sleep in a 1910 frame house surrounded by the 200-acre corn and soybean farm that Mary, her husband, Ray, and their son, Dave, operate. Mary named the inn for her mother and the guest rooms for her favorite aunts. The Beda is a "tomboy" room, bathed in soft apricot and green with walnut furniture. It also has a whirlpool. Elisabeth boasts bird's-eye maple furniture and an antique white iron tub complete with rubber ducks. Louella, the smallest room, is decorated in shades of red, including the clawfoot tub.

The Nicholses have recently added another historic home, The Carl Gustav House, to the lodging options. It is used primarily for lunches, dinners, and business meetings and also houses additional guests. Its Lamplighter's Room is decorated in an English mystery theme. Mary says (with tongue firmly in cheek) that Sherlock Holmes actually spent the night here. You will find some of his items still in the room.

Mary may send recent guests a tea bag with instructions for making a perfect cup of tea, as well as a hearty invitation to return.

The full breakfast here can cater to dietary needs. Afterward, you can relax on the wide-planked front porch or grab a parasol or walking stick (provided by the inn) to explore the farm.

Michigan

Northern Michigan
& the
Upper Peninsula

Copper Harbor

Sault Ste. Marie

Mackinac I.

Traverse City

Southern
Michigan

Saginaw

Dearborn

Kalamazoo

St. Joseph

Lower Michigan

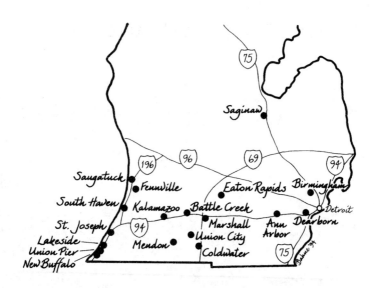

Best Bed and Breakfast Inns

Ann Arbor
  Reynolds House at Stonefield Farm
Battle Creek
  Greencrest Manor
Coldwater
  Chicago Pike Inn
Fennville
  The Crane House
Kalamazoo
  Stuart Avenue Inn
Lakeside
  The Pebble House
Marshall
  McCarthy's Bear Creek Inn
  The National House Inn
Mendon
  Mendon Country Inn
New Buffalo
  Sans Souci
Saugatuck
  Maplewood Hotel
  The Park House
South Haven
  A Country Place
  Yelton Manor
Union Pier
  The Inn at Union Pier

Best Full-Service Country Inns

Eaton Rapids
  Dusty's English Inn
Saginaw
  The Montague Inn
Union City
  The Victorian Villa Guesthouse

Best Hotels

Birmingham
  The Townsend Hotel

Dearborn
The Dearborn Inn

Best Budget Stay

St. Joseph
Snow Flake Motel

From the minute you pass the border from Indiana on I-94, you'll find tiny communities that take full advantage of the scenic beauty of the Great Lakes State. The summer cottage communities of **Union Pier, New Buffalo,** and **Lakeside** all sport art galleries, restaurants, and access to Lake Michigan watersports.

Saugatuck, farther up the coast along I-196, is a summer place, where the beaches are dotted with sun worshipers shading their eyes for a glimpse of rainbow sails on Lake Michigan. A bustling downtown offers antiques and specialty stores. In the evening, Kilwin's candy shop sends a sweet aroma to after-dinner strollers. Saugatuck has long been known as an artist's retreat, so you'll find it a mecca for fine art galleries and the Ox-Bow Art Workshop.

Though it's hard to pinpoint quality lodging in the city proper, Detroit has unique attractions that make it well worth a visit: Greektown, the magnificently restored Fox Theatre, and the Detroit Institute of Arts. The Motown Museum, where "The Sound of Young America" was launched in the late 1950s, is also open for tours. A Motor City tradition since 1981, the Detroit Grand Prix runs each June. Detroit is also just a bridge away from Canada.

A drive west on I-94 leads to **Dearborn** and the world-famous Henry Ford Museum and Greenfield Village. Here you'll find a reconstructed turn-of-the-century village, including Thomas Edison's laboratory and the Wright Brothers' bicycle shop. The Museum has a phenomenal Auto in American Culture exhibit, a fitting tribute to the Motor City.

Ann Arbor, home of the University of Michigan and about 45 minutes from Detroit, is a quintessential college town with coffeehouses, fine ethnic restaurants, and an overwhelmingly cultural atmosphere. **Kalamazoo,** another pleasant college town, lies halfway between Chicago and Detroit off I-94.

ANN ARBOR

Reynolds House at Stonefield Farm

5259 West Ellsworth Road
Ann Arbor, MI 48103
313-995-0301

*Quiet romance
off a country road
near the university*

Innkeeper: Laurel Reynolds. **Accommodations:** 3 rooms sharing 1 bath. **Rates:** $60 single, $70 double. **Included:** Buffet breakfast; served breakfast on Sundays. **Minimum stay:** No. **Added:** 6% tax. **Payment:** MasterCard, Visa, cash, check. **Children:** Yes. **Pets:** No. **Smoking:** No. **Open:** Year-round.

Situated on ten acres of rolling farmland, Reynolds House is an idyllic hideaway just minutes away from the student rush of downtown Ann Arbor and the University of Michigan. The surrounding fields are alive with sheep, hens, and a rooster that crows at the dawn. Hummingbirds buzz in the formal English gardens. The cottage, shaded by tall pine trees, is a comfortable exercise in community living with three guest rooms sharing a kitchen, living room, and bath.

Reynolds House caps its small-town feel with a white picket fence planted with well-tended rose bushes. Flowers overflow from window boxes.

The inn is named after a Pennsylvania hostelry from the early 1800s. Sinclair Lewis mentioned it in one of his books, along with then-owner Harry Reynolds, whom he considered among the world's foremost innkeepers. Laurel Reynolds retained a few pieces of her great-great-grandfather's legacy, including silverware and two desks, when she opened her own unique lodging.

All rooms are furnished with antiques, hardwood floors, and a Laura Ashley motif. Jimmy's Room is a favorite, with a converted rope feather bed and a window facing the fields. The living room has a small black and white television and lots of windows.

Mondays through Saturdays, breakfast is self-serve in the

fully stocked kitchen. Farm-fresh eggs, cereal, hot rolls and scones, juice, and coffee are there for the making. On Sundays, Laurel invites guests to a full breakfast served in the main house dining room or on white wicker underneath a maple tree. The freewheeling menu might include a Mexican breakfast with eggs ranchero, or an egg dish with herbs lined with edible nasturtiums from one of several gardens on the property.

Guests enjoy moonlit or daytime strolls by the crescent-shaped pond, or relaxing in the adjoining gazebo where they can peck out a "wish you were here" letter on the manual typewriter. Bicycles are available for surveying fall colors. In winter, Laurel urges guests to pack cross-country skis.

BATTLE CREEK

Greencrest Manor

6174 Halbert Road
Battle Creek, MI 49017
616-962-8633

> *A touch of French countryside in Cereal Town, USA*

Innkeepers: Kathy and Tom Van-Daff. **Accommodations:** 5 rooms, 3 with private bath. **Rates:** $80–$180 single or double. **Included:** Full breakfast. **Minimum stay:** No. **Added:** 7% tax. **Payment:** Visa, MasterCard, American Express. **Children:** Yes. **Pets:** No. **Smoking:** No. **Open:** Year-round.

Greencrest Manor, a mansion in the French-Normandy style, is quickly gaining a reputation as one of the most romantic spots in Michigan. Quite a feat for a bed-and-breakfst located near the very unromantic sounding "cereal capitol of the world" in Battle Creek. Looking out over St. Mary's Lake, sipping lemonade on the stone porch, it doesn't take much to imagine yourself in the French countryside.

The innkeepers cultivate this image, but not without considerable effort. The mansion was a mess when they arrived, with a huge hole in the roof and frogs hopping in several inches of water in the basement. The home was originally built on the favorite picnic spot of lumber baron George R. Burt, who passed away before its completion in the mid-1930s. The Catholic Church took over in the 1960s, using the mansion as a monastery for the next 20 years.

The innkeepers were lucky enough to locate the original blueprints for both the home and the garden. The end result is a knockout, with marble floors, a spiral staircase, a ballroom-sized living room, and a cherry-pan-

> **Breakfasts are served on Wedgwood china with silver and crystal. Not surprisingly, Kellogg's cereal is among the breakfast choices.**

eled library decorated in soft chintzes. The kitchen is accented with jade green marble splash boards. Fresh and elegant silk flowers line virtually every room. Even the bird house here is elaborate.

Guest rooms are decorated in country French and English style. Down comforters and handwoven or hand-quilted throws dress the beds. The Geranium Room has a sink in the room and a bath down the hall, while the VIP Suite has a Jacuzzi bath. Greencrest Manor has plenty of space to expand, and more guest rooms are planned.

Business travelers appreciate the cable television, telephone jacks, and in-room safes. A private breakfast room is the site of many a job offer or business deal. For dinner, the innkeepers recommend the Aries Cafe about a half-hour's drive to Plainwell. The Marywood Country Club and Bedford Country Club are both nearby, with meals available as well as golf. Cross-country ski trails are only minutes away, though the estate's surrounding acreage is ideal for some winter activites.

BIRMINGHAM

The Townsend Hotel

100 Townsend Street
Birmingham, MI 48009
313-642-7900
800-548-4172 outside Michigan
Fax: 313-645-9061
Telex: 798502

*A small hotel
with gracious
accommodations
outside Detroit*

General manager: Otto Haensler.
Accommodations: 35 rooms, 51 suites. **Rates:** Rooms $179 single, $189 double; suites $199 single, $209 double; executive suites $479 single or double; packages available. **Minimum stay:** No. **Added:** 7.5% tax. **Payment:** Major credit cards. **Children:** Yes. **Pets:** No. **Smoking:** Nonsmoking rooms available. **Open:** Year-round.

The Townsend Hotel offers fine accommodations in the upscale suburban community of Birmingham, just 20 minutes northwest of downtown Detroit.

Floral patterned chairs and overstuffed couches grace both the paneled lobby and traditionally furnished guest rooms. The color scheme throughout is a tasteful blend of blue, red, and ivory. Marble-lined baths, terrycloth robes, French soaps, Belgian pillows, and fluffy down comforters are standard amenities here. The concierge speaks nine languages, and room service is offered around the clock. Ask about transportation from the airport.

**Special-function rooms
provide elegant facilities
for larger gatherings of up
to 400 or banquets for 200.**

Three exclusive corner suites offer separate living and dining areas, butler pantries, and double balconies. Some include VCRs.

Marley's Boutique, which sells clothing and gifts from Europe and Asia as well as utilitarian travel items, is located right in the hotel. Step out the front door, and you are in the center of one of the area's fanciest shopping districts. Fine restaurants also abound, including the hotel's Rugby Grill, which remains a popular breakfast spot with the locals.

COLDWATER

Chicago Pike Inn

215 East Chicago Street
Coldwater, MI 49036
517-279-8744
Fax: 517-278-8597

> *Bright touches in*
> *a somber mansion*

Innkeepers: Becky and Jane Schultz. **Accommodations:** 5 rooms, 1 suite, all with private bath. **Rates:** Rooms $80–$165 double, suites $140 double. **Included:** Full breakfast. **Minimum stay:** No. **Added:** 4% tax. **Payment:** Major credit cards. **Children:** 12 years and over. **Pets:** No. **Smoking:** Downstairs. **Open:** Year-round.

As a teenager, Jane Schultz worked weekends in her father's paint and wallpaper store. As an inn owner, Jane drew from her knowledge of fine materials — Schumacher and Waverly wall coverings, borders, and fabrics — to brighten the somber ambience of the Colonial Reform mansion's dark paneling.

The reception room has a canine theme, with a pair of ceramic Staffordshire dogs, an overstuffed armchair boasting carved canine heads on its arms, and vintage oil paintings in this handsome paneled entryway with Oriental rugs and a cherry double-mantel fireplace. An original Kokomo stained glass window (from Kokomo, Indiana) illuminates the landing that leads to the guest rooms upstairs.

Jane and her daughter Becky, a trained hotelier, avoided creating a museum when they appointed the mansion for guests. The towels are thick, the beds are comfortable, the toiletries are luxurious. A pot of coffee awaits early risers on a buffet upstairs.

A favorite room is the Grandchildren's Room, a confection of pink walls, gingham fabrics, and Battenberg lace. Victorian prints of children hang on the walls, wicker rockers create an oasis for reading, and twin iron and brass headboards are swagged with antique lace curtains.

Decorated with black pillow-ticking paper and red Cranston plaid fabric, the Hired Girl's Room features a cozy sitting area and sleeping alcove with a wrought iron bed and a small bathroom. The furnishings include an antique oak washstand, a pine wardrobe, and carefully coordinated collectibles.

> In the carriage house, two new rooms have been added, both with private balconies, sink-refrigerator mini-bars, and Jacuzzi baths.

Miss Sophia's, a spacious suite with its own balcony, includes a lavish ensemble of velvet chairs and sofa and a large table for a conference or private breakfast. Be warned, however: this room overlooks Chicago Street, which is busy by day but fairly quiet at night.

In the carriage house, the Stableman's Room is done in black, red, and white, furnished with a black pencil post bed, old plank bottom chairs, and primitive tables. The Garden Room, in pink and green, has a Medallion-style canopy bed.

For breakfast, Becky may serve homemade peach sorbet and muffins, French toast made with pound cake, and an aromatic chocolate-raspberry coffee. Guests can enjoy breakfast in the formal dining room or, in summer, in the gazebo. Elegant dinners are offered to guests on Friday nights from January through March or at other times by arrangement.

Nearby is a well-known summer theater (ask about the inn's weekend theater packages). If you want to explore the neighborhood and the center of town, the inn has 12 bicycles to loan to guests. Antiques hounds will want to visit Allen, just minutes away; Shipshewana Amish country is less than an hour to the south.

DEARBORN

The Dearborn Inn

20301 Oakwood Boulevard
Dearborn, MI 48124
313-271-2700
800-228-9290
Fax: 313-271-7464
Reservations: 800-228-2800

> *Henry Ford's presence still permeates this historic lodging*

General manager: Yves J. Robin.
Accommodations: 222 rooms, including 23 suites in the main building, motel units, and Colonial homes. **Rates:** Rooms $130 single, $145 double; suites $145–$175 single or double; packages available. **Included:** All meals available. **Minimum stay:** No. **Added:** 11% tax. **Payment:** Major credit cards. **Children:** Yes. **Pets:** By arrangement. **Smoking:** Nonsmoking rooms available. **Open:** Year-round.

In 1929, Henry Ford was watching passengers arrive at the airport he had built across the street from his auto manufacturing headquarters in Dearborn, Michigan. Realizing that there was nowhere to eat or sleep closer than Detroit, 20 miles away, he decided to build a hotel. Opened in 1931 and renovated in 1989, the Dearborn Inn continues to welcome business travelers as a Marriott hotel.

Working closely with Ford, the architect Albert Kahn designed the traditional Georgian structure with red brick and white trim. The lobby has elegant black and white marble floors and groupings of comfortable chairs and couches, with a portrait of Ford watching over the proceedings from above the fireplace. Adjacent is a small brick-lined sun porch with wicker furniture.

> **Business travelers fill the inn during the week, and weddings are often held here on weekends. The formal, 3,444-square-foot Alexandria Ballroom features a cathedral ceiling and period crystal chandeliers. It was inspired by similar ballrooms that Ford admired in Virginia.**

The detailing and furnishings in the recent addition blend seamlessly with the original rooms. You can hardly tell the difference, except for the deep porcelain tubs found in the older units. The guest rooms are decorated in two schemes — some in conservative stripes, the others in a blue ribbon theme. The premium rooms on the second and third floors have their own gathering room with concierge service. The other rooms are across the street, in colonial-style motel units added in 1960.

Offering bed-and-breakfast accommodations, five 18th- and 19th-century homes, all replicas of famous Americans' homesteads, form a semicircle behind the hotel. The largest of these, the Patrick Henry House, has six suites and two rooms decorated with bright floral wallpapers and antique prints. The white clapboard Poe Cottage can be rented as an individual unit, making it appealing to honeymooners.

Lunch and dinner here can be enjoyed in the Early American Room, which has tall windows, crystal chandeliers, and an excellent menu that includes plank roasted salmon, prime rib, and veal scaloppine. Brunch here is a Sunday tradition for both tourists and Detroit residents. Three meals are served daily at the Ten Eyck Tavern, which is rustic and informal, with dark wood Windsor chairs and tables surrounded by turn-of-the-century photographs. The Fat Man's Buffet, all-you-can-eat Prime Rib and Shrimp, is a tradition Monday through Friday in the Golden Eagle Lodge. Local entertainment and dancing are also featured here Tuesdays through Saturdays.

You'll also find tennis courts and a pool on the Inn's 28 acres. The Dearborn Inn is just down the street from the world-famous Henry Ford Museum and Greenfield Village.

EATON RAPIDS

Dusty's English Inn

728 South Michigan Avenue
Eaton Rapids, MI 48827
517-663-2500

A cow-country inn with the amenities of an English country hotel

Innkeeper: Clarence "Dusty" Rhodes. **Accommodations:** 5 rooms, 1 suite, all with private bath. **Rates:** Rooms $65–$90 single, $75–$100 double; suite $145 single, $155 double. **Included:** Full breakfast; lunch and dinner available. **Minimum stay:** No. **Added:** 4% tax. **Payment:** MasterCard, Visa. **Children:** Discouraged. **Pets:** No. **Smoking:** No. **Open:** Year-round.

Dusty's English Inn offers lots of surprises, not least of all its location. Set on 15 acres in the middle of Michigan cow country, the 1927 Tudor mansion offers a stately yet comfortable stay in an authentic English country house.

Dusty Rhodes is an important part of that stay. He grew to appreciate country inns while working in England, where he still resides part of the year. He purchased the home's centerpiece, the white stag portrait at the top of the stairs, years ago in Scotland. Only now does he have a grand enough place to display it properly.

Dusty relates with a hearty laugh the often unusual history of the mansion. The original owner, Irving Reuter, was an Oldsmobile president who routinely smashed his cars while careening up the narrow drive past the entrance gate. He would simply have them hauled away and replaced. Dusty also recalls a time when the estate was owned by a Catholic bishop, who turned the downstairs pub into a chapel. The watering hole, now called the Crossed Guns Pub, is up and running again, serving bar food and good British ale.

While Dusty faces the ongoing challenge of buying back from neighbors the elegant statuary that once occupied the grounds, many of the mansion's original touches remain. Ivy still creeps up brick walls toward a slate roof. Wrought-iron chandeliers hang from detailed plastered ceilings. The rarest touch remains the dining room's matchbook quilted paneling, which required splitting a tree in such a way that it opened up in a mirror image of the grain.

> **Breakfast can be enjoyed in the Thames Room, where you can glimpse canoes paddling down the Grand River, meandering gently behind the property.**

The Brighton Room (the guest rooms are named for English towns) has some of the home's original furniture. It includes a bedroom set that the Reuters purchased in France but, to their shock, was actually manufactured in nearby Grand Rapids. Black border wallpaper is from the Natchez collection, and yellow and black tile highlights the bathroom.

Guests love the Somerset Room because its windows face the sunset over a farmer's field. Lavender tile complements the stained glass window in the bathroom. An English cottage feel pervades the Avon Room, a pink and green confection with geraniums peeking up outside the leaded windows. The Bath Room's bathroom is appropriately larger than the bedchamber.

A refurbished pool and gazebo is now open, along with a small croquet court. Dusty is still working on the grounds, bringing the rose garden back into bloom.

The full breakfast of omelettes, eggs and bacon, or French toast is always served with fresh fruit. Lunch and dinner are served daily in the dining room.

Conference facilities can presently be found on the inn's lower level. The inn attracts a good deal of its clientele from Dusty's alma mater, Michigan State University, and the capital in Lansing, both just 20 minutes away.

FENNVILLE

The Crane House

6051 124th Avenue (M-89)
Fennville, MI 49408
616-561-6931

A century-old farmhouse serving famous pies

Innkeeper: Nancy Crane McFarland. **Accommodations:** 5 rooms, some with shared showers. **Rates:** $60–$90 double. **Included:** Full breakfast. **Minimum stay:** No. **Added:** 6% tax. **Payment:** MasterCard, Visa, Discover. **Children:** Yes. **Pets:** No. **Smoking:** No. **Open:** Year-round.

Guests have been flocking to the Pie Pantry Restaurant since 1972 to sample Lue Crane's homemade fruit pies. Now they can spend the night in her family's century-old farmhouse.

Dwight and Lydia Crane pioneered the property in the early 1870s. The homestead has remained in the Crane family ever since and now includes a popular restaurant, cider mill, U-pick fruit farm, and bed-and-breakfast inn on 300 acres. Lue's daughter Nancy has taken over the innkeeping responsibilities, and you will likely see other family members during your visit, perhaps one of the 14 grandchildren busing tables.

Farmhouse guest rooms, decorated in country primitive style with handmade quilts, iron-and-brass beds, and wall stenciling, are named after ladies who have lived here. Lydia is the largest, highlighted by a tin tub painted candy apple red. Hattie is decorated in light pink hues complementing the blossoming peach trees outside the windows.

A 1900 wood-burning stove warms the inviting first-floor

parlor, which has the home's only television. The Cranes will laughingly refer to the backyard outhouse (complete with catalog), but there are actually facilities in each room. Two rooms share showers.

> **Plan your trip around picking time; the orchards yield red raspberries and cherries in early July and apples in late September, and you can pick your own.**

The Pie Pantry Restaurant across the street has evolved over the years into one of the Midwest's most charming family-run eateries. Burlap sacks paper the ceiling, and animated apple characters have been painted on the cement floors. Old clothing, magazine covers, straw boaters, and farm implements line the walls, along with Bob Crane's growing collection of Charles Lindbergh memorabilia.

The restaurant serves primarily soup and sandwiches on homemade bread, though some diners skip the main course entirely and dig into the award-winning fruit pies. Seasonal fruit also figures prominently in the full breakfast that comes with an overnight stay.

The Crane House is within easy driving distance of Lake Michigan and the hopping summer haven of Saugatuck.

KALAMAZOO

Stuart Avenue Inn

229 Stuart Avenue
Kalamazoo, MI 49007
616-385-3442

> *Victorian touches and a spectacular garden*

Innkeepers: Bill and Andy Casteel. **Accommodations:** 16 rooms, all with private bath. **Rates:** $45–$110 single, $55–$120 double. **Included:** Continental breakfast. **Minimum stay:** No. **Added:** 8% tax. **Payment:** Major credit cards. **Children:** Yes. **Pets:** No. **Smoking:** No. **Open:** Year-round.

The Stuart Avenue Inn had become a bit unwieldly, with overnight stays offered in a handful of restored Victorians spread over a city block in downtown Kalamazoo. Innkeepers Bill and Andy Casteel have streamlined the operation, making it a wonderful place to stop between Detroit and Chicago.

The inn now offers rooms in the Bartlett-Upjohn House, the Chappell House next door, and a spacious carriage house behind. Built by newspaper publisher James Bartlett, the main building was purchased in 1907 by James T. Upjohn, the youngest of the four brothers who founded the pharmaceutical company. It's a stunning example of Eastlake Queen Anne Victorian architecture, a dream of gables and turrets, painted a dark blue. Breakfast is served here on a long harvest table. A favorite room here is the Mayor's Room with Bradbury and Bradbury wallpapers, burled walnut accents, and a queen-size bed.

> **The Chappell House, built in 1902, has a heavy Arts and Crafts influence reflected in the many beamed ceilings and fireplaces. Tall guests will be pleased to discover that the home was specially crafted for the original owners, who were well over six feet tall.**

Rooms in the carriage house are comparatively modest, considerably smaller, but quite a bargain at $45 for a single.

VIP Suites are offered in the Chappell House, with the added luxury of a Jacuzzi, VCR, and sound system. A dozen of the rooms have fireplaces. The enclosed sleeping porch, with valuable twig furniture, overlooks the elegant garden and other homes in the historic district. Check out the secret room off the back staircase.

Among the framed prints and photos that line the walls you'll find a letter to Bill's grandfather from President Taft. Many of the pictures in the house are genuine Casteel ancestors. Others the innkeepers call "garage sale relations."

A vacant lot until just a few years ago, the inn garden is now a Kalamazoo showcase. The site was formerly a nationally recognized Shakespearean garden that Alice Louise McDuffee nurtured in the 1920s and '30s. Footpaths meander through an acre of flower beds and past a gazebo, pergola, fountain, and lily pond. Weddings and anniversary parties are often held here on weekends.

LAKESIDE

The Pebble House

15093 Lakeshore Road
Lakeside, MI 49116
616-469-1416

Museum-quality Arts and Crafts furnishings

Innkeepers: Jean and Ed Lawrence. **Accommodations:** 4 rooms, all with private bath, 2 suites, house. **Rates:** Rooms $96–$101 double, suites $101–$130 double, house $200. **Included:** Full breakfast. **Minimum stay:** 2 nights on weekends, 3 nights on holiday weekends. **Added:** 6% tax. **Payment:** MasterCard, Visa. **Children:** Limited. **Pets:** No. **Smoking:** On decks, balconies only. **Open:** Year-round.

The Pebble House has earned a national reputation for its museum-quality collection of Arts and Crafts furniture. Straight-lined Mission oak furniture and art glass–shaded lamps, the most popular and well-known representations of this aesthetic, are found throughout the inn.

If you're interested in learning more about the Arts and Crafts movement, a number of books are available for guests. There are also antiques shows and special weekend packages devoted to Arts and Crafts education.

The building was constructed of concrete with small embedded stones in 1912. The quiet summer village of Lakeside has long attracted vacationers from Chicago, an hour and a half away. The beach is just across the street, while restaurants, shops, and state parks lie only a short drive away.

Seven guest rooms are in three buildings, separated by a series of wooden walkways. The rooms are decorated in either Victorian or Mission style. In the main house, the bright Buttercup Room is decorated with oak furniture and flowered borders. A huge bathroom has a clawfoot tub and shower. The Peach Room features flowered wallpaper, an alcove study, and a deck overlooking the yard.

The Coach House contains three guest rooms. The Blueberry House, usually offered as a single unit, has two bedrooms, two baths, a living room, a sitting room, and a freestanding fireplace.

Guests gather at large round tables in the main dining room for a Scandinavian breakfast featuring fresh fruit, cheese, cereal, herring, homemade breads and muffins, and such main dishes as baked apple pancakes, soufflés, or quiche. Breakfast can also be enjoyed on the screened porch, a popular spot during warmer months.

The inn offers plenty of extras, including cookies upon arrival. There is even a tennis court on the property.

MARSHALL

McCarthy's Bear Creek Inn

15230 C. Drive North
Marshall, MI 49068
616-781-8383

*Antique charm
with modern
comforts*

Innkeepers: Beth and Michael McCarthy. **Accommodations:** 14 rooms, all with private bath. **Rates:** $63–$93 double; $59 on Sundays. **Included:** Full breakfast. **Minimum stay:** No. **Added:** 7% tax. **Payment:** Major credit cards. **Children:** Yes. **Pets:** No. **Smoking:** Limited. **Open:** Year-round.

Robert Maes, a wealthy agricultural inventor, built his Williamsburg-style Cape Cod house on a knoll just a mile from downtown Marshall. He built the fieldstone fences that meander around century-old burr oaks and outbuildings. He named the estate Bear Creek Farm, for its view of the water.

Beth and Michael McCarthy have filled the the old house with comfortable overstuffed furniture and subtle country accents, along with with big brass beds, balconies, and bay windows that take full advantage of their prime location.

The popular Library Room has a queen-size brass bed and a bay window overlooking Bear Creek. It's the only guest room with a fireplace. The gentle running of the creek is best heard from the Guest Room, furnished with a bedroom set that belonged to Michael's great-grandparents. Originally the mud room, the Garden Room has an appealing private entrance.

> **Guests can enjoy hiking, fishing, or cross-country skiing on the inn's 14 acres of farmland or shop in Marshall's myriad antiques and crafts shops.**

The Creek House, formerly the dairy barn, offers seven rooms on three floors. The original stone foundation has been preserved, giving the ground-floor rooms a wonderful rustic quality. Michael duplicated the trim from the main house and also made many of the furnishings. One of the most stunning pieces is the cherry pencil-post bed in the Green Room. The Stone Room provides a Southwest flair in its washed pine bed, stone walls, and antique wicker. The building is roofed with slate shingles that were removed in the late 1950s and carefully stored in another barn on the property.

Breakfast here is a generous spread of fruit, baked goods, cereals, and an egg dish served buffet-style on the 1880s Dutch cupboard.

The National House Inn

102 South Parkview
Marshall, MI 49068
616-781-7374
Fax: 616-781-4510

> *A historic stagecoach inn*

Innkeeper: Barbara Bradley. **Accommodations:** 13 rooms, 3 suites, all with private bath. **Rates:** Rooms $64–$82 double, suites $91–$115 double. **Included:** Continental breakfast. **Minimum stay:** No. **Added:** 7% tax. **Payment:** Major credit cards. **Children:** Yes. **Pets:** No. **Smoking:** Yes. **Open:** Year-round.

As Michigan's oldest operating inn, the National House has a reputation for history and hospitality that it works hard to maintain. Built in 1835 as a stagecoach stop, the Greek Revival building was also, according to legend, once a stop on the Underground Railroad. In 1868, it was converted to a wagon and windmill factory and, later, apartments. In 1976, it reopened as an inn.

The guest rooms range from the elegant Victorian Ketchum Suite to pleasant country rooms with folk art portraits. Some beds are gleaming brass, others hand-carved wood. The Andrew Mann Room is decorated entirely around an antique quilt of cream and green. The second-floor rooms open onto a sitting room with a fireplace surrounded by paneled cabinets.

> **The historic town of Marshall has been called the Williamsburg of the Midwest, and thousands flock to the annual tour of 19th-century homes in September. Candlelight tour weekends are held from January through April.**

Downstairs, a massive beam and brick fireplace dominates the lobby. The dining room has salmon-hued woodwork and antique oak tables, where guests enjoy a light Continental breakfast. The Tin Whistle Gift Shoppe overflows with unusual Victorian reproduction pieces and hand-crafted country gift items.

Authenticity exacts a price, however. The old road in front of the inn, once a stagecoach route, is now a busy intersection, where trucks rumble by through the night. When making reservations, ask for a room overlooking the garden.

MENDON

Mendon Country Inn

440 West Main Street
Mendon, MI 49072
616-496-8132

> *The innkeepers' enthusiasm is contagious*

Innkeepers: Dick and Dolly Buerkle. **Accommodations:** 18 rooms, 9 suites, all with private bath. **Rates:** Rooms $50–$85 double, suites $125–$150. **Included:** Continental breakfast. **Minimum stay:** 2 nights on weekends.

Added: 6% tax. **Payment:** Major credit cards. **Children:** Over 12 years. **Pets:** No. **Smoking:** Limited. **Open:** Year-round.

Dick Buerkle, the bearded innkeeper of Mendon Country Inn, greets you like a friendly old bear. His enthusiastic descriptions of his inn and nearby Amish attractions, as well as his recommendations for antiques shops and ice cream parlors, come so fast and furious that they may catch the weary traveler off guard. But after a night here, you'll understand why he gets so excited about the country haven he and his wife, Dolly, have created in lower Michigan.

> A well-worn saddle sets the cowboy theme of the Sundance room. There is an old-fashioned chain pull for the toilet and a bucket propped above the shower. Dick chuckles as he reveals the outhouse-style hole cut into a wooden plank that fits over the toilet.

The inn first opened as a frontier hotel in the 1840s. Over the years it housed a bakery, restaurant, storage space, and even a cow barn, before the Buerkles took over and started welcoming guests in 1987. The inn now features rooms in the main house, cottage suites, and candlelight lodge suites.

Some of the unusual decorating touches would appear corny just about anywhere else. The Sea Captain's Room, with a 15-foot ceiling, has a heavy fisherman's net draped over the bed. The Riverbend Room has a cigar-shaped duck boat stretched over the fireplace.

The inn also offers traditional rooms, such as the elegant first-floor Adams Wakeman Room, with 12-foot ceilings, eight-foot windows, and fine country Empire furnishings. It opens onto a shaded porch overlooking a creek.

For an extra-special stay, try one of the renovated suites in a converted house on the property. Each offers a Jacuzzi and fireplace and is decorated in the style of a different Native American tribe. The attractive Kiva Room was inspired by a trip the innkeepers made to New Mexico. The suites share a spacious living room, where a panoramic view of the parklike property can be enjoyed through picture windows.

Native American artifacts and crafts also decorate the living room in the main house. Some can be purchased, along with Amish quilts and woodcarvings, in the inn's gift room.

A light buffet breakfast is served in the Puddleman Room, whose vintage signs advertise Mendon shops from long ago. Small meetings and weddings are sometimes held in this history-filled room.

The inn is on the edge of Amish country. During the winter, there are Amish sleigh rides, cross-country skiing, and a country Christmas celebration. In spring, the monthly Centreville Antique Market attracts more than 600 dealers. The inn also schedules such events as quilting retreats and mini-folk festivals, which attract musicians from across the country to the rooftop garden.

Canoes can be rented on the property for a paddle down the St. Joseph River. Deer, foxes, groundhogs, and raccoons are frequently spotted on the inn's 14 acres.

NEW BUFFALO

Sans Souci

19265 South Lakeside Road
New Buffalo, MI 49117
616-756-3141
Fax: 616-756-5511

> *Pampering European touches highlight a converted farm*

Innkeeper: Angelika Siewert. **Accommodations:** 6 rooms, 2 suites, all with private bath, 2 cottages, vacation homes. **Rates:** Rooms $98 single or double; suites $168 single or double; cottages $175; weekly rate available. **Included:** Full breakfast. **Minimum stay:** 2 nights on weekends. **Added:** 4% tax. **Payment:** Major credit cards. **Children:** Yes. **Pets:** No. **Smoking:** Restricted to rooms with fireplace. **Open:** Year-round

Sans Souci ("without a care") is a family farm that has been converted into three crisp white guest buildings on 50 acres. From one of the upstairs decks, you can glimpse turtles sunning themselves on logs in the river. Hummingbirds, raccoons, ducks, and blue and green herons also pay visits.

In the guest rooms, Angie Siewert subscribes to a European

aesthetic of hardwood floors and spotless white walls. The amenities are anything but sparse, however. Most feature fireplaces with imported tiles from Angie's native Germany. All the wood used here is oak and walnut harvested right on the property.

> **Few lodgings blend so perfectly with their surroundings as do those at Sans Souci.**

The Kingfisher Suite is decorated in dusty rose and has a river view. Both it and the Green Heron Suite have kitchen areas with a refrigerator and microwave, along with wood floors and Jacuzzis. Binoculars are provided to help you watch the wildlife. Room telephones are available.

Breakfast, which can be delivered to your room, includes homemade baked goods, a fresh fruit plate, meat and cheese, soft-boiled eggs, assorted cereals, and a bread platter with butter, cream cheese, marmalade, and honey. Guests have their choice of morning newspapers from Chicago, Detroit, and Indiana, since the inn's location in the southwestern corner of Michigan appeals to travelers from three states.

Angie has thought of everything. Ice skates and skis are supplied in the winter, as the area is frequented by cross-country skiers. In summer, she provides fishing rods for catching bass and bluegills in Lake Sans Souci, a private spring-fed lake on the property. Guests sometimes build a late-night bonfire on its banks.

SAGINAW

The Montague Inn

1581 South Washington Avenue
Saginaw, MI 48601
517-752-3939

*An ivy-covered inn
recalls an English
country manor*

Innkeeper: Willy Schipper. **Accommodations:** 15 rooms, 2 with shared bath, 1 suite. **Rates:** Rooms $55–$105 single, $65–$115 double; suites $140 single, $150 double. **Included:** Continental breakfast; lunch and dinner available. **Minimum stay:** No. **Added:** 8% tax. **Payment:** Major credit cards. **Children:** Yes. **Pets:** No. **Smoking:** In some common rooms. **Open:** Year-round.

Providing the atmosphere you'd expect in the English countryside, the eight landscaped acres of the Montague Inn, shaded by hickory, pear, walnut, and oak trees, slope down to a small lake. The inn is the creation — or re-creation — of Norm and Kathryn Kinney, veteran innkeepers and Montague co-owners, who have restored the 1929 Georgian home to its former standing in the parklike neighborhood called the Grove.

Its original owner, Robert Montague, was so intent on recreating a 200-year-old mansion that he insisted on handmade bricks instead of the machine-cut variety. The resulting ivy-covered exterior, with a slate roof, forest green shutters, and cream-colored trim and dormers, pulls off the illusion splendidly.

Traditional Georgian furnishings set the tone throughout the interior, accented by brass chandeliers, fine fabrics, Oriental rugs on hardwood floors, and period wallpapers. A winding staircase leads to the bedrooms, many named after historical figures from the Saginaw area. The guest rooms, including five in the former chauffeur's quarters and five-car garage, are decorated with a comfortable mix of antiques and reproductions. Some even have marble fireplaces and Pewabic tile bathrooms.

Weddings are frequently held on weekends. The inn also holds a grand New Year's Eve party, special Valentine's Day dinners, and a Fourth of July picnic.

The Montague also boasts one of the best dining rooms in mid-Michigan. The menu changes seasonally, but salmon is a specialty, baked with white wine and herbs and topped with hazelnut butter. A sorbet precedes the main course, and cheesecake, mousse, and tortes highlight the dessert menu. You can also enjoy dinner, by special arrangement, in a secret alcove behind a bookcase.

A 30-person conference facility is downstairs, though smaller groups often prefer the inviting upstairs library, with its maroon swag draperies over bay windows.

The grounds now include an abundant herb and vegetable garden used by the chef. The Kinneys have also unearthed a stone path leading to the lake and plan to cultivate a formal English garden over the next several years.

SAUGATUCK

Maplewood Hotel

428 Butler Street
Saugatuck, MI 49453
616-857-2788
Fax: 616-857-1773

> *The Maplewood has been a small hotel for most of its 130 years*

Owners/innkeepers: Catherine L. Simon and Sam Burnell. **Accommodations:** 10 rooms, all with private bath, 5 suites. **Rates:** Rooms $75–$105 double, suites $130–$155; ask about off-season rates. **Included:** Continental or full breakfast. **Minimum stay:** 2 nights on weekends, May–October. **Added:** 6% tax. **Payment:** Major credit cards. **Children:** Yes. **Pets:** No. **Smoking:** Yes. **Open:** Year-round

Though built as a stately private residence, the Maplewood has been serving as a hotel for most of its 130 years. The Greek Revival building with 25-foot wooden pillars required considerable sprucing up when Catherine Simon and Sam Burnell purchased it in the spring of 1991. They are slowly bringing the place back to its understated grandeur and have already created a special small hotel in the summer haven of Saugatuck.

The guest rooms include a Bridal Suite with a sitting area, canopy bed, fireplace, and double Jacuzzi tub. Complimentary champagne is also provided here. Though less formal, Room 215 offers a country flair with a rustic pine floor in the bathroom and a bay window overlooking the village square. Catherine's collection of Weller and Roseville pottery is found in many of the rooms.

> **Two porches (one screened, the other glassed-enclosed) are excellent spots to relax, read, and play cards in the evening.**

The variety of comfortable common areas sets the Maplewood apart from other area lodgings. The Butler Library, with an antique fireplace and dark wood paneling, faces the main street. French doors lead to a spacious living room with a fireplace and player piano, a popular spot for meetings, receptions, and private parties. More collectible pottery is displayed here in a cabinet.

The Burr Tillstrom Dining Room (named for a former Saugatuck resident and the creator of Kukla, Fran, and Ollie) is the site of a light breakfast of fresh fruit, juice, coffee, and homemade date and prune muffins. On weekends, the menu is filled out with entrées like quiche and sausage and biscuits.

Dinner is not served here, but many excellent restaurants are just steps from the front door. Catherine has a basket of menus in the reception area, but if pressed she'll recommend the English pub atmosphere of Checkers, just two blocks over, for excellent hamburgers or fish. Toulouse, under the same management, offers more formal dining just a half block from the hotel. Catherine notes that even at the best Saugatuck restaurants, casual attire is always acceptable.

The Park House

888 Holland Street
Saugatuck, MI 49453
616-857-4535
800-321-4535
Fax: 616-857-1065

*Saugatuck's
oldest residence
is also one of its
most popular inns*

Innkeepers: Joe and Lynda Petty.
Accommodations: 5 rooms, all with private bath, 3 suites, 2 cottages. **Rates:** Rooms $75–$95 double; suites $120–$140; cottages $120–$160. **Included:** Continental breakfast. **Minimum stay:** 2 nights on weekends in May, June, September, October; 3 nights on weekends in July and August. **Added:** 6% tax. **Payment:** Major credit cards. **Children:** Yes. **Pets:** No. **Smoking:** No. **Open:** Year-round.

This two-story white clapboard home, built in 1857 from original timbers on the property, is the oldest residence in Saugatuck. In the 1880s, it served as the Park Club House, with pool tables and guest rooms. In 1984, Joe and Lynda Petty saw the potential of what had become a dilapidated house and restored its original country warmth with wide-planked floors, throw rugs, fireplaces, and a bounty of craft-work, ranging from needlepoint and wall stencils to tin punch and grapevine wreaths.

Legend has it that Susan B. Anthony once slept here. Her namesake room, on the first floor, is the inn's most splendid, a Victorian study in dark wood and lace with a mahogany bedroom set. Winnie's Room has burgundy wallpaper, lace-edged drapes, a queen-size bed, a twin four-poster daybed, and French sliding doors opening onto a balcony for two. Most unusual is the Lumberman's Room, with burlap walls, patch-work accents, and a large saw over the handmade bed.

In the morning, fruit, muffins, granola, sweet breads, and a special blend of coffee are set out on a sideboard in the inviting country kitchen. After breakfast, guests retreat to the parlor or adjoining garden room. Lynda often sends them home with herbs and recipes.

SOUTH HAVEN

A Country Place

79 North Shore Drive North
South Haven, MI 49090
616-637-5523

*A congenial
family-style inn
and cottages*

Innkeepers: Lee and Art Niffenegger. **Accommodations:** 5 rooms, all with private bath, 3 cottages. **Rates:** Rooms $50 weekday single, $65–$85 double; cottages $75–$100; weekly rates available. **Included:** Full breakfast. **Minimum stay:** 2 nights on summer weekends. **Added:** 6% tax. **Payment:** Major credit cards. **Children:** In cottages only. **Pets:** No. **Smoking:** In cottages only. **Open:** Year-round for inn; cottages May–October.

An added dose of hospitality sets A Country Place apart from the countless other small bed-and-breakfast inns that dot this section of the Lake Michigan shoreline. Lee and Art Niffenegger are constantly fine-tuning their century-old Greek Revival home for the enjoyment of guests.

You can tell this is a family place when you go up the staircase lined with photographs of the innkeepers' families. There's Art at 16, on the South Haven High School basketball team, and a shot of the old Niffenegger Handy Market. At the top of the stairs is Lee's grandparents' ornate marriage certificate from 1905.

The four guest rooms upstairs are furnished with country touches like stuffed lambs and bears, but they aren't overdone. In the Garden Room, with

> **Two cottages down the street are all that remain of South Haven's popular Belvedere Beach Resort. They have been redone with painted boxcar siding and full kitchen facilities.**

two double beds and pine floors, a Shaker rake serves as a towel rack. The Terrace Room has a double bed with folk art prints of cats. The Windsor Room, on the main floor, features a jet tub and television. Some of the baths have old-fashioned wooden commodes.

The cottage on the property has a great room, a small loft, a Franklin fireplace, an enclosed front porch, and a back deck overlooking the woods.

Breakfast, included with main house stays only, features homemade muffins, breads, fresh fruit, and special entrées like peach crêpes. It is served in the formal dining room or, during warmer weather, on the deck or enclosed sun porch. The innkeepers will gladly point you toward attractions in downtown South Haven.

Yelton Manor

140 North Shore Drive
South Haven, MI 49090
616-637-5220
Fax: 616-637-4957

> *South Haven's*
> *premier B&B*

Proprietors: Robert Kripatis and
Elaine Herbert. **Accommodations:** 12 rooms, all with private
bath, 5 suites. **Rates:** Rooms $90–$135 single or double, suites
$145–$185. **Included:** Full breakfast, treats throughout the
day. **Minimum stay:** 2 nights on weekends May–October.
Added: 6% tax. **Payment:** Major credit cards. **Children:** No.
Pets: No. **Smoking:** No. **Open:** Year-round.

Elaine Herbert and Robert Kripatis loved their overnight stay
at Yelton Manor so much that they never left. They bought
the place lock, stock, and barrel and now run it with the same
blend of hospitality and
services that made it the
town's premier B&B.

> **The inn is just across from
> a public beach, so the
> sounds of Lake Michigan
> can lull you to sleep.**

The guest rooms are
furnished with king-size
beds covered with Amish
quilts and no fewer than
eight pillows. Lily, Snap-
dragon, and Magnolia are
just some of the rooms named after flowers in the inn's Victorian garden. Victorian and Amish furniture decorate the
house, along with plenty of stained glass. Honeymoon and anniversary suites, both with whirlpool baths, are tucked be-

neath slanted ceilings. The common rooms include a third-floor library for reading and writing.

The Manor Guest House, with additional suites, recently opened on the property. The six suites are named after popular South Haven resorts of yesteryear and boast panoramic lake views and walk-out balconies, along with romantic flourishes like fireplaces and Jacuzzis. The guest house also features a wraparound porch and guest parlors.

The inn may soon see an increased number of business meetings and conferences. But for now it's a delightful summer getaway.

ST. JOSEPH

Snow Flake Motel

3822 Red Arrow Highway
St. Joseph, MI 49085
616-429-3261

> *A funky motel
> designed by
> the Frank Lloyd
> Wright Foundation*

Managers: Isobel and Calvin Magil. **Accommodations:** 57 rooms, all with private bath. **Rates:** $38 single, $48 double. **Included:** All meals available. **Minimum stay:** No. **Added:** 4% tax. **Payment:** Major credit cards. **Children:** Yes. **Pets:** Negotiable. **Smoking:** Yes. **Open:** Year-round.

In 1962, the Frank Lloyd Wright Foundation was commissioned to create a lodging that incorporated a flavor of the countryside in a modern motel facility. It takes an aerial view to fully appreciate the resulting Snow Flake Motel, whose rooms are arranged in a snowflake design.

Like many of Wright's own works, the Snow Flake has generated its own controversy. Some architecture buffs consider it an abomination that would have Wright spinning in his grave. Yet a growing number of young Chicagoans make regular pilgrimages here to enjoy the kitschy accommodations.

Some Wright touches remain, including soaring ceilings in some rooms (quite a change from a claustrophobic Motel 6) and modern desks. The rooms offer everything from a pair of single beds to a king-size waterbed, and include amenities like remote-control cable television and direct-dial phones.

> Don't expect furnishings designed by Wright in the standard motel rooms, which feature painted cinder block walls and brown and gold carpeting.

All the rooms have direct access to the grassy courtyard through sliding glass doors.

The Snow Flake Restaurant and Lounge are next to the office, as is the octagonal pool, which is covered by a six-ton open steel dome. It is accessible only through the office or across the courtyard. The motel is just a mile off I-94 and a brisk walk from Lake Michigan.

UNION CITY

The Victorian Villa Guesthouse

601 North Broadway Street
Union City, MI 49094
517-741-7383
Fax: 517-741-4002
800-34-VILLA

> *A Victorian valentine in the middle of nowhere*

Innkeeper: Ron Gibson. **Accommodations:** 8 rooms, all with private bath, 2 suites. **Rates:** Rooms $95 double, suites $125 double. **Included:** Full breakfast; dinner available. **Minimum stay:** No. **Added:** 4% tax.

Payment: Major credit cards. **Children:** Yes. **Pets:** No. **Smoking:** No. **Open:** Year-round.

At his Victorian Villa, Ron Gibson has brought all the excess of Victoriana to lower Michigan. The home has been lovingly restored to the grandeur it enjoyed when it was built as the home of a prosperous doctor in 1876.

The guest chambers are decorated with prime Victorian antiques. A complete set of Brooks furniture is the highlight of the Master Bedchamber. The Rococo Country Bedchamber features Civil War–era furnishings with deep carvings in elegant walnut. The circa 1850s Empire Bedchamber has a massive carved armoire and four-poster bed. The

> **The inn upholds several Victorian-inspired traditions: a summer croquet tournament, Sherlock Holmes mystery weekends in the fall, and an elaborate Dickensian Christmas, complete with authentic 19th-century feasts and decorations.**

two Tower Suites, separated by a private parlor, are especially popular with honeymooners. They are decorated with exposed brick and have a Victorian country feel.

To enhance his Victorian time capsule, Ron frequently plays recordings of antique music boxes and Reginaphones in his red velvet-swagged parlor. On crisp winter evenings, he lights a fire here and serves hot cider and mulled wine.

Recently equipped with a commercial kitchen and spacious dining room, the Villa now offers popular 19th-century dinners Thursday through Saturday. The seven-course meal may include English roasted loin of boar, Chinook salmon, or French trussed game hens.

Breakfast is equally elaborate. It features imported herbal teas and coffees, chilled orange juice, pastries, toasted English muffins, homemade preserves, Amish butter and cheese, seasonal Michigan fruit, and an egg and cheese puff soufflé.

Ron will also stage elegant high teas, featuring his own fancy pastries and finger sandwiches. He'll even pack a picnic lunch in a wicker basket, which guests can enjoy during a ride in the country on the inn's bicycle built for two.

The popularity of the Victorian Villa testifies to Ron's love of Victoriana and his ability to capture so much of it in one place — and virtually in the middle of nowhere! Union City certainly isn't a drawing card, but antiques shops and other attractions are a comfortable drive away.

UNION PIER

The Inn at Union Pier

P.O. Box 222
9708 Berrien
Union Pier, MI 49129
616-469-4700

> *Summer guests flock to this 1920s lakefront retreat*

Innkeepers: Joyce Erickson Pitts and Mark Pitts. **Accommodations:** 15 rooms, all with private bath. **Rates:** $105–$150 double. **Included:** Full breakfast. **Minimum stay:** 2 nights on weekends; 3 nights certain holidays. **Added:** 6% tax. **Payment:** Major credit cards. **Children:** Over 12 years. **Pets:** No. **Smoking:** No. **Open:** Year-round.

Union Pier and the other communities wedged into the southwestern corner of Michigan have experienced a new popularity with Chicagoans. While the Inn at Union Pier shines in all seasons, summer is the time when guests flock to this 1920s lakefront retreat, just 200 steps from Lake Michigan.

The inviting reception area is decorated in a comfortable mix of Scandanavian country and lakeside cottage touches. It also has an antique Swedish wood-burning fireplace called a Karelugn. Eleven of the guest rooms also feature these unusual ceramic tile fireplaces. Many were imported from Sweden more than 80 years ago.

The Scandinavian aesthetic continues with hand-painted signs reminiscent of the work of Carl Larsson over the guest room doors. The Captain's Quarters recalls a British officers' club, appointed in dark woods with a cherry sleigh bed, private balcony, and a two-person whirlpool. Madeleine's Room is decorated in relaxing blue and gray and features original art of birds and flowers.

> **Energetic guests will find the staff more than happy to arrange wind-surfing, fishing, canoeing, horseback riding, golf, and bicycling.**

The separate Cottage of the Four Seasons celebrates the changing year with charming theme rooms. In Fall, shafts of wheat on a spread cover a pencil bed encircled with grapevines. Grandma Moses prints line the walls. Spring uses white wicker furniture and pastel greens.

The inn's three buildings are connected by a long wooden deck. Guests enjoy breakfast overlooking a yard filled with flowering redbud and cherry trees. The meal may include muffins and fruit with omelettes, Belgian waffles, or eggs Florentine. In the evening, guests can soak in the eight-person hot tub in another corner of the deck and relax in the adjacent sauna.

The check-in area is well stocked with articles and brochures about restaurants and attractions in the area. While the inn is a natural for a weekend stay, it has grown increasingly popular with businesspeople, who drive the quick hour and a half from Chicago for retreats and conferences. The inn has no restaurant, though there are numerous restaurants — from formal to country casual — within a 10-minute drive.

Northern Michigan
and the
Upper Peninsula

Best Bed-and-Breakfast Inns

Big Bay
  Big Bay Point Lighthouse
Harbor Springs
  Kimberly Country Estate
Lewiston
  LakeView Hills Country Inn
Mackinac Island
  Metivier Inn
Michigamme
  Michigamme Lake Lodge
Northport
  The Old Mill Pond Inn
Pequaming
  The Bungalow
Traverse City
  Cherry Knoll Farm

Best Full-Service Country Inns

McMillan
  The Helmer House Inn
Petoskey
  Stafford's Bay View Inn

Best Hotels

Bay View
  The Terrace Inn
Mackinac Island
  Hotel Iroquois
Petoskey
  The Perry Hotel
Sault Ste. Marie
  Ojibway Hotel

Best Lodges and Resorts

Copper Harbor
  Keweenaw Mountain Lodge

Glen Arbor
  The Homestead
Lewiston
  Garland Resort
Mackinac Island
  Grand Hotel
Traverse City
  Grand Traverse Resort

Traverse City is Michigan's Cherry Capital. In July, the National Cherry Festival features parades, races, and fireworks. Located on Grand Traverse Bay and near many inland lakes, Traverse City remains a haven for fishing and water sports, while abundant lake-effect snow draws snowmobilers, skiers, and ice fishermen in winter. The Cherry County Playhouse, Old Town Playhouse, and Traverse City Players all stage community theater. The Con Foster Museum has programs on Grand Traverse history, while the Music House, located in an old granary, showcases automatic musical instruments from the turn of the century. The Sleeping Bear Dunes National Lakeshore, about 25 miles west of town, towers some 500 feet above Lake Michigan at some points. Legend states that the dune is a mother bear waiting for her cubs — the Manitou Islands — to return. If you don't feel like climbing the dunes, the Pierce Stocking Scenic Drive has great views of the dunes and water.

  Petoskey, a scenic drive north from Traverse City on Highway 31, is highlighted by fishing, sailing, and sandy beaches. The downtown Gaslight District features numerous specialty shops, even some devoted to the state Petoskey stone. Neighboring **Bay View** began as a religious retreat, then grew into a thriving summer Chautauqua devoted to cultural and educational pursuits. The program is still there, along with the well-tended Victorian summer homes that line the residential streets.

  Harbor Springs, on the other side of Little Traverse Bay, is an upscale resort community. Championship golf can be enjoyed at Boyne Highlands, while downhill and cross-country skiers head for Nub's Nob. The 31-mile drive on Country Road 77 from Harbor Springs to Cross Village affords beautiful glimpses of Lake Michigan shoreline and virtual tunnels of trees.

  Mackinac Island is the state's best-loved tourist attraction. Located in the Straits of Mackinac at the top of Michigan's geographic mitt, the island is reached by plane or by high-speed hydroplanes from ferry companies in either Mackinaw City or St. Ignace. Because no cars are allowed here, the island presents a real step back in time, with a bustling main street full of restaurants and gift and fudge shops in restored store-fronts. Horse-drawn carriages can be commandeered for a nostalgic trip downtown. Bikes can be rented for the eight-mile trip around the island. During the summer, Mackinac swells with tourists, or "fudgies," so it's much more pleasant (and cheaper) to visit in the off-season. Try to spend a night here, when the less populated streets give you an entirely different feel for the place.

It costs a five-spot to walk the long front porch of the landmark Grand Hotel. Splurge on a meal here instead. It's an expensive but memorable island treat. About 80 percent of the island is state park land, including Fort Mackinac, which is preserved as a living history museum. Costumed guides conduct tours through 14 buildings, all dating from 1780 to 1855. There are natural wonders to take in as well, including dramatic Arch Rock.

Sault Ste. Marie is the state's oldest settlement. Visitors are still fascinated by the Soo Locks. This engineering marvel, created to allow traffic through once-dangerous rapids and waterfalls, raises or lowers ships to meet different plateaus in the channel. A two-hour boat ride gives you a closer look.

Much of the upper peninsula is dotted with rustic, often economically depressed, small towns. **Big Bay** and Grand Marais, both at the top of the state and overlooking Lake Superior, appear much as they did 30 years ago — and that's part of their charm. Marquette, meanwhile, is the bustling home to Northern Michigan University. While touring the areas between Grand Marais and Munising, take the three-hour cruise to Pictured Rocks. These sandstone cliffs are colored by iron, limestone, and copper deposits.

The Keweenaw peninsula, Michigan's northernmost point, is actually an island accessible by bridge. While here, visit the Calumet Theater, which once hosted turn-of-the-century greats like Douglas Fairbanks, Lillian Russell, and Sarah Bernhardt. Mine tours are still part of the experience at **Copper Harbor,** though the town is long past those days when copper was king. Fishing, however, is still a popular draw.

Take an unforgettable trip through the Porcupine Mountains State Park. This is the site of Lake of the Clouds, a scenic overlook high above the lake.

BAY VIEW

The Terrace Inn

216 Fairview
Bay View, MI 49770
616-347-2410
Reservations: 800-CLARION

A historic hotel surrounded by Victorian cottages

Innkeepers: Patrick and Mary Lou Barbour. **Accommodations:** 44 rooms. **Rates:** $66–$99. **Included:** Continental breakfast. **Minimum stay:** No. **Added:** 6% tax. **Payment:** Major credit cards. **Children:** Yes. **Pets:** No. **Smoking:** Nonsmoking rooms available. **Open:** Year-round.

Bay View was founded a century ago because of its annual summer Chautauqua festival. Visitors to this educational and spiritual program of lectures, concerts, and dramatic performances initially slept in tents. Later they built gingerbread-trimmed cottages. Bay View's summer residents still keep their coveted Victorian cottages immaculate, and many of the homes are passed from generation to generation.

It is amazing, then, that in 1910, the banker W. J. DeVol was able to talk the pious residents of Bay View into building a rambling resort hotel right in the middle of the residential area. Demolishing several cottages in the process, he built the Terrace Inn for $26,000 — and visitors are glad he did.

In the spring of 1987 another set of bankers, Patrick and Mary Lou Barbour, reopened the inn after renovating the lobby, dining room, and guest rooms. The building came with much of its old furniture — mostly solid oak dressers, rockers, and chairs — which mingle with curvy Victorian pieces and potted ferns.

Prospective guests may wander through the halls and peek into empty guest rooms, many with Victorian reproduction wallpapers and framed 19th-century prints. Black wallpaper contrasts dramatically with white wicker rockers, painted dressers, embroidered linens, and white tieback curtains in many rooms. There are no televisions or telephones, though some rooms have air conditioning.

A dining room, whose dusty rose and forest green decor was inspired by a swatch of the home's original wallpaper, is open during the summer for lunch and dinner. Entrées include northern Michigan whitefish broiled on natural wood planks (a house specialty), lobster Alfredo, and pork tenderloin with pecan mustard sauce. Breakfast pales by comparison: a light Continental offering of fruit, muffins, coffee, and tea set out in a gathering room.

> **Hiking trails and swimming are within easy walking distance; Petoskey and Harbor Springs and Petoskey State Park are just minutes away by car.**

Children enjoy the ice cream parlor in the lower level, though plans for a nostalgic retro-decor have apparently fallen by the wayside.

The front desk staff can answer questions about Chautauqua events, held daily between June and August. Many guests simply enjoy walking around Bay View, admiring the houses' delicate scrollwork and elaborate gardens. The inn's long back porch is the perfect spot to relax and imagine that, just for a moment, you are one of the privileged Bay View cottagers with the entire summer stretching before you.

BIG BAY

Big Bay Point Lighthouse

No. 3 Lighthouse Road
Big Bay, MI 49808
906-345-9957

> *Spend the night in a Lake Superior lighthouse*

Innkeepers: Linda Gamble. **Accommodations:** 6 rooms, some with private bath. **Rates:** $85–$165 single or double. **Included:** Full breakfast, all taxes. **Minimum stay:** 2 nights on weekends July–October. **Payment:** Personal checks and cash. **Children:** No. **Pets:** No. **Smoking:** No. **Open:** Year-round.

Upon arriving at the Big Bay Point Lighthouse in Michigan's Upper Peninsula, you will discover a pink sheet of paper taped to the door. On it, innkeeper Linda Gamble has typed a tongue-in-cheek description of your duties. An attached button, to be worn at all times during your stay, identifies you as a Keeper's Helper. You soon realize that your real responsibilities are few, outside of hiking, rock hunting, and taking in the scenic beauty of the lighthouse's full mile of Lake Superior shoreline.

> At sunset, guests climb to the top of the tower, 120 feet above the lake, where the lighthouse casts its beam. You can't imagine a more romantic setting as the sun sinks slowly from view.

According to the innkeeper, Big Bay Point is one of only a few privately owned and operating lighthouses in the country that allows guests to sleep right on the premises. The historic 1896 brick structure opened as an inn in 1980. Since the word got out, an empty room on weekends has been hard to find.

Conversation is especially lively during the family-style breakfast, which begins at 8:00 A.M. Guests feel so at home here that they've been known to pitch in with the dishes. Since there aren't a multitude of fine dining establishments in the area, guests often prefer to bring in their own groceries and take over the kitchen.

After breakfast, you can hike the scenic trail around the property. Linda also recommends the 4½–hour Big Bay van trip and hike led by naturalist Jeff TenEyck. For $25, you can scale cliffs, hop slippery stones over flowing rivers, and sample a trail lunch of northern Michigan pasties.

After dark, activity moves to the first-floor living room, where a fire can take a bite out of the cold lake wind. Conversation invariably turns to William Pryor, the original Big Bay Point lighthouse keeper, who died under mysterious circumstances in 1901 and whose ghost reportedly roams the bluffs.

You can also drive into the tiny town of Big Bay, where the movie *Anatomy of a Murder* (based on an actual UP murder case) was shot in 1959. You can even visit the bar where the killing happened, and there's usually at least one denizen who will tell you "the real story" and show you the bullet holes behind the bar. Before the arrival of the lighthouse inn, the movie connection was the area's main claim to fame.

COPPER HARBOR

Keweenaw Mountain Lodge

Copper Harbor, MI 49918
906-289-4403

General manager: Chuck Abe. **Accommodations:** 34 cottages, 8 motel rooms. **Rates:** Motel rooms $46; cottages $49–$59; packages available. **Included:** All meals available. **Minimum stay:** No. **Added:** 7% tax. **Payment:** MasterCard, Visa. **Children:** Yes. **Pets:** No. **Smoking:** Yes. **Open:** Mid-May–mid-October.

> *A premier vacation site on the Upper Peninsula*

The Keweenaw Mountain Lodge was established by the federal government in the 1930s to bring work to an area hard hit by the Depression. By the end of World War II, the lodge had become one of the premier vacation destinations in Michigan's Upper Peninsula.

Now run by Keweenaw County, it carries on that tradition, attracting families and bike tour groups to reasonably priced accommodations in renovated cabins and motel units. One- to three-bedroom cottages offer hardwood floors and stone fireplaces in comfortable living rooms.

> **Copper Harbor is at the tip of a Michigan peninsula that once mined copper for the world. It now welcomes tourist traffic, with the Brockway Mountain Drive, Fort Wilkins State Park, and tours of old copper mines among the major draws.**

The furnishings include overstuffed chairs and firm mattresses. The spacious motel rooms have cathedral ceilings and dark wood paneling.

The Grand Lodge dining room serves American-style beef, roasted chicken with country dressing, and seafood specialties, including Lake Superior trout. All dinners include trips to the salad bar, where potato salad and hearty beef stew soup could make a meal by themselves. There's also an adjoining cocktail lounge with a 40-foot-tall fireplace.

The lodge sits on its own 500 wooded acres, and it's surrounded by thousands of acres of primeval forest. It also includes an 18-hole golf course, tennis courts, shuffleboard, and hiking trails.

GLEN ARBOR

The Homestead

Wood Ridge Road
Glen Arbor, MI 49636
Reservations: 616-334-5100
Information: 616-334-5000
Fax: 616-334-5120

Comfortable accommodations with four seasons of activities

President: Robert Kuras. **Accommodations:** 140 rooms, 14 suites, number of condominiums varies. **Rates:** Rooms $77–$120; suites $102–$145; condominiums $109–$350; packages and weekly rates available. **Included:** All meals available. **Minimum stay:** No. **Added:** 6% tax. **Payment:** Cash, check, credit cards. **Children:** Yes. **Pets:** No. **Smoking:** Yes. **Open:** Mid-May–October, Christmas–mid-March.

You can strap on your Rossignols and ski right out the door of your room at this classic Midwestern resort in the heart of Michigan's Leelanau Peninsula. With 16 miles of slopes and 42 holes of golf, the Homestead now attracts visitors of all ages in all seasons. Built as a boys' camp in 1929, the resort lies on 500 wooded acres with three miles of shoreline on Lake Michigan.

The original sleeping quarters are now a formal dining

room. Most of the accommodations have been built since the 1980s to enhance their newfound popularity with families.

Hotel-style rooms are available above attractive shops and restaurants in the Village, the hub of activity in the ski season. At the Pinnacle Place condominiums, you are literally on top of the slopes.

Standard rooms have queen-size beds and sitting areas. Deluxe rooms add fireplaces and spa tubs. Some suites have three-sided fireplaces and televisions built in behind mirrors above Jacuzzis for two.

> **Families can climb the famous Sleeping Bear Dunes or tour a restored Coast Guard station. The Leelanau Peninsula also has a number of excellent wineries.**

The condominiums, privately owned but often available to guests, sit on ridges high above the bay, at the Golf Academy, along the river, and on the beach. They are fully equipped units tastefully decorated with exposed wood, folk art prints, quilts, and four-poster beds.

For children, a summer stay here includes access to beaches, pools, paddleboats, bikes, and nature trails on the property. Daytime and evening programs, for an additional fee, offer different age groups tennis, treasure hunts, arts and crafts, and nature walks. More sports activities, dinner, and movies are scheduled most evenings.

HARBOR SPRINGS

Kimberly Country Estate

2287 Bester Road
Harbor Springs, MI 49740
616-526-9502
616-526-9740

Luxury and attention to detail still live in Harbor Springs

Innkeepers: Ronn and Billie Serba. **Accommodations:** 6 rooms, 2 suites, all with private bath. **Rates:** Rooms $135–$155 double, suites $165–$225. **Included:** Continental breakfast. **Minimum stay:** 2 nights on weekends; 3 nights on holidays. **Added:** 4% tax. **Payment:** Major credit cards. **Children:** 12 years and older. **Pets:** No. **Smoking:** No. **Open:** Year-round.

In the comfortable summer community of Harbor Springs, Kimberly Country Estate was built in 1961 with the elegance and attention to detail you probably thought died with the Victorians. Lavish crown moldings are found in many rooms. The 8,000-square-foot home, in the Colonial plantation style, is surrounded by fields and farms and overlooks a swimming pool, a duck pond in the backyard, and a golf course beyond.

The designers wanted both men and women to feel comfortable with the elegant English country decor. The library, for instance, is lined in North Carolina black walnut and has English armchairs, an old drop-leaf table, and paisley fabric on the ceiling. Other rooms blend pastel hues, Battenberg lace, oil paintings, and chintz-covered chairs for an almost impressionistic feel. The owners once ran a flower shop in Grosse Pointe, so, not surprisingly, fresh flowers decorate each room.

Le Soleil, with a queen-size canopy bed and several windows, is the most popular room. Honeymooners can enjoy breakfast in their room and complimentary champagne in the Verandah Suite, with a canopy bed and a Jacuzzi overlooking the fireplace. Four rooms open onto the back porch. Notice the stately column in the Lexington Suite's bathroom. Baskets of Gucci soaps, shampoos, and body lotions are supplied in all the rooms.

In the kitchen you'll find a cast-iron chandelier and a handsome marble-topped table with Queen Anne claw-and-ball-foot legs. Here the Serbas prepare a generous Continental breakfast, which includes whole-grain cereals, yogurt, fresh fruit, and muffins. On Sundays (and occasional Saturdays), an egg dish is served, with perhaps a slice of smoked turkey replacing ham or bacon as a side dish. Iced lemonade is available by the pool; high tea is served on the terrace.

> **After shopping in Harbor Springs, you will enjoy returning to the inn, where deer, wild turkeys, and rabbits are often spotted on the property. There is also a golf course, Wequetonsing, nearby.**

LEWISTON

Garland Resort

Route 1, Box 364–M
County Road 489
Lewiston, MI 49756
517-786-2211
800-968-0042
Fax: 517-786-2254

> *Golf and other
> activities attract
> guests to Garland*

General manager: Barry Owens. **Accommodations:** 55 rooms, 5 suites, 60 villas. **Rates:** Rooms $137–$180 midweek, $137–$202 weekend; suites $208–$242 midweek, $242–$334 weekend; villas $242–$508 midweek and weekend; packages available. **Included:** All meals available. **Minimum stay:** No. **Added:** 6% tax. **Payment:** Major credit cards. **Children:** Yes. **Pets:** No. **Smoking:** Yes. **Open:** Closed in late fall and early spring.

Garland began in the early 1950s, when Herman Otto, a businessman originally from Germany, built a 9-hole golf course for family, friends, and employees of his Detroit company, Garland Manufacturing. When a fire destroyed the original clubhouse in 1985, Herman's son Ron decided not only to rebuild but also to add guest rooms and conference facilities to the property.

Over the years, Garland has retained its family-run atmosphere. The late owner's children and grandchildren work at the resort, which is still primarily known for its excellent golf facilities on tree-lined fairways. Gradually, new courses have been added for a total of 72 championship holes. You may even see a bald eagle nesting in the trees. There is also tennis, a fully equipped weight room, and a large pool.

The main lobby has an Italian marble floor, stained glass windows, and a soaring cut-stone fireplace. The polished oak woodwork continues into the guest rooms, which are clean, well equipped, and tastefully decorated with floral wallpaper and four-poster beds. All rooms have fireplaces. Some baths have Jacuzzis, mirrored ceilings, and multiple shower heads.

> **Hiking trails cut through a portion of the resort's 3,500 acres. Winter guests can enjoy cross-country skiing, sleigh rides, or the glass-enclosed whirlpool, which is open year-round and actually looks like an igloo when steam freezes on the glass.**

Golf-minded businessmen, used to plastic cards instead of keys, will be most at home here. The third-floor executive level of the main lodge, with its cathedral-beamed ceiling and marble-lined bathrooms, should satisfy even the most persnickety company president. The conference facilities feature a large main area with vaulted ceilings and four adjoining smaller rooms.

Herman's, the dining room, serves such dishes as breast of Michigan pheasant roasted in a corn husk with wild mushrooms. Try one of the fish entrées, including hardwood planked salmon with hazelnut and chives or pan-fried walleye with fresh herbs, lemon, and brown butter. Caesar salad and bananas Foster are prepared at your table.

Ask about Garland packages, including the popular "Zhivago Night" package with a romantic 45-minute sleigh ride to Garland's Buckhorn Lodge. Guests are treated to a five-course meal with wine and wild game entrée, while serenaded by strolling minstrels.

Garland has quickly moved up the ranks of Michigan business and golf retreats. Though it has missed out on some of the rustic charm it tries so hard to replicate, it delivers the same atmosphere promised by its founder, catering to businesspeople seeking relaxation on and off the links.

LakeView Hills Country Inn and Resort

1 Fleming Road
P.O. Box 365
Lewiston, MI 49756
517-786-2000
517-786-3445

> *A place for
> antiques lovers,
> croquet players,
> and skiers*

Owner/innkeeper: Shirley Chapoton. **Accommodations:** 13 rooms, 1 suite, all with private bath. **Rates:** Rooms $120 double, suite $135 double. **Included:** Full breakfast. **Minimum stay:** 2 nights on peak weekends. **Added:** 6% tax. **Payment:** MasterCard, Visa. **Children:** 12 years and older. **Pets:** No. **Smoking:** Limited. **Open:** Year-round.

Shirley Chapoton could have easily renovated an old building after deciding to open a country inn in Michigan. She opted instead for the flexibility of a new structure, and the resulting LakeView Hills Country Inn and Resort showcases the antiques collected over the years.

Shirley, an antiques dealer and auctioneer, has decorated each room to reflect northern Michigan's history. The Mitchelson-Hanson Bunkhouse recalls Lewiston's rough-and-tumble logging camp days, with rustic bunk beds. The C. W. Comstock Room has hand-painted flowers on the queen-size Eastlake bed. Bradbury and Bradbury wallpaper and country blue accents add to its charm. The Otsego Room has a Radio City Music Hall microphone among its art deco and '50s furnishings, such as a blond wood bedroom set and black and white tile in the bathroom.

An exercise facility offers fitness equipment, a hot tub, and a sauna. The room is decorated with a dart board from an English pub, a 1907 Maytag washer (with its brochure), a Western mail pouch, and game tables from the 1800s.

Outdoor activities include downhill and cross-country skiing, hiking, and guided bike tours. Two of Michigan's great trout streams, the Au Sable and the Black, are nearby, and 72-hole Garland, one of the state's best golf courses, is just down the road. A regulation croquet court, one of only two sanctioned in the state, sits behind the inn. Shirley is convinced that the sport will soon rival golf as a favorite American pastime.

Breakfast at LakeView Hills includes fresh fruit with yogurt, quiche or French toast, muffins,

> **Shirley took full advantage of the inn's location on a 355-acre tract of pine and hardwood forest, at 1,442 feet the highest point in Michigan's lower peninsula. The best view is from the fourth-floor observatory; the 35-mile panorama takes in East Twin Lake and the village of Lewiston.**

and homemade granola. Throughout the day, a guest refrigerator is kept stocked with fresh lemonade and homemade baked goods.

MACKINAC ISLAND

Grand Hotel

Mackinac Island, MI 49757
906-847-3331
800-33-GRAND

> *A true step back in time*

President and General Manager: R. D. Musser. **Accommodations:** 317 rooms. **Rates:** $210–$400 single, $260–$450 double. **Included:** Breakfast, afternoon tea, and dinner. **Minimum stay:** No. **Added:** 18% service charge, 4% tax, $4 per person baggage handling. **Payment:** MasterCard, Visa. **Children:** Yes. **Pets:** No. **Smoking:** Yes. **Open:** Mid-May–October.

The Grand Hotel is synonymous with lodging on Mackinac Island; islanders simply call it "the hotel." While the rates border on the outrageous, this old venerable resort has enough freewheeling style, grandeur, and history to make a stay here worth the expense.

Built in 1887 by steamship and railroad barons, the Grand capitalizes on its ideal location on historic Mackinac Island. As a guest of the Grand, you will be greeted at dockside by a red-jacketed driver in an antique horse-drawn carriage. The view is splendid as you clip-clop up the long driveway of the big white Greek Revival hotel, high on a bluff and surrounded by colorful blooms on 50 acres.

> **The Grand has the facilities of a world-class resort. Its serpentine pool is named for Esther Williams (who made a film here), and an 18-hole golf course is aptly called the Jewel. There is also a croquet court.**
>
> **On the lower level are several elegant boutiques, including clothing stores, gift shops, and hair salons.**

It remains one of the world's largest summer hotels, with the verandah alone measuring some 660 feet. A battery of white wicker rockers stretches along the verandah, offering a spectacular view of the Straits of Mackinac. Visitors must pay $5 to simply stroll across if they're not staying or eating here.

The interior, which was redecorated for the hotel's centennial, blends cabbage rose fabric and wallpaper with bold colors in a breezy summer style. Three categories of guest rooms are decorated not too differently from a hotel's, with reasonably plush furnishings and the lobby's penchant for summer-bright colors. While not all views were created equally, some are truly unforgettable. The mist rises from the golf course to reveal a sunny day with horses clopping by.

Named rooms, distinctively appointed luxury rooms, are the hotel's most expensive. The Lodge of Teddy Roosevelt, for instance, has an antelope head and an elephant-foot table. The China Suite is a lush Oriental emporium complete with an elaborately carved opium bed.

   Breakfast is a six-course showcase of more than 30 choices, from omelettes to pastries. Dinner is a formal affair, a five-course feast that typically includes seafood cocktail with mustard sauce, smoked salmon, whitefish (caught the same day), and aged prime rib of beef. It's served by nattily dressed waiters, many of whom spend the winter season in Jamaica. The popular lunch buffet covers ten tables. Box lunches can also be provided for guests who want to plan a picnic.

   Outside the hotel, you can tour historic Fort Mackinac or embark on the eight-mile bike ride around the island. Your sweet tooth won't escape the tempting aroma of 13 shops offering homemade fudge, the reason that Mackinac's tourists have long been called "fudgies."

Hotel Iroquois

P.O. Box 456
Main Street
Mackinac Island, MI 49757
906-847-3321
616-247-5675 in winter

> *Generations have enjoyed this family-run hotel*

General manager: Mary K. McIntire. **Accommodations:** 41 rooms, 6 suites. **Rates:** Rooms $98–$315, $68–$285 off-season; suites $315, $285 off-season; packages available. **Included:** All meals available. **Minimum stay:** No. **Added:** 4% tax. **Payment:** Discover, MasterCard, Visa. **Children:** Yes. **Pets:** No. **Smoking:** Nonsmoking rooms available. **Open:** Mid-May–mid-October.

Cool evening breezes blow from the waterfront as guests sip cocktails on the verandah. The view is unforgettable, as pleasure boats and freighters dot the white-capped Straits of Mackinac. Similar views can be enjoyed from many of the brightly decorated accommodations. Owned and run for more than 30 years by the McIntire family, the Hotel Iroquois has never wavered in its quality or service.

Despite regular additions and renovations, the hotel retains its turn-of-the-century charm. Floral wallpapers, sparkling white trim, and comfortable beds provide the summer hotel feeling. The most popular rooms have cathedral ceilings, sitting rooms, or large bay windows.

Phil Kromer, the chef, specializes in fresh northern Michigan whitefish and sautéed perch as well as soups and pasta. Breakfast, available through room service, can be served in the room or on the wicker-filled front sun porch.

> **Even if you don't stay overnight, you'll want to sample lunch or dinner at the hotel's Carriage House Restaurant.**

The hotel is pricey but highly rated. The most meaningful recommendations come from guests who summer here year after year, generation after generation. It's not uncommon to find young parents who can't imagine staying anywhere else.

Metivier Inn

P.O. Box 285
Market Street
Mackinac Island, MI 49757
906-847-6234
616-627-2055 in winter

> *A turreted inn offers a haven from the bustling street*

Innkeepers: Jane and Mike Bacon, Diane and Ken Neyer. **Accommodations:** 19 rooms, 2 efficiencies. **Rates:** High season $125–$165, low season $98–$145. **Included:** Continental breakfast. **Minimum stay:** No. **Added:** 4% tax. **Payment:** Major credit cards. **Children:** Yes. **Pets:** No. **Smoking:** Yes. **Open:** May–October.

Louis Metivier built the turreted Victorian house in 1877, and, like many island homes, it remained in the family until the current owners took over in 1984. Additional guest rooms were quickly built and now a new third floor offers even more. Antique wicker chairs and settees line the front porch, where guests congregate on summer nights.

The small but well-decorated guest rooms fall into two categories. A country room may contain a four-poster whitewashed pine bed, antique prints, and straw hats. Summer cottage rooms feature floral wallpaper, wicker chairs, and iron and brass headboards.

Breakfast is served buffet-style downstairs and includes fruit, muffins,

> **The most popular accommodations are the many-windowed Turret Rooms, with splendid views of island rooftops and the sounds of horses from the stables across the street. The rooms at the back of the inn are quieter and feature garden views.**

and juices. Most guests enjoy it on the porch or in the cozy dining room. Though the inn stresses comfort, this isn't the sort of place to linger over coffee with a friendly innkeeper.

The Metivier Inn is on historic Market Street, which parallels the main street just a block behind. It's close to historic sites and accommodations for horseback riding, swimming, and, of course, biking the eight miles around the island.

MCMILLAN

The Helmer House Inn

Country Road 417
McMillan, MI 49853
906-586-3204

> *Fine food and solitude are worth the search*

Innkeepers: Guy and Imogene Teed. **Accommodations:** 5 rooms, all shared bath. **Rates:** $32–$46 single, $36–$55 double. **Included:** Full breakfast. **Minimum stay:** No. **Added:** 4% tax. **Payment:** MasterCard, Visa. **Children:** Yes. **Pets:** No. **Smoking:** Yes. **Open:** May–February.

The simple white clapboard structure welcomed its first guests in 1887, when Gale Helmer turned the former Presbyterian mission into a general store and resort hotel. The current owners arrived in 1978. In Michigan's upper peninsula, towns are separated by dense forests and long two-lane roads, and the Helmer House is a little hard to reach. But once you experience the solitude and excellent food at such reasonable prices, you'll be glad you made it.

> **Boats can be rented at the inn for fishing on Manistique Lake, which abuts the inn's nine acres.**

The feeling of an old-fashioned bed-and-breakfast fills the upstairs guests rooms. They are small, comfortable, and casually decorated with twin and double brass and iron beds and marble-topped antique tables. They all share a second-floor tub and shower, though most have their own vanities. The two attic rooms are air-conditioned. The high-backed oak bed with a lace bedspread and views of both the adjoining creek and Lake Manistique make Room 2 the most popular. At $32 for one person, the closet-size Salesman's Room, with an iron-rail bed and oak dresser, is the inn's best bargain.

The restaurant, which follows the path of an L-shaped porch around the building, is famous for its grilled breast of chicken, barbecued ribs, and Lake Superior whitefish. Portions of the latter are so generous that the kitchen feels safe in inviting you to have more if you're still hungry. The restaurant comfortably seats 40. During busy summer weekends, diners waiting for a table retreat to the parlor, where they find some of the building's original red velvet settees and a piano. After dinner, you can stroll on the lighted boardwalk by the creek.

Following a generous country breakfast of omelettes, quiche, pancakes, or French toast along with toast, muffins, juice, and coffee, you can explore nearby Tahquamenon Falls, Devil's Slide, Pictured Rocks, Fayette State Park, and the historic fishing town of Grand Marais. Less than a mile away, Luce County Park offers sandy beaches and hiking trails.

The large room that once housed the general store is now called the Osprey Nest. With country crafts and antiques on the original store shelves behind a long maple display counter and tins, scales, and a safe original to the building, this becomes the inn's most nostalgic spot.

MICHIGAMME

Michigamme Lake Lodge

P.O. Box 97
Champion, MI 49814
906-339-4400 in summer
906-225-1393 in winter

*An inn of native
materials and
rustic simplicity*

Innkeepers: Frank and Linda Stabile. **Accommodations:** 9 rooms, 3 with private bath. **Rates:** $100–$125. **Included:** Continental breakfast. **Minimum stay:** No. **Added:** 7% tax. **Payment:** MasterCard, Visa. **Children:** Yes. **Pets:** No. **Smoking:** No. **Open:** Year-round.

Michigamme Lake Lodge, surrounded by ancient birch trees, is a fine example of the great retreats that once flourished in the upper Michigan wilderness. The 1934 lodge was inspired by the Adirondack style, which emphasized native materials and rustic structural simplicity.

The light fixtures suspended from the ceiling were made from electrified cedar stump roots.

The interior continues this aesthetic, with a massive stone fireplace reaching up to cathedral ceilings in the main hall. The hand-hewn stairways lead to twin balconies. Bearskin rugs and mounted wolf and deer heads line the walls. The guest rooms have excellent views and contain all of the lodge's original twig and maple furniture. A guided tour is offered to nonguests at 2:00 P.M. daily.

The property offers 1,700 feet of private shoreline on Lake Michigamme and the Peshekee River. The parklike grounds rise some 25 feet for a panoramic view of the lake. You can follow the walkways to beaches for swimming, boating, and fishing in the summer. Winter brings cross-country skiing and snowshoeing. The innkeepers also own the Days Inn in Marquette, about 30 miles east of the lodge, so they often leave the day-to-day operation to a manager.

NORTHPORT

The Old Mill Pond Inn

202 West Third Street
Northport, MI 49670
616-386-7341

> *Eccentric touches add to the experience at Old Mill Pond*

Innkeeper: David Chrobak. **Accommodations:** 4 rooms, 2 with full bath. **Rates:** $75–$100, $50–$75 off-season. **Included:** Full breakfast. **Minimum stay:** 2 nights on summer weekends. **Added:** 4% tax. **Payment:** MasterCard, Visa. **Children:** Allowed but restricted. **Pets:** No. **Smoking:** Limited. **Open:** Closed for a month in early spring.

David Chrobak doesn't mind being considered a bit eccentric when it comes to his circa 1895 summer cottage. He has filled the place with a crazy collection of stuff from around the world, some of it valuable, some junk, but each piece has its own fascinating history.

Shelves on one wall in the parlor display a paperweight collection, and art deco lamps and knickknacks fill the tables. Mannequins model vintage clothing that changes with the season. A rare "reproducing" player piano actually simulates the strength used to depress the keys at the time of recording. David has always liked the 1832 English oil portrait that hangs here because it reminds him of his mother.

The four second-floor guest rooms lean toward cluttery

Victorian, though there is also a country-style room with quilts on the walls. A canopy bed was cleverly crafted from old house pediments, and an entire room is devoted to Princess Di memorabilia (ask David about the time he met her). The two rooms at the front of the house, overlooking the inn's namesake pond, are favorites. Hats, including a pair from the original Broadway production of *A Chorus Line*, fill the hall here.

A private third-floor room uses its peaked ceiling to great effect. A loft built above the bed is decorated with things you'd find in a family attic, including old trunks, vintage clothing, a bird cage, and Mickey Mouse and Donald Duck caps. There's only one problem: with no air conditioning, this room gets mighty hot during the summer.

> **The inn is filled throughout with colorful blooms, not surprising since David ran a flower shop in the Virgin Islands for several years. Flower baskets hang on the porch and the backyard gazebo, and the garden beds overflow with well-tended perennials.**

This is primarily a summer haven, where plastic pink flamingos have been known to congregate on the front lawn. David goes all out at Christmas, when larger-than-life Santas and reindeer land on his front lawn, and countless yards of garlands and twinkling lights envelop the house.

David serves an artful breakfast of scrambled eggs, omelettes, French toast, and banana pancakes. Three blocks away is tiny Northport, and a 30-mile drive along Lake Michigan takes you to the bustling summer resort town of Traverse City.

PEQUAMING

The Bungalow Bed and Breakfast

Ford Drive
Pequaming, MI 49946
Mailing address:
Route 1, Box 123
L'Anse, MI 49946
906-524-7595

> *Henry Ford's grand*
> *social experiment*
> *still lives*

Innkeepers: Lora Westberg and Pat Osterman. **Accommodations:** 6 rooms, 3 with private bath, 1 suite. **Rates:** Rooms $65–$85, suite $100. **Included:** Full breakfast. **Minimum stay:** No. **Added:** 4% tax. **Payment:** Cash only. **Children:** Yes. **Pets:** No. **Smoking:** Restricted. **Open:** Year-round.

In 1923, Henry Ford purchased the tiny lumber town of Pequaming in Michigan's upper peninsula to produce the wooden siding and floorboards for his "woodies." Following his own strict code of living, he turned the town into something of a social experiment, with strict rules that forbade alcohol and sloppiness. Thomas Alva Edison and Harvey Firestone were among the famous guests who visited the Bungalow, the home where he entertained.

The Ford Motor Company abandoned the sawmill and town in the 1940s, and the 75 workers' homes and the downtown were later torn down; only the faded Ford symbol on a water tower reminds the casual traveler of its former use. Spend the night at the Bungalow and you will find not only unusual history but also an inn that ranks as one of the Upper Peninsula's best overnight stays.

The home had been wracked by seven years of neglect and vandalism when the innkeepers sought to create their magnificent inn. The stark white walls and dark-stained pine wood downstairs hold firm to the Ford aesthetic. The Victorian sofa in the living room is on loan from the local historical society.

Ford's former suite has a magnificent view of the lake. Two rooms here are separated by French doors and can be rented singly. His bodyguard apparently stayed in the smaller room when the auto tycoon was in ill health. Other rooms incorporate lavender, pastel pink, and light blue with bright white-painted trim. Unique touches include an old Morris chair and beds so high you need a stepstool to clamber into them at night.

A formal English garden now graces the property, brought back to the specifications set up by Clara Ford. The innkeepers believe that many of her original plantings, including stunning peonies, still flourish here. Wooden steps lead to a wooden deck that overlooks the rocky beach where a surprising number of guest swimmers brave the chilly Lake Superior waters. Guests enjoy strolling the beach, playing with the family dog, Greta, or lounging in one of the spacious sitting rooms or great rooms.

> **Hiking trails wind through inn property, and there are also cross-country skiing and snowmobiling trails nearby. Gambling occurs nightly at the Ojibwa Casino Resort, about 12 miles away.**

PETOSKEY

The Perry Hotel

Bay and Lewis Streets
Petoskey, MI 49770
616-347-4000
800-456-1917
Fax: 616-347-0636

> *Stafford Smith's downtown hotel*

General manager: Shawn Gray. **Accommodations:** 80 rooms, 3 suites. **Rates:** Rooms $59–$140, suites $135. **Included:** All meals available. **Minimum stay:** No. **Added:** 6% tax. **Pay-**

ment: Major credit cards. **Children:** Yes. **Pets:** No. **Smoking:** Nonsmoking rooms available. **Open:** Year-round.

It's no surprise that the Perry Hotel was renovated with considerable charm and historic character. It was purchased by Stafford Smith, the owner of the popular Stafford's Bay View Inn a mile away, who has added some of his own decorating touches to the place while keeping the room rates reasonable.

> **Many rooms have a balcony overlooking Little Traverse Bay.**

The rooms here are spacious, clean, and well decorated. Tired pine furniture, some of it original to the hotel, has been painted with floral details. Some rooms feel decidedly masculine, with deep greens and blues and dark wood reproduction furniture. Some have rose-patterned wallpaper in bed chambers and bathrooms.

Among the several nice amenities are telephones, room service, writing desks, and televisions attractively tucked into armoires.

The specialty at both of the hotel restaurants is the fresh whitefish. While breakfast is available here, there are other restaurants close to the hotel, in Petoskey's Gaslight District. The hotel's Noggin Room, an English-style pub, also serves lunches and light dinners and has nightly entertainment. The town hops all year, especially in summer, when the Chautauqua educational and entertainment programs are held in neighboring Bay View.

Stafford's Bay View Inn

P.O. Box 3, U.S. 31
Petoskey, MI 49770
616-347-2771
800-456-1917
Fax: 616-347-3413

A northern Michigan institution

Innkeeper: Reg Smith. **Accommodations:** 26 rooms, all with private bath, 8 suites. **Rates:** Rooms $88–$175 double, suites $45–$175 double. **Included:** Full breakfast; dinner available. **Minimum stay:** No. **Added:** 6% tax. **Payment:** Major credit cards. **Children:** Yes. **Pets:** No. **Smoking:** Nonsmoking rooms available. **Open:** Mother's Day through October; winter weekends.

Stafford Smith entered the hotel business as a Bay View Inn desk clerk in 1958. Three years later, the enterprising young man purchased the tired lodging, spruced it up, and added his name to the shingle. The inn has changed plenty over the years, adding new and more luxurious rooms, but it has yet to lose its unpretentious appeal.

A large part of that appeal centers on the food, which is served in the Roselawn Porch main dining room, featuring a knockout view of Little Traverse Bay. Specialties include Lake Michigan whitefish baked in parchment, baby rack of lamb basted in herbs, and medallions of beef tenderloin dressed with morel mushroom or Dijon mustard sauce. Breakfast is ordered from the menu. If you stay on a Saturday night, the popular Sunday brunch will be included with your room. Stafford's caters meals outside the inn and also stages elaborate Christmas dinners.

During his Tauck Tours, Stafford or his son Reg (who has taken over innkeeping responsibilities), relates a colorful history of the inn and the Bay View area to visiting groups. You will often see Stafford, identified by his friendly manner and flaming red hair, talking with guests who have been coming here for decades.

> **Still want to dine with Stafford but wish a change of scenery? Try one of his other nearby restaurants, including Stafford's Pier in Harbor Springs, the Weathervane in Boyne City, One Water Street in Charlevoix, and Petoskey's Perry Hotel.**

In the guest rooms, antiques and wicker furnishings blend with carefully chosen wallpapers and fabrics. Most of the beds are reproductions, with the exception of an antique mahogany sleigh bed and a New England cannonball bed. Stafford has recently reclaimed the third floor, which now has six suites with Jacuzzis and fireplaces. None of the rooms has television or a telephone. On the first floor, guests gather in a bright wicker-filled sun room and enjoy the crafts in the gift shop.

SAULT STE. MARIE

Ojibway Hotel

240 West Portage
Sault Ste. Marie, MI 49783
906-632-4100
800-654-2929
Fax: 906-632-4100

> *A 1920s brick hotel overlooking the Soo Locks*

General manager: Robert Rodenroth. **Accommodations:** 71 rooms. **Rates:** $70–$100 double; packages available. **Included:** All meals available. **Minimum stay:** No. **Added:** 7% tax. **Payment:** Major credit cards. **Children:** Yes. **Pets:** No. **Smoking:** Nonsmoking rooms available. **Open:** Year-round.

The Ojibway Hotel overlooks one of Michigan's most fascinating attractions: freighters and other vessels lined up as they wait to pass through the locks. You'll probably want a closer look at this engineering marvel, constructed over what was once a waterfall.

Opened in 1928, and totally refurbished in the mid-1980s, the Ojibway offers modern, comfortable hotel rooms. The bathrooms are spacious, with one offering a whirlpool tub. The work of a local artist, Pat Norton, decorates and is for sale in the downstairs lobby. A small blue tile pool area, along with a sauna and spa, is on the lower level. Built to serve corporate guests, the brick hotel continues this tradition by offering conference and meeting facilities.

Boat watchers will love the views of the ships from Freighters, the hotel restaurant. It offers all three meals, including the specialty of the house, Lake Superior whitefish served broiled, pan-fried, or blackened.

TRAVERSE CITY

Cherry Knoll Farm

2856 Hammond Road East
Traverse City, MI 49684
616-947-9806
800-847-9806

A cherry farm with a fruitful decor

Innkeepers: Dorothy and Percy Cump. **Accommodations:** 3 rooms sharing 2 baths. **Rates:** $55 single, $65 double. **Included:** Full breakfast. **Minimum stay:** No. **Added:** 4% tax. **Payment:** MasterCard, Visa. **Children:** Yes. **Pets:** No. **Smoking:** No. **Open:** May–October.

Dorothy Cump fears that she overdoes the cherry theme at her bed-and-breakfast, but guests don't mind a bit. Decor at her century-old Victorian farmhouse includes cross-stitched place mats and cherry napkin rings, along with a picture or two of framed fruit. Breakfast often features cherry nut bread, pancakes, or waffles. In July, guests can pick cherries from 1,200 trees which stretch across 12 of the farm's 115 acres.

A rustic tool shed and a three-story barn add to the country charm. Lemonade and other cold drinks are always waiting upon guests' arrival, and beds are always turned down. Fresh flowers typically greet birthday or anniversary guests.

Add to this a superb location, about 15 minutes from downtown Traverse City, and you've got an unforgettable stay. The inn has three bedrooms, containing country antiques and family heirlooms like Dorothy's grandmother's bedspread, which dresses the bed in the Oak Room. Other rooms include vintage wood and tin toys among the furnishings.

The common areas here include a family room with fireplace, though guests often head for the wide wood porch. There are plenty of board games, but Dorothy admits that guests are usually too busy exploring Traverse City or the Sleeping Bear Dunes, about 45 minutes away. Closer to the inn is the Music House (a museum of turn-of-the-century automatic musical instruments) and myriad antiques shops.

Grand Traverse Resort

6300 U.S. 31 North
Grand Traverse Village, MI 49610
616-938-2100
800-748-0303
Fax: 616-938-2035

Every amenity for the active traveler

Managing Director: Kim Chappell.
Accommodations: 750 rooms. **Rates:** In high season, hotel $170, tower suites $235, condominiums $125–$325; packages available; $15 for extra person. **Included:** All meals available.

Minimum stay: No. **Added:** 6% tax. **Payment:** Major credit cards. **Children:** Free under age 18. **Pets:** No. **Smoking:** Non-smoking rooms available. **Open:** Year-round.

The 17-story glass tower that houses much of the Grand Traverse Resort looks more like a modern office complex than a northern Michigan hideaway. But you won't mind a bit once you've sampled 36 holes of championship golf, special restaurants and shops, and elaborate conference rooms at this largest of all Midwest resorts.

> **The Bear, one of two par-72 golf courses here, was designed by Jack Nicklaus and features terraced fairways, four lakes, ten water hazards, and tiered greens nestled among hardwood forests. The other course winds among rolling hills overlooking the bay.**

Only six miles from downtown Traverse City, the resort's accommodations include such amenities as wet bars, refrigerators, and cable television. The bathrooms come complete with hair dryers, makeup mirrors, and heat lamps. Some have fancy whirlpool tubs.

Two restaurants are in the main building. Trillium, at the top of the glass tower, offers American regional dining, fine wines, and a spectacular view of the bay. Downstairs, Paparazzi serves casual Italian cuisine. There are other restaurants and lounges in the sports complex and in the Shores condominium village. Specialty shops in the main tower sell everything from fancy chocolates to designer sportswear.

In the winter, guests ice skate, cross-country ski, and take horse-drawn sleigh rides. Good downhill skiing is 30 minutes away. "The Max," the resort's health and racquet club, has four outdoor and five indoor tennis courts, an aerobic workout studio, indoor and outdoor swimming, and a whirlpool.

While Grand Traverse Resort lacks some of the history and charm of its counterparts, it offers everything an active vacationer could conceivably desire.

Minnesota

Northern Minnesota

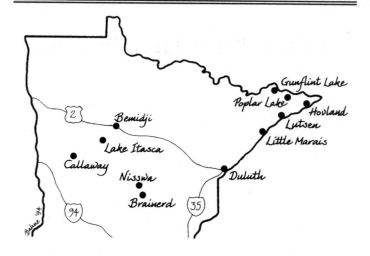

Best Bed-and-Breakfast Inns

Duluth
  Barnum House
  The Mansion
Little Marais
  The Stone Hearth Inn

Best Hotel

Duluth
  Fitger's Inn

Best Resorts and Lodges

Bemidji
  Ruttger's Birchmont Lodge
Brainerd
  Kavanaugh's Resort
Gunflint Lake
  Gunflint Lodge
Hovland
  Naniboujou Lodge
Lake Itasca
  Douglas Lodge
Lutsen
  Lutsen Resort
Nisswa
  Grand View Lodge
Poplar Lake
  Rockwood Lodge

Best Ski Retreats

Callaway
  Maplelag
Poplar Lake
  Young's Island Bed and Breakfast

Duluth is Minnesota's fourth largest city and a major U.S. seaport. The Canal Park Marine Museum, with models and shipwreck relics on display, is a popular attraction at the lakefront. Depot Square, in the St. Louis County Heritage and Arts Center, has an ice cream parlor, trolley rides, and a silent movie theater. Here, too, are the city's Ballet, Art Institute, and Playhouse. Several historic sites are open for touring, including the Jacobean-style Glensheen mansion. A shopping mall and hotel have been constructed in an old Duluth brewery, and the Holiday Center has restaurants including Grandma's Saloon and Deli, with old-fashioned atmosphere and pop culture decoration spanning the past century.

The drive north from Duluth on Highway 61 brings you to Grand Marais and the start of the Gunflint Trail. Originally an Indian footpath, the 60-mile automobile route now meanders over rocky ridges and land inhabited by moose. There are a number of jumping-off points, including the Boundary Waters Canoe Area, which is loaded with excellent canoeing outfitters. This is also home to cross-country skiing in winter, including the yurt-to-yurt trips offered by Boundary Country Trekking. On the way back down, check out the Split Rock Lighthouse and Gooseberry Falls State Park.

Minnesota's northwest region also boasts popular vacation destinations, including **Bemidji,** Detroit Lakes, and **Brainerd.** Lake Itasca State Park, Minnesota's oldest, is a 32,000-acre tract known for excellent birding. The area is also dotted with blacktop bicycle paths that follow the paths of former rail lines. Canoeing is popular on Crow Wing River, Red Lake River, Pine River, and even on parts of the Mississippi.

Bemidji is Paul Bunyan country, represented by the mammoth statues in the center of town of the mythical lumberjack and his blue ox, Babe. Check out the collection of tools that once supposedly belonged to Paul. They're housed at Bunyan House Information Center.

You'll find more Bunyan stuff at the Paul Bunyan Amusement Center in nearby Brainerd and at Lumbertown USA, with replicas and restorations of 19th-century logging-related buildings.

BEMIDJI

Ruttger's Birchmont Lodge

530 Birchmont Beach Road N.E.
Bemidji, MI 56601
218-751-1630
800-726-3866
Fax: 218-751-9519

> *Family recreation
> since the 1920s*

General manager: Randy Ruttger. **Accommodations:** 63 rooms, 7 suites. **Rates:** Rooms $48–$66 single, $62–$78 double; suites $84–$118 single or double; packages available. **Included:** All meals available. **Minimum stay:** 2 nights during peak seasons. **Added:** 6.5% tax. **Payment:** Major credit cards. **Children:** Yes. **Pets:** Allowed in cabins at $4 per day. **Smoking:** Yes. **Open:** Year-round.

Situated on 1,700 feet of sandy beachfront, Ruttger's attracts families with excellent recreational facilities for both children and adults. The active youth program, available six days a week, includes fishing, treasure hunts, sandcastle contests, water olympics, dinner parties, group bonfires, and movies. Rowboats are provided free, and fishing boats, a 16-foot Hobie Cat, a 28-foot pontoon, sailboards, and water skiing are available.

> **Ruttger's has tennis courts, an outdoor pool, and an indoor recreation center with a heated pool, sauna, whirlpool, exercise room, and game room. An 18-hole golf course is just a mile away at the Bemidji Town and Country Club.**

Ruttger's was built in the 1920s, though nostalgic touches remain only in the spacious, sunny lobby, presided over by a stuffed moose head. The lodge rooms range in size but have similar amenities and decor, with twin or double beds, cable television, and modern motel atmosphere. The frame beachfront cottages are preferable, with refrigerators, fireplaces, desks, and screened porches. Pricier units have kitchenettes; meal plans are offered at $24 per adult per day and $4–$14 for kids. New town homes have also been added to the property.

Staffed primarily by teenagers and college students, Ruttger's has a friendly, casual atmosphere. The staff falls short in some areas, however, such as maintaining the fleet of mountain bikes and replacing broken oars on rowboats. Workers too often shrug their shoulders when dealing with disappointed guests. However, there's no problem with the Garden Court dining room, where the staff is consistently attentive and professional. The excellent meals here include meat and vegetables cooked over sugar maple hardwood embers. Be sure to sample Lucy's lemon bread, available with all meals.

After dinner on Wednesday through Sunday, adults will enjoy the Paul Bunyan Playhouse, the region's oldest summer professional theater, which is right on the grounds. Paul Bunyan figures prominently in the scheme of things here, since legend has it that his blue ox, Babe, created the area's many lakes with his massive hooves. Be sure to have your picture taken in front of their towering statues in downtown Bemidji.

BRAINERD

Kavanaugh's Resort

2300 Kavanaugh Drive S.W.
Brainerd, MI 56401
218-829-5226
800-562-7061

A thriving, family-run summer resort

General manager: John Kavanaugh. **Accommodations:** 80 rooms. **Rates:** $90–$185 in peak season. **Included:** Dinner available. **Minimum stay:** 3 nights on reservations. **Added:** 6.5% tax; 15% on winter package. **Payment:** Major credit cards. **Children:** Yes. **Pets:** No. **Smoking:** Yes. **Open:** May–October; weekends in winter.

Established in 1969, this friendly, modern resort has thrived under three generations of Kavanaughs, and more than 15 relatives work here during the busy summer months. Though no specific children's activities are offered, the family spirit here is contagious.

Swimming, fishing, croquet, and golf are all part of the summer fun at Kavanaugh's, the only resort on Lake Sylvan. Kayaks and paddleboats are provided free of charge; other boats can be rented. A pair of tennis courts (also free) are on the main property next to a recreation building housing an indoor pool. Three golf courses are nearby. The resort has also become popular with cross-country skiers.

> **Couples without children will likely choose the scenic beauty of the Oaks, a group of five cottages on beautifully landscaped grounds. A creek trickles through here and flows into a small waterfall.**

Kavanaugh's Resort has modern cottages, most of them built in the past decade in the fashion of attractive condominiums or town houses. All have fireplaces and decks overlooking the lake. Large families like the Woods villas, which have two or three bedrooms, two baths, spacious front lawns, and beachfront access. Fully equipped kitchens, cable televisions, and telephones are standard here.

Still extremely popular is the quartet of original cabins, simply called the Cottages. With knotty pine interiors and rock fireplaces, they are rented as single units and provide a refreshing north woods touch.

Kavanaugh's restaurant, open from Memorial Day through Labor Day, is decorated in hardwoods and light colors, and its tables are covered with crisp white cloths. Walleye is the specialty of the house, broiled or deep-fried and perhaps topped with a lobster-based cream sauce. The restaurant overlooks the lake and colorful flower gardens. There is also a conference center here, making the resort wonderfully self-contained.

You are also near several family attractions. Paul Bunyan Amusement Park and Deer Forest are both within a 10-minute drive, and shopping is found in nearby Nisswa and Brainerd. Back at Kavanaugh's, children enjoy the recreation room with video games and pool tables, along with candy, soda, and popcorn for sale.

CALLAWAY

Maplelag

Route 1
Callaway, MI 56521
218-375-4466
800-654-7711

Rustic accommodations with top-notch skiing

Innkeepers: Jim and Mary Richards. **Accommodations:** Room for 175 in 20 buildings. **Rates:** $154 per person, 2-night weekend; $194 per person, 3-night weekend; $54 per person, midweek. **Included:** All meals and facilities. **Minimum stay:** 2 nights on weekends. **Added:** 6.5% tax. **Payment:** Major credit cards. **Children:** Yes. **Pets:** No. **Smoking:** Not permitted in lodge; limited in cabins. **Open:** Labor Day to Memorial Day.

Jim and Mary Richards came up with the name Maplelag as a pseudo-Scandinavian term meaning "maple community." Their imagination doesn't end here. This upper Minnesota resort has been consistently ranked among the finest places in the Midwest to go cross-country skiing. It may also be the most unusual.

Talent shows are held on the weekends, in a big room with a mirrored ball. The disc jockey plays everything from rock 'n' roll to polkas.

There are no longer rooms in the main lodge, so overnight guests head for the cabins, which sleep up to 35. You must furnish your own sleeping bags and sheets for these lodgings, most brought here from old Finnish settlers' homesteads. One was actually made from an old chicken coop. They are constantly updating these units and adding baths within. In some, you'll still have to use the facilities in the main lodge.

There are 35 miles of trails here, both for skiers and snowshoers. Ice skating is also popular. Skiers can warm up on the Rootin' Tootin' or Sap runs, used for hauling maple sugar in the spring. They will progress to the 10-kilometer Roy's Run, with challenging hills in remote woods north of the resort. After skiing, they may enjoy a steamy sauna or a soak in what

Jim calls "the Rolls-Royce of hot tubs." It can hold up to ten people.

Maplelag likes big eaters and proves it during the Sunday Scandinavian smorgasbords, wahich include an egg soufflé, homemade breads, pickled herring, a dozen imported cheeses, and lefse. For snacks, there is a bottomless cookie jar.

In the main lodge, stained glass sets off the rusticity. Jim has filled the place with everything from old maple sugar arti-facts to one-of-a-kind neon and metal advertising signs, some bearing the names of long-gone products and motels. His pride and joy are a series of original Burma Shave signs, which line the walls on the way to the outdoor hot tub. A collection of metal lunchboxes has now reached 400, with contributions coming from regular guests. A collection of Norwegian duck decoys could populate a small pond. Ask him about his grow-ing collection of Minnesota fish decoys.

DULUTH

Barnum House

2211 East Third Street
Duluth, MI 55812
218-724-5434
800-879-5437

> *A beautifully appointed family home*

Innkeepers: Dick and Dorothy Humes, Susan Watt. **Accommoda-tions:** 5 rooms, all with private bath. **Rates:** $95–$115. **In-cluded:** Full breakfast. **Minimum stay:** No. **Added:** 10.5% tax. **Payment:** MasterCard, Visa. **Children:** No. **Pets:** No. **Smok-ing:** No. **Open:** Year-round.

After raising nine children, Dick and Dorothy Humes found themselves clattering around a house much too large for just the two of them. Dick wanted to hit the open road in *Miss Behavin'*, his 35-foot-long motor home; but Dorothy didn't want to leave Duluth or their home. She won, and so will you.

A collection of tins from long-closed Duluth businesses sits on the fireplace in the enclosed porch and reception area. A signed photograph of Buffalo Bill with Sitting Bull hangs here too. There are also toys in a glass display case, among them an immaculate tin produce truck and a circa 1915 wind-up Santa.

Entrepreneur George G. Barnum built the house in 1910 to showcase his extensive collection of art objects from around the world. While few of them remain, the Humes have filled the place with their own impressive finds.

The ornate oak dining set came from a mansion in Long Island but looks like it was made for the place. Mythological figures, including griffins holding up ends of the sideboard, are carved throughout this stunning three-piece set. A mahogany Federal secretary was purchased from Paul Otis, who was once the oldest living professional baseball player before he died at age 100.

While all the guest rooms are spacious and comfortable, the Barnum Suite is the most impressive. Its furnishings include an 1880s walnut bedroom set, including a pair of eight-foot-tall armoires. It has a private bath and a fireplace and shares a deck.

Breakfast, served in the beamed dining room, is a treat, and is often presided over by Dick or Dorothy at the head of that impressive 1880s table. Served on fine china with Victorian napkin rings, the meal may include homemade pumpkin muffins, a fresh fruit plate, and quiche with ham and hash browns.

The Humes are truly gracious hosts, eager to help with dinner or entertainment suggestions. On chilly nights (common even in summer), they'll keep a fire blazing in front of the living room's deep leather sofa for your return.

Though the inn is in a residential section near downtown

Duluth, you feel far removed from the city. The house is insulated by towering pines and birches and overlooks a brook running through a ravine. Ask Dick to show you the photograph of the hungry bear who tips over neighborhood trash cans or to tell you about the double take he gave to a misguided moose on the corner.

Fitger's Inn

600 East Superior Street
Duluth, MI 55802
218-722-8826
800-726-2982
Fax: 218-727-8871

Duluth's brewery-turned-hotel

Hotel manager: Jim Makitalo. **Accommodations:** 42 rooms, 6 suites. **Rates:** Rooms $70–$90, suites $110–$175. **Included:** All meals available. **Minimum stay:** No. **Added:** 12.5% tax. **Payment:** Major credit cards. **Children:** Yes. **Pets:** Occasionally permitted. **Smoking:** Yes. **Open:** Year-round.

Fitger's Inn successfully incorporates its history into its current design. The ten-building complex, once a brewery, now houses a restaurant, shopping mall, and hotel. The original copper circuit-breaking box has been left along one wall in the lobby.

The rooms are spacious and decorated with wing chairs and Victorian reproduction beds and armoires. Many have excellent views of Lake Superior, while the rooms on the street side compensate by offering split-level accommodations. The management promises that some of the rough edges, like the occasional tattered edge on a bedspread, will soon be smoothed out.

Augustino's has a fine Italian menu that includes home-made pasta, mesquite-grilled steaks and seafood, fresh northern lakes fish, and a tempting dessert called Death by Chocolate. Some shops remain vacant, but there are gift and clothing stores, one of which features an old brewing kettle in its decor. A lake walk behind the building follows the water's edge.

> **Guests check in at the old wrought-iron cashier's cage, and wood beams and exposed brick find their way into some of the rooms.**

The Mansion

3600 London Road
Duluth, MI 55804
218-724-0739

> *A richly appointed Tudor mansion*

Innkeeper: Sue Monson. **Accommodations:** 8 rooms, 6 with private bath; 2 suites; carriage house. **Rates:** Rooms $85–$155 double; suites $155–$195 double; carriage house $155. **Included:** Full breakfast. **Minimum stay:** 2 nights on weekends. **Added:** 10.5% tax. **Payment:** MasterCard, Visa. **Children:** By prior arrangement. **Pets:** No. Smoking: In library only. **Open:** May through October and most winter weekends.

Moat lanterns from an English castle line the gallery walls. A shining suit of armor stands at attention atop the grand staircase. Wooden beams outside the stately stone exterior bear intricately carved miners' symbols. One thing is clear: the Mansion in Duluth is true to its name, a richly appointed Tudor mansion on sweeping grounds facing Lake Superior.

The house was built in 1929 for Harry Dudley, a millionaire mining engineer. His wife, Marjorie, was one of six children born and raised in the neighboring Glensheen mansion. Sue Monson opened the house to guests in 1983, making it Duluth's first bed-and-breakfast inn. Because of its location, city officials only allow it to operate six months a year.

The guest rooms aren't as spectacular as the common areas. Most are carpeted, with king- or queen-size beds with antique headboards, and spectacular lake views. The rooms vary greatly in size as well, from a pair of sunny maids' rooms that share a bath to the grand Master Suite, which has a marble walk-in shower and two dressing rooms. The carriage house can comfortably hold a family of six.

> **Guests have access to over 500 feet of shoreline, accessible by a wood-and-stone staircase. They're also free to roam over the seven acres, which include rainbow gardens of lilies, peonies, tulips, and irises and a pond near the driveway.**

When you want to explore, start with the upstairs Trophy Room and its mounted bear and wolf heads, gun racks, airplane propeller, and leaded windows offering yet another million-dollar view of the lake. Be prepared for that suit of armor (his name is Mortimer) on the way upstairs. The Library has comfortable leather chairs in front of a roaring fire and plenty of good books.

If you want more of the same on an even grander scale, stop by Glensheen, which is open for tours. You are also only ten minutes from downtown Duluth.

GUNFLINT LAKE

Gunflint Lodge

HC64, Box 750
Grand Marais, MI 55604
218-388-2294
800-328-3325
Fax: 218-388-9429

> *A historic resort
> at the end of
> the Gunflint Trail*

Manager: Jennifer Walsh. **Accommodations:** 23 cottages in summer, 14 in winter. **Rates:** Summer $79–$189 double, winter $69–$179 double; packages and fall and early spring discounts available. **Included:** Firewood, canoes; meals available. **Minimum stay:** 2 nights. **Added:** 7% tax plus a service charge of 5% to 12%. **Payment:** Major credit cards. **Children:** Yes. **Pets:** Yes. **Smoking:** Not permitted in the dining room. **Open:** Year-round.

Gunflint Lodge was started as a fishing camp at the end of Minnesota's Gunflint Trail. Fishing is still a major attraction, though over the years resort activities have been added to make a stay here even more enjoyable for families. The lodge offers canoes, kayaks, and rafts to explore the surrounding Boundary Waters Wilderness. Children can splash at the small sand beach on the waterfront, play in the tree fort in the recreation area, or go on a hobo hike with a naturalist. The ducks arrive each morning for the kids to feed them.

The main lodge has big rock fireplaces, a collection of carved birds, and voyageur artifacts. A nice touch here are the Polaroids of guests with their catches. Since the capacity here is only 50 or 60 guests, you'll never find things too crowded.

Summer activities are focused on the adjacent wilderness country. They include hikes, cookouts, animal searches, birding trips, and a hike to an old Indian cave. Guides can take guests out for walleye and lake trout fishing.

Gunflint Northwoods Outfitters, based at the lodge, schedules canoe trips and even provides a picnic lunch for day trips. You will likely encounter moose and beavers during your voyage.

Scattered along the lakeshore are cabins with living room fireplaces and

> **The primary winter activity at Gunflint is cross-country skiing; over 100 kilometers of groomed trails lace the forest behind the lodge. There's even a lighted trail for night skiing. Gunflint also has over 20 "mushers" on staff for unforgettable dog sled trips.**

one to four bedrooms. They mix rustic and modern decorating touches, and some have kitchens and even their own saunas. Only the newer units are used in the winter; they have whirlpool tubs, popcorn poppers, coffeemakers, microwave ovens, and even washers and dryers.

Gunflint has earned a reputation for food as well. When you're on a meal plan, you can have anything you want from the dining room menu. Lunch can be taken in the dining room or as a picnic. After a morning with your rod and reel, you can enjoy your catch prepared by the chef.

The resort has long been owned by the Kerfoot family, whose matriarch, Justine Kerfoot, has written two well-known books about her life on the Gunflint Trail. Gunflint has the highest tariff in the area, but their services literally define lodging on the Gunflint Trail.

HOVLAND

Naniboujou Lodge

HC-1, Box 505
Grand Marais, MI 55604
218-387-2688

> *Diners and overnight guests still flock to Naniboujou*

Innkeepers: Tim and Nancy Ramey. **Accommodations:** 23 rooms, all with private bath, 4 suites. **Rates:** $45–$79 single, $59–$79 double. **Minimum stay:** No. **Added:** 6.5% tax. **Payment:** Discover, MasterCard, Visa. **Children:** Yes. **Pets:** No. **Smoking:** No. **Open:** May 20–October 20.

Babe Ruth, Jack Dempsey, and Ring Lardner were all charter members of this private club on the banks of Lake Superior. Plans to increase the membership to 1,000 were scrapped by the stock market crash in 1929, and while the lodge never realized its plans to add a golf course, tennis courts, and hunting lodge, it still attracts visitors with its excellent meals and ongoing redecoration of guest rooms.

> **The Arrowhead Room, an enclosed porch that runs the length of the Great Hall, is a popular spot to play board games, watch movies on a VCR, or simply relax and read.**

Some rooms have been combined to create larger family units. The attractive modern decor features pastel walls or print wallpaper and firm mattresses with paisley comforters. Others have been recently remodeled, replacing nicked dressers with classic reproduction pieces. The communal bathrooms upstairs have made way for private baths in all the rooms. Some rooms have fireplaces.

The undisputed highlight of Naniboujou remains the Great Hall, whose lofty ceilings and walls are decorated in brilliant oranges, yellows, greens, reds, and blues in a motif inspired by Cree Indian mythology. At one end of the hall sits Minnesota's largest native rock fireplace, weighing some 200 tons. All three meals are served here; dinner entrées include moderately priced Lake Superior trout, walleye pike, and apricot roast chicken.

A basketball court and volleyball net are on the property, which also offers hiking and trout fishing along the Brule River. Grand Marais, where the Gunflint Trail begins, is only 15 miles away.

LAKE ITASCA

Douglas Lodge

Itasca State Park
Lake Itasca, MI 56460
Information: 218-266-3654
Reservations: 800-765-CAMP

> *Cabins and hotel rooms on 32,000 acres*

General manager: James Keller. **Accommodations:** 80 rooms, suites, and cabins, some with private bath; 10-unit clubhouse. **Rates:** Rooms and suites $27–$33 single, $33–$50 double; cabins $55–$85; packages available. **Included:** All meals available. **Minimum stay:** No. **Added:** 6.5% tax. **Payment:** Discover, MasterCard, Visa. **Children:** Yes. **Pets:** No. **Smoking:** Yes. **Open:** Memorial Day weekend through Labor Day weekend.

Itasca is the only Minnesota state park that offers overnight accommodations. Douglas Lodge, constructed in 1903, has two dining rooms and a lobby on the main floor. Upstairs are guest rooms with utilitarian twin and double beds. Most units share two baths and a shower, though three suites have private baths. The feel is slightly institutional but old-fashioned.

Less historic but more comfortable, neighboring Nicollet Court offers 18 motel-style units on two floors. They're away from the hustle and bustle of the main building and also have twin or double beds. All have private showers. A lounge and a conference room with a fireplace are on the main floor.

Instead, choose one of the park's rustic cabins. To reach them, you can walk over a bridge, where chirping birds and squirrels can be heard in the woods below. The cabins, most built after 1920, have the perpetual north woods aroma of burning logs.

Housekeeping cabins with fireplaces and full kitchens are at the nearby campground. At the Squaw Lake cabins, about 10 miles from the main lodge, guests must provide their own linens.

While the Itasca State Park, which celebrated its centennial in 1991, is open year-round, meals and lodgings are only offered seasonally. It's decorated with Native American artifacts and offers specialties like Itasca walleye pike and herbed chicken breast over Minnesota wild rice. The restaurant proves very popular in the summer, so plan to wait for a table.

> There are no televisions here, but the screened porches on some cabins offer a great wildlife show and superb views of Lake Itasca. Deer, ospreys, bald eagles, and beavers are often spotted on the property.

Hikers and bikers will enjoy the 32,000 acres of parkland, including virgin stands of pine, balsam, fir, and tamarack. Anglers will delight in catching largemouth bass and walleye in a number of lakes that, surprisingly, aren't heavily fished. In fact, much of this wonderful park is still a well-kept secret.

LITTLE MARAIS

The Stone Hearth Inn

1118 East Highway 61
Little Marais, MI 55614
218-226-3020

> *A cozy inn on the Lake Superior shore*

Innkeepers: Charlie and Susan Michels. **Accommodations:** 5 rooms in main house, 2 rooms and 1 suite in boathouse, all with private bath. **Rates:** $65 single, $75 double. **Included:** Full breakfast. **Minimum stay:** No. **Added:** 6.5% tax. **Payment:** MasterCard, Visa. **Children:** No. **Pets:** No. **Smoking:** No. **Open:** Year-round.

Talk about romantic. Charlie Michels was a confirmed bachelor when he opened this inn on the Lake Superior shore in 1990, and Susan was one of his first guests. A few months later, they were married.

The Stone Hearth Inn began as a log cabin, built in 1893 by Benjamin Fenstad, who singlehandedly started the town of Little Marais. He raised nine children and ran a post office and even a school from the family home. In 1924, an addition transformed the cabin into the Lakeside Inn, one of the first resort hotels on Minnesota's North Shore.

> **There are lots of outdoor activities nearby, including hiking, canoeing, and a scenic drive north to Grand Marais and the start of the Gunflint Trail.**

Charlie, a contractor and carpenter from St. Paul, has preserved that 1920s style. A Mission oak rocker and chair can be found in the living room, which also has a beamed ceiling, maple floors, a mounted fish, and a massive fireplace built of Lake Superior stones. The player piano is the only remnant from the old days.

In painting the guest rooms, Charlie chose solid blues, pinks, and greens more evocative of the period. The rooms are small, impeccably clean, and simply decorated, with antique armoires, bedside tables, reading lamps, and sitting chairs. Fancy black and white hex tiles decorate some of the bathrooms. Most of the rooms retain their original hardwood floors. The old boathouse has now been renovated into two additional rooms and a suite.

Breakfast is served in the grenadine-colored dining room on the sprawling handmade oak table that Charlie designed. It includes entrées like stuffed French toast, sausage quiche, and Norwegian or blueberry pancakes. Fresh lake trout also shows up on the morning menu in sausage form. Note the vintage photographs in a frame made from a wood window the innkeepers found outside the boathouse.

Guests enjoy the 50-foot-long back porch, where they relax on Adirondack furniture (also made by Charlie) and listen to the waves roll in.

Most nights see a bonfire down by the lake. The inn also offers a bed-and-breakfast hiking package, in which it becomes a stop on a three-day trek along the Superior Hiking Trail.

LUTSEN

Caribou Lake B&B

P.O. Box 156
Lutsen, MI 55612
218-663-7489

> *A dream home
> on a golden lake*

Innkeepers: Leanne and Carter Wells. **Accommodations:** 1 suite, 1 cabin. **Rates:** Suite $85, cabin $103. **Included:** Full breakfast. **Minimum stay:** No. **Added:** 9.5% tax. **Payment:** MasterCard, Visa. **Children:** Yes. **Pets:** No. **Smoking:** No. **Open:** Year-round.

Remember the movie *On Golden Pond?* Rumor has it that Caribou Lake was considered as a shooting site. You can see why as you head down the raspberry-lined path that leads to the dock, where the still water beckons you to swim out to the raft or cast a line.

> **Leanne uses lots of seasonal fruit, especially when the raspberries are in season. Dinners and trail lunches are available with notice.**

The Wellses moved to the red cedar log home in 1990, converting the main house rooms and adding a guest cabin. The cozy suite has two queen-size brass beds, TV/VCR, and a sauna on the inn's lower level. The two-bedroom cottage has a full kitchen and a wood-burning stove.

Leanne's elegant breakfast is served on fine china with silver and may include Austrian apple or Swedish pancakes or lake trout sausage and wild rice quiche.

Trails leading to White Sky Rock and Honeymoon Rock are only a mile or so away. From these romantic summits, you can often spot the inn's dock across the lake.

Lutsen Resort

Lutsen, MI 55612
218-663-7212
800-346-1467
Fax: 218-663-7212

> *Hospitality
> stretching back
> four generations*

General manager: Diane Loh. **Accommodations:** 33 lodge rooms, 17 motel rooms, 50 townhouses and villas, 3 log cabins. **Rates:** Lodge rooms $56–$115 single, $66.50–$130 double; motel rooms $46–$65 single, $53–$75 double; townhouses and villas $102–$145 single, $116–$195 double; log cabins $175–$225 double; packages available. **Included:** All meals available; MAP $25 per person. **Minimum stay:** 2 nights August, September, and peak ski weekends. **Added:** 9.5% tax. **Payment:** Major credit cards. **Children:** Yes. **Pets:** In certain sea villas. **Smoking:** Nonsmoking rooms available. **Open:** Year-round.

At most resorts, the lobby is used solely for checking in. At Lutsen Resort, on Minnesota's North Shore, guests can be found lounging, playing cards, building Lego castles, and even napping amid the comfortable overstuffed furnishings. The owners consider the lobby simply an extension of the guest rooms.

> **Summer activities include tennis, fishing, hiking, and mountain bike rental, while the enclosed pool, hot tub, and sauna offer recreation year-round. Ski buffs can enjoy easy access to adjacent ski facilities.**

Though the main lodge was built in 1952, hospitality at Lutsen Resort stretches back four generations. Turn-of-the-century travelers would arrive by boat, wagon, dog team, or on horseback and often stayed with Charles Alex Nelson and his family. The Swedish immigrant, who worked here as a fisherman, logger, and trapper, put guests up in the spare bedroom, family room, and sometimes the hayloft before building a proper rooming house. The complex that now makes up Lutsen remained in the Nelson family until 1988, when it was purchased by a group of investors.

The present Swedish-style main lodge, with its heavy hewn

pine timbers, now offers guest rooms with Scandinavian-style furnishings. Lakeside dining is offered here in the Lutsen dining room, which, like most North Shore lodgings, prides itself on having the best Lake Superior trout and salmon, prepared either broiled or pan-fried. Light appetites will appreciate the thoughtful vegetarian and pasta selections on the menu.

Just a stone's throw from the lodge, the Cliff House offers rooms decorated similarly with superb lake views. All the rooms have televisions and telephones. Sea Villa town houses, about three miles south of the complex, have complete kitchens, high ceilings, and access to all Lutsen facilities. The newest additions are the Lutsen log cabins, built high on bluffs on the surrounding Lutsen property. All have hardwood floors, wood-burning stoves, and decks with superb lakeside views.

Lutsen has long had a par 3 golf course. In 1991, 18 holes of considerably more challenging golf opened across the street, with the winding Poplar River coming into play on two holes.

NISSWA

Grand View Lodge

South 134 Nokomis
Nisswa, MI 56468
218-963-2234
800-432-3788 in Minnesota
800-345-9625 elsewhere

> *A well-run resort, perhaps Minnesota's best*

General manager: Mark Ronnei.
Accommodations: 12 lodge rooms, 60 cottages, ranging from single-room studios to 4-bedroom cabins. **Rates:** $150–$945 double. **Included:** Two meals on MAP. **Minimum stay:** No. **Added:** 6.5% tax. **Payment:** Major credit cards. **Children:** Yes. **Pets:** No. **Smoking:** Yes. **Open:** April 15–October 15.

Grand View Lodge has thrived since 1919 as an unpretentious and rustic place to stay, yet "rustic" almost belittles the service and luxury found here. On the shore of a picturesque Minnesota lake, shaded by birch and pine trees, Grand View is everything a midwestern resort lodge should be.

There used to be 20 rooms. Now there are 12 remodeled main lodge rooms, all spacious and well equipped with beamed ceilings, comfortable couches and beds, and televisions. In the lobby, firewood is stacked high beside the stone fireplace, moose heads are mounted on the walls, and cushy seating surrounds a big-screen television. The dining room serves breakfast, lunch, and dinner. The Totem Pole Lounge has live music and dancing nightly.

> **The 27 holes of golf and 11 tennis courts have been ranked among the finest in the Midwest. Pros are available at both, with daily instruction for children, teens, and adults offered.**

Nestled between the main lodge and the lake are 60 charming cottages and luxury town houses, many facing the lake. The oldest ones were built in the 1940s and have knotty pine interiors and vaulted ceilings. The largest and one of the newest, Loon Lodge is extremely flexible because it can be used as eight units (with private entrances and baths) or as one big house. All the cottages have one or more bathrooms, carpeting, air conditioning and heat, refrigerators, picture windows, and spacious decks. Some units have kitchenettes and fireplaces.

An overnight stay is pretty pricey but almost a bargain when you take advantage of the many programs. Water skiing, pontoon cruises, aerobic classes, and evening nature walks are offered to all guests, as are canoes and fishing boats.

The popular children's program has both day and evening sessions for children 6 through 12. It meets at the Kids' Club House, with arts and crafts classes, scavenger hunts, mini-olympics, and movie nights among the scheduled fun. Aside from a lunch fee, the program is offered free for families on the modified American plan and for a nominal hourly charge to other guests. After dark, you'll find older children (and a few adults) in the lively game room, downstairs in the main lodge. It has modern video and pinball machines, along with air hockey, pool, and Ping-Pong.

Grand View Lodge has also developed a reputation for the elegant gardens that line the property. Every day you'll see a small battalion of employees keeping them fresh. There's even a greenhouse here. Many of the blooms are rare and have small signs to identify them.

Other ambitious plans are in the works. The old boathouse has been razed, making room for a new indoor heated swimming pool and sauna. And while vintage cabins arc slowly being modernized, don't worry about the charm being renovated out of the place. Grand View Lodge is savvy enough to realize that folks who come here year after year don't appreciate dramatic change in their home away from home.

POPLAR LAKE

Rockwood Lodge

HC 64, Box 625
Grand Marais, MI 55604
218-388-2242
800-942-2922

*A classic lodge
on the
Gunflint Trail*

Owners: Dana and Tim Austin; Rick and Lori Austin. **Accommodations:** 7 housekeeping cabins. **Rates:** $90–$125 double; packages available. **Included:** All meals available. **Minimum stay:** 3 nights. **Added:** 6.5% tax. **Payment:** Major credit cards. **Children:** Yes. **Pets:** No. **Smoking:** Yes. **Open:** Mid-May through early October.

Many folks head up the Gunflint Trail for some of the best canoeing in the Midwest. Rockwood Lodge is a great place not only to rent gear but to spend the night as well. Surrounded by the Boundary Waters Canoe Area, the lodge is just 30 miles north of Grand Marais and four miles from the Canadian border.

You may see a moose or two fording the lake. The owners say more moose live here than anywhere else in the country.

Built in 1926, the cedar building is one of the few original log lodges on the trail. At the heart of the lodge is the restaurant, with its moose head mounted on the massive stone fireplace. Fresh lake trout and roast duck are served here on red and white tablecloths and rustic furniture.

Guests sleep in one-, two-, and three-bedroom cabins, tucked along the lakeshore and surrounded by towering pines. A number of plans, combining canoes and meals, are available. Most guests stay longer than the minimum — often for a week or month.

Mountain bikes can be rented for touring, or you can set off on foot to explore the rugged acreage. Lake Poplar, with a sandy bottom, offers excellent swimming.

Young's Island Bed and Breakfast/ Boundary Country Trekking

590 Gunflint Trail
Grand Marais, MI 55604
218-388-4487
800-322-8327
Fax: 218-388-4487

> *Yurt-to-yurt skiing,*
> *with fine dining*

Hosts: Barbara and Ted Young. **Accommodations:** 1 housekeeping cabin, 3 yurts. **Rates:** Cabin $105 double in summer, $125 midweek, $140 on weekends; yurt-to-yurt $115–$125 per person with 2–4 night packages. **Included:** Meals available with packages. **Minimum stay:** 2 nights in cabin. **Added:** 7.5% tax plus 2% tax on lodging. **Payment:** MasterCard, Visa. **Children:** Yes, in cabin. **Pets:** Yes, in cabin. **Smoking:** No. **Open:** Year-round in cabin; winter only for yurts.

For centuries, the people of the Mongolian plateau have resided in round, peaked-roof huts called yurts. The yurts offered by Boundary Country Trekking are a bit grander — canvas-covered, with Plexiglas skylights, and heated by a wood-burning stove. A night with other skiers (and an experienced host) in one of these ancient dwellings is part of the adventure in yurt-to-yurt skiing.

> **On Boundary Country Trekking trips, you ski while the staff carries your gear and the food.**

The meals are memorable, especially the Mongolian fire pot, a delicious fondue of vegetables and meats cooked in a savory broth heated by a charcoal-fueled fire pot and served over rice. Also available are glazed maple-cranberry roast duck and stuffed and grilled rainbow trout with shish kebabs. Bag lunches are provided for the trail.

While yurts are by far the most unusual lodgings the Youngs offer, you can also stay in the Young's housekeeping cabin, Little Ollie Lake Cabin, near the yurts. A two-mile drive from the Gunflint Trail, Little Ollie rests on a hill overlooking a small lake. It features a full kitchen, free-standing fireplace, full bath, sauna, and, during the summer, free use of a canoe. The cabin is accessible by road from mid-April to late October, but beware: the mosquitoes can be murder. Save the experience for arrival by ski or snowmobile, when the only thing biting is the brisk winter wind.

Southern Minnesota

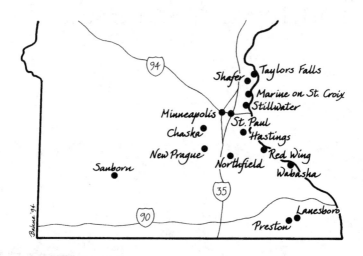

Best Bed-and-Breakfast Inns

Chaska
  Bluff Creek Inn
Hastings
  Rosewood
Lanesboro
  Cottage House
Marine on St. Croix
  Asa Parker House
Minneapolis
  Inn on the Farm
Preston
  The Jail House Inn
Sanborn
  Sod House on the Prairie
Shafer
  Country Bed and Breakfast
Stillwater
  The William Sauntry Mansion
Taylors Falls
  The Old Jail Company Bed and Breakfast

Best Full-Service Country Inns

Lanesboro
  Mrs. B's Historic Lanesboro Inn
New Prague
  Schumacher's New Prague Hotel
Wabasha
  The Anderson House

Best Hotels

Minneapolis
  Nicollet Island Inn
Minneapolis
  The Whitney Hotel
Red Wing
  St. James Hotel
St. Paul
  The St. Paul Hotel

Best Budget Stay

Northfield
  The Archer House

Located on the banks of the Mississippi, **Minneapolis** and **St. Paul** offer world-class hospitality and sights. At Minneapolis's Hubert Humphrey Metrodome, football and baseball fans have seen more than their share of action in recent seasons. Not only did the Twins clinch the World Series in 1991, but Superbowl XXVI was held here the following year.

Performing arts centers like the Ordway Music Theatre in St. Paul and the Guthrie Theatre in Minneapolis further the Twin Cities' reputation as a major Midwest cultural center. Though the winters get mighty cold here, Minneapolis is often cited as one of the most desirable places to live in the Midwest, particularly for raising families.

While in St. Paul, visit Rice Park, an urban oasis of trees and fountains surrounded by brick-lined streets. During the summer, local brown-baggers enjoy their lunch here while others rely on the hot dog vendors. This is also the spot in winter where ice sculptures for the city's Winter Carnival are created. Mickey's Diner, on the National Register of Historic Places, is a classic 1930s greasy spoon. The Science Museum of Minnesota offers exhibits on archeology, technology, and biology. Also in this half of the Twin Cities is the World Theater, home to many years of the *Prairie Home Companion* radio show. Native son Garrison Keillor has since left for the Big Apple, but the renovated theater still schedules regular plays and concerts.

The University of Minnesota is part of your tour of Minneapolis. Aside from an enrollment of more than 50,000 students, it also houses the James Ford Bell Museum of Natural History and the University Art Museum. The Minneapolis Institute of Arts has a world-renowned collection of fine and decorative arts spanning 4,000 years. Rembrandt's *Lucretia*, the Roman statue *Doryphos*, and an impressive photo gallery are among the highlights here. For modern art, try the Walker Center, whose permanent collection focuses on important 20th century works. It's located next to the Minneapolis Sculpture Garden. The Minnesota Zoo, in suburban Apple Valley, resembles a natural habitat for wild animals, with over 1,700 animals living there.

The Mall of America has become a popular tourist destination since its unveiling in 1992. Twenty minutes south of downtown Minneapolis, the "Mega Mall" features 400 stores surrounding Knott's Camp Snoopy amusement park.

Just a short drive east of the Twin Cities is the spot where Minnesota began. **Stillwater,** founded in 1848, nestles beneath the bluffs formed by the St. Croix River. It looks like a town you'd see along the Rhine River of Germany, with church spires, the cupola of a historic courthouse, and businesses and homes that look much as they did a century ago. Stillwater is just one of a number of historic communities (**Taylor's Falls** and **Marine on St. Croix** among them) that thrive on both sides of the River, which flows into the Mississippi farther south.

Red Wing, home of the famous Red Wing Shoes, is a delightful limestone-bluffed river port. Aside from perusing the town's well-preserved historic homes and buildings, you can tour the still-thriving Red Wing Shoes plant or catch a play or concert at the T. B. Sheldon Auditorium Theatre.

Lanesboro, about two hours from the Twin Cities, is reached by taking Highway 52 south, then following 16 east shortly after hitting **Preston.** Lanesboro is still Minnesota's best-kept travel secret, though its location off the scenic Root River Trail bicycle path is helping to spread the word. Antiques shops and hardware stores blend effortlessly here in preserved 19th-century storefronts. The annual Buffalo Bills celebration has dances, live music, and even a live buffalo on display. The Commonweal Theater has taken over the local movie house and stages professional-quality productions. Restaurants are noticeably lacking here, but you can still stop by the Chat and Chew for the local lowdown.

CHASKA

Bluff Creek Inn

1161 Bluff Creek Drive
Chaska, MN 55318
612-445-2735

> *Innkeepers carry
> on a tradition
> of pampering
> and hospitality*

Innkeepers: Gary Delaney and Anne Karels. **Accommodations:** 5 rooms, 3 with private bath. **Rates:** $75–$150. **Included:** Full breakfast; dinner possible. **Minimum stay:** No. **Added:** 6.5% tax. **Payment:** MasterCard, Visa. **Children:** 12 years and older. **Pets:** No. **Smoking:** No. **Open:** Year-round.

As the first bed-and-breakfast in Minnesota, this circa 1860 farmhouse established high standards for the state. The original innkeeper, Marjorie Bush, has since moved on to the Asa Parker House in Marine on St. Croix. Gary Delaney and Anne Karels carry on her tradition of pampering and hospitality.

They recently added a private hideaway called Hollyhock Cottage to the accommodations. Country English garden prints by Waverly adorn the king-size bed, which is tucked under a cathedral ceiling in a room over the carriage house. A sliding glass door opens onto a massive deck that faces west for a lovely sunset view. A double whirlpool, fireplace, and the option of having breakfast brought to your door make this a most romantic and memorable stay.

The main house has four equally charming guest rooms, some with exposed brick and most with Laura Ashley linens and quilts. May's Room has a queen-size hand-carved pine bed and a splendid view of towering pines in the valley. Elizabeth's Room offers a tester bed surrounded by dusty rose and dark green accents. My Sister's Room has green carpeting, soft pink walls, and white wicker details.

During summer, guests gather for breakfast on the white, brick-lined sun porch. Served on old English china with Bavarian crystal, it might include fruit, muffins, puff pancakes, French toast, blueberry blintzes, or eggs Florentine. Peach cobbler or mandarin orange cake follow for dessert. In the winter, the meal moves to the dining room, where the conversation piece is the home's framed land grant, signed by President Lincoln.

> **Along with its Scandinavian decor, Emma's Room has a small gnome. According to the innkeepers, he collects your unpleasant thoughts and tucks them under his tall red hat. When you leave, your worries will have disappeared.**

Dinner can be served if enough guests request it, especially on busy summer weekends. The innkeepers also hold several weddings each year on the porch.

Though just 30 minutes from Minneapolis, the inn's location on a gravel road, just a half mile from a major thoroughfare, successfully creates the illusion of being far out in the country. The inn is set on just over an acre, but there are plenty of places to hike nearby. Other attractions include the Chanhassen Dinner Theatre, the Minnesota Renaissance Festival, and Canterbury Downs just minutes away.

HASTINGS

Rosewood

620 Ramsey
Hastings, MN 55033
612-437-3297
800-657-4630
Fax: 612-437-4125

> *Fireplaces and whirlpools set the scene for luxury*

Innkeepers: Dick and Pam Thorsen. **Accommodations:** 6 rooms, all with private bath, 1 suite. **Rates:** Rooms $75–$195 single, $69–$189 double; suite $195 double. **Included:** Full breakfast; dinner available. **Minimum stay:** 2 nights on weekends. **Added:** 6.5% tax. **Payment:** Major credit cards. **Children:** By prior arrangement. **Pets:** No. **Smoking:** No. **Open:** Year-round.

Dick and Pam Thorsen know that fireplaces and whirlpools have become the most requested elements of a romantic stay. As a result, Rosewood, their elegantly restored and furnished bed-and-breakfast inn, features a number of two-sided fireplaces that can be viewed from both an elegant bath and a queen-size featherbed in the spacious guest rooms.

> **Hastings has more than 60 buildings on the National Register of Historic Places, including storefronts run by third- and fourth-generation shopkeepers.**

The St. Croix Room, the original master suite of the 1880 mansion, has a bay window, yards of cream-colored lace, and roses on deep teal wallpaper. The bed in Rebecca's Room is on a four-season porch with shuttered windows. The room has two fireplaces. Most spectacular is the 1,200-square-foot Mississippi under the Stars, where six skylights brighten the paisleys and muted burgundies and grays that line the walls. The bathroom has a rounded tiled shower and antique copper soaking tub; interior touches include a baby grand piano and walls of bookcases.

Every room offers cushy towels, rose-scented hand soap, and unusual Victorian wallpapers. The common areas downstairs are also special, including two large parlors with their own fireplaces and love seats. The library offers an eclectic collection of books, from romantic fiction to photography, most donated by former guests.

Breakfast includes fruit pastry and an entrée, perhaps wild rice quiche or a coddled egg with Havarti cheese and a biscuit. Dinners are served nightly at 7:00 P.M. to guests only. The set menu features either a three- or six-course meal. Cornish hen with an orange sauce is served with salad and French bread. Dessert is turtle cheesecake or rum cake. More elaborate meals add an appetizer, soup, and sorbet, and dessert may be raspberry mousse in a chocolate shell. Dinners and breakfast can also be enjoyed in the room.

Hastings is on the banks of three rivers just 25 miles from the Twin Cities. There are eight golf courses in the area, seven of which are available to guests. In winter, you are near two downhill ski facilities and cross-country trails. Thor-wood, another antiques-filled B&B owned by the Thorsens, is just six blocks from Rosewood.

LANESBORO

Cottage House Inn

P.O. Box 2227
209 Parkway N.
Lanesboro, MN 55949
507-467-2577

> *New construction exudes old-town charm*

Innkeepers: Waldo and Marilyn Bunge. **Accommodations:** 6 rooms, all with private bath. **Rates:** $45 Sunday–Wednesday; $55 Thursday–Saturday. **Included:** Continental breakfast. **Minimum stay:** No. **Added:** 9.5% tax. **Payment:** MasterCard, Visa. **Children:** Yes. **Pets:** No. **Smoking:** No. **Open:** Year-round.

Though constructed in the summer of 1993, the Cottage House Inn fits seamlessly with other restored buildings in downtown Lanesboro. It's one of the more ambitious projects in this small Minnesota town bitten by the tourism bug.

The inn, which resembles a turn-of-the-century storefront with rooms for rent upstairs, overlooks the Commonweal

Theatre. The repertory theater, once the town movie house, has proven so popular with summer visitors that its schedule of plays now runs through Christmas. Eric Lorentz, artistic director, is one of the Cottage Inn owners. Day-to-day operations of the inn, however, are handled by his parents.

> **Guest rooms offer early American antiques. Four have queen-size beds covered with Amish quilts.**

The spacious lobby, the inn's sole common room, is decorated with a copper boiler and stove, crocks, and coffee pots from frontier days. The room, which also sports a chintz davenport and wine-colored easy chair, is the site of afternoon coffee (by reservation only) complemented by Norwegian and German pastries and homemade bread. Guests often gather on the long front porch.

Favorite accommodations include the Walnut Room, the Primitive Room, and the Indian Room with watercolors and papier-mâché artifacts from the Far East. There are also rooms for rent in the Trailside Cottage, a fully-equipped duplex with two bedrooms in each unit.

Breakfast is light (coffee and rolls), but the lack of fuss has kept costs down in a town whose reputation as an unpretentious getaway is growing with each passing season.

Mrs. B's Historic Lanesboro Inn

101 Parkway
P.O. Box 411
Lanesboro, MN 55949
507-467-2154

*A homey hostelry
in a popular
hamlet*

Innkeepers: Bill and Mimi Serme-us. **Accommodations:** 10 rooms, all with private bath. **Rates:** $55–$65 weekdays; $85–$95 weekends and holidays. **Included:** Full breakfast; dinner available. **Minimum stay:** No. **Added:** 9.5% tax. **Payment:** Personal checks, cash. **Children:** Yes, with restrictions. **Pets:** No. **Smoking:** Restricted to several rooms. **Open:** Year-round.

Keep an eye on Lanesboro, a tiny farming community that may be the best-kept travel secret in the Midwest. Walled by limestone bluffs, the Root River valley could easily have been created by Grandma Moses, with its pastures, trout streams, and Queen Anne homes. There are some antiques shops here, but the 1870s storefronts in Lanesboro primarily peddle farm implements and feed. A leg of a 30-mile bike trail runs right through town.

The high-ceilinged parlor welcomes guests with its baby grand piano, comfortable furniture, and cozy fireplace.

At the heart of this is Mrs. B's Historic Lanesboro Inn, the best-established lodging in town. The 1872 limestone structure served as a furniture store and mortuary before becoming an inn in 1985. Its rooms are decorated in country Victorian style, with queen-size canopy beds, air conditioning, carpeting, and access to balconies. A leg of the Root River winds behind the inn.

Guests can enjoy a hearty breakfast with blueberry buttermilk pancakes or French toast with a slab of cottage bacon, and dinners are also served here. The five-course fixed price meal relies heavily on the bounty of local meat and fish as well as the inn's herb garden.

Life does exist after five o'clock in Lanesboro. You just have to look for it. The movie house has become the Commonweal Theater, offering truly exceptional plays featuring actors from New York and the West Coast. Afterward, head to the Chat and Chew on the edge of town for a piece of pie.

MARINE ON ST. CROIX

Asa Parker House

17500 St. Croix Trail North
Marine on St. Croix, MN 55047
612-433-5248

Marjorie Bush knows how to make guests feel at home

Innkeeper: Marjorie Bush. **Accommodations:** 4 rooms, 1 suite, all with private bath. **Rates:** Rooms $89–$125 single, $99–$135 double; suite $135 double. **Included:** Full breakfast. **Minimum stay:** 2 nights during peak weekends. **Added:** 6.5% tax. **Payment:** Discover, MasterCard, Visa. **Children:** Age 12 and older. **Pets:** No. **Smoking:** No. **Open:** Year-round.

You don't just drive by the Asa Parker House, you drive under it. The white mansion with green shutters perches on a bluff high above the street, overlooking the St. Croix River. It was built in 1856 by Asa Parker, the man credited with launching Minnesota's lumber industry. Marjorie Bush thinks he patterned it after a stately home in Vermont so he could catch a proper wife.

Marjorie, who used to own the Bluff Creek Inn in Chaska, renovated the Asa Parker House in 1986 and knows how to make guests feel at home. She makes what she calls a Minnesota breakfast, which means if she doesn't pack 5,000 calories into it, it's not worth serving. Her morning casserole is made with eggs, bacon, and wild rice.

China tea setups are displayed throughout the downstairs common rooms. A grape-embossed buffet and a wine cupboard highlight the country Danish antiques in the double parlors, which are brightly decorated and smell of sweet potpourri.

The guest rooms are named for historic village women, including Isabella Parker, Asa's wife, whose name you will not find in the history books. Pink wallpaper and white wicker accent this room, which has an attractive pedestal sink and a claw-foot tub. Beds in all the rooms have down comforters on firm mattresses and six pillows.

> **The village of Marine on St. Croix, just an hour from Minneapolis, has a marina with canoe rentals. The William O'Brien State Park, with miles of paved paths for biking, walking, and cross-country skiing, is just out the kitchen door. The Stillwater–Taylors Falls bicycle path also winds through here.**

A heart-shaped whirlpool tub is in the Alice O'Brien Room, once the maid's quarters and now the most splendid room. The three-room suite is tucked under the eaves and has a large, private, flower-filled deck with Adirondack chairs.

The grounds feature a tennis court and a screened gazebo. Marjorie used to have a vegetable garden. But since guests so enjoy watching animals graze on her herbs and carrots, she now calls the backyard plot her rabbit and deer garden.

Before you go, stop at Marjorie's dried flower workshop in the carriage house. Throughout the year, she prepares for her two booths at the Minnesota Renaissance Festival and even arranges flowers for magazines and fancy Minneapolis hotels.

MINNEAPOLIS

Inn on the Farm

6150 Summit Drive North
Brooklyn Center, MN 55430
612-569-6330
800-428-8382
Fax: 612-569-6320

*A historic farm
in the reflection
of Minneapolis
skyscrapers*

General manager: Judith Bergeland.
Accommodations: 10 rooms, all
with private bath, 1 suite. **Rates:** Rooms $80–$110; suite
$120–$130; packages available. **Included:** Full breakfast. **Minimum stay:** No. **Added:** 12.5% tax. **Payment:** MasterCard,
Visa, American Express. **Children:** 12 years and older. **Pets:**
No. **Smoking:** Nowhere in the inn. **Open:** Year-round.

In the reflection of glass high-rises in a busy Minneapolis-area
office park sits Inn on the Farm, a gracious lodging with an
unusual history. Earle Brown — successful farmer, horse
breeder, and sheriff — bequeathed his 750-acre farm to the
University of Minnesota in 1963. The school quickly parcelled it off for home, office, and mall development, although
the farmhouse and its surrounding outbuildings miraculously
remained standing, eventually falling into the hands of the
City of Minneapolis. With the prodding of the local historical
society, the City spared no expense to turn the farmhouse and
its remaining eight acres into a bed-and-breakfast inn and
conference center.

A glass-enclosed grape arbor now connects the main house
and three outbuildings. Beds are firm and high in the guest
rooms, which are named after workers on the old Brown
farm. There's the Jess Howe room, which occupies the second
floor of the foreman's house. Beautifully restored pine furnishings from the 1800s are offset by such niceties as
whirlpool tubs, dimmers for the bedside lights, and remote
control televisions hidden in armoires.

Brown's own room displays his own simple, utilitarian
tastes. Decorated in darkwood tones, it has overstuffed
chairs, a brass bed, and a knockout view of the duck-filled
pond. As if the rooms weren't spacious enough, there are several sitting areas, including a gazebo off of the main porch.

A framed photograph in the sitting room served as a blueprint for remodeling the rooms, and the decorators tried to restore as many details as possible, including an airplane propeller and snow shoes on the walls and a moosehead over the fireplace. Most of the original furnishings were auctioned off after Brown's death, and the City bought some of them back. Old calendars Brown gave to family and friends show the white-haired farmer on horseback surrounded by fields of cattle. Photographs with stories to tell

> **Cookies and tea are set out in the late afternoon, before or after a trip to downtown Minneapolis, which is only a 10-minute-drive down I-94. There are shopping centers and biking trails nearby.**

can be found throughout the place, including one of Brown with houseguest Judy Garland. Legend has it that Alfred Hitchcock filmed scenes for one of his movies here.

Breakfast is a real treat, and includes homemade muffins, fruit with yogurt topping, and French toast. You can enjoy it in a sun room overlooking fields, with office towers beyond.

Conference facilities are located across from the inn, in the massive barn-style building once used to show horses. The conference center does big business, with 13,500 square feet of banquet room, lots of break-out facilities, and a fully-equipped kitchen built underneath. Aside from closed corporate affairs, guests might find antiques markets, crafts and collectors shows, and art exhibits.

You need to look closely to see the historic touches that have survived the renovations at the Inn on the Farm, including old safes that now house cleaning supplies and a room that served as the birthplace of the Minnesota Highway Patrol. Horses once exercised their teeth on the rough-edged posts in the conference center. A tunnel that runs the length of the grape arbor hallway is regularly used by the inn staff. The deep claw scratches near the front entrance were made by one of Brown's many dogs. Homemade animal gravestones are still here, though the City keeps them in storage, convinced that a view of Brown's pet cemetery at breakfast might curb some appetites.

Nicollet Island Inn

On Nicollet Island
95 Merriam Street
Minneapolis, MN 55401
612-331-1800
Fax: 612-331-6528

*A small hotel
on a Mississippi
River island*

General manager: Chuck Paton.
Accommodations: 24 rooms, all with private bath. **Rates:**
$110–$145. **Included:** Continental breakfast Sundays only.
Minimum stay: No. **Added:** 10% tax. **Payment:** Major credit
cards. **Children:** Yes. **Pets:** Yes. **Smoking:** Nonsmoking rooms
available. **Open:** Year-round.

Though rooms on both sides offer views of the Mississippi,
don't expect a secluded hideaway at this inn, for the teardrop-
shaped island, reached by bridge, lies between downtown and
northeast Minneapolis. The 1893 limestone building spent a
good part of its life as Salvation Army head-quarters before its trans-formation in 1982.

> **Nico's Bar, on the lobby
> level, has a 30-foot counter
> decorated with carved
> figureheads, stained glass,
> and inlaid seashells. An
> outdoor patio can be
> enjoyed in the summer.**

The guest rooms offer
standard hotel amenities
and Victorian touches in
the decor. Reproduction
brass or four-poster beds,
armoires, wing chairs, fox
and hound or flowered
wallpapers, and exposed
stone walls add to the antique appeal. Two rooms have
Jacuzzis. Corner rooms overlook both the river and a park. All
include morning coffee, juice, and a newspaper delivered to
your room.

The Nicollet's steak, pasta, and seafood restaurant is open
daily for all three meals. Guests may sit near the antique oak
fireplace or on the glassed-in porch overlooking the Mississippi.

Business guests enjoy the hotel's location and its friendly,
accommodating staff. You can walk to nearby restaurants,
movie theaters, and night spots in the River Place entertainment and dining complex. And, unlike most lodgings in the
Twin Cities, the Nicollet Island offers free parking.

The Whitney Hotel

150 Portland Avenue
Minneapolis, MN 55401
612-339-9300
800-248-1879
Fax: 612-339-1333
Reservations: 800-248-1879

> *Midwestern
> sincerity mixed
> with downtown
> panache*

General manager: Bertrand Weber.
Accommodations: 54 rooms, 43 2-level suites, 3 penthouse suites. **Rates:** Rooms $90–$160, suites $125–$225; packages available. **Included:** All meals available. **Minimum stay:** No. **Added:** 12% tax, $5 nightly parking charge. **Payment:** Major credit cards. **Children:** Yes. **Pets:** No. **Smoking:** Nonsmoking rooms available. **Open:** Year-round.

A sunny front desk clerk welcomes you by name. A concierge helps you plan a trip to a museum while the hotel limousine waits to take you there. Room attendants leave fancy chocolates during the evening turndown. In the morning, tea and coffee greet you in a shining silver setup in the lobby. The Whitney Hotel in Minneapolis pulls these touches off with a sophisticated but sincere style that keeps its reputation solid and its guests coming back.

> **The ceilings are high (usually 12 to 14 feet), even in the standard rooms, while bi-level suites soar even higher, with loft bedrooms reached by spiral staircases.**

Built in 1878 as a flour mill and transformed into a hotel in 1987, the Whitney's exterior retains its brick-lined prosaic quality. You might think that wheat is still ground here. Inside is another story entirely. The elegant European-style lobby boasts marble floors, crystal chandeliers, and a grand staircase that winds up to meeting rooms and second-floor accommodations.

The guest rooms are furnished with Thomasville Queen Anne pieces and offer such amenities as terrycloth robes, bathroom telephones, and 24-hour room service.

The penthouse, comprising three bedrooms and two living rooms, features a grand piano, fireplaces, whirlpools, and a deck with a spectacular view of the Mississippi River.

Five meeting rooms, richly appointed with polished mahogany tables and upholstered armchairs, can hold receptions or dinners of up to 200 people. Though the Whitney has the slightly sterile aura of a modern hotel, special decorating touches are found throughout, like the framed Victorian handbags, gloves, and lace collars decorating some hallways.

The Whitney Grille, on the lower level, offers classic American cuisine. It feels like a private club with its paneled walls, intimate booths, and austere classical music just audible above hushed conversation. Entrées of lavender peppered shrimp or filet mignon are served on fine china with polished silver. In warmer weather, you can also dine on the more casual garden plaza.

NEW PRAGUE

Schumacher's New Prague Hotel

212 West Main Street
New Prague, MN 56071
612-758-2133
612-758-2400

A German restaurant is the highlight of this popular inn

Innkeepers: John and Kathleen Schumacher. **Accommodations:** 11 rooms, all with private bath. **Rates:** $105–$125 weekdays; $130–$155 weekends; packages available. **Included:** All meals available. **Minimum stay:** No.

Added: 6.5% tax. **Payment:** Major credit cards. **Children:** Yes. **Pets:** No. **Smoking:** Discouraged in guest rooms. **Open:** Year-round.

The varied menu and eclectic decor at Schumacher's New Prague Hotel has placed it among the most popular full-service inns in Minnesota. The European authenticity at this Bavarian-style hotel stems from John and Kathleen Schumacher, who head to Germany or Czechoslovakia when they want new dining or decorating ideas.

> You will want to explore the small, unpretentious town of New Prague, which still has a large German and Czech population.

The 1898 Georgian Revival hotel was built by Cass Gilbert, who also designed the Minnesota capitol and the Supreme Court building in Washington, D.C. John Schumacher bought the building in 1974, when it was a flophouse offering rooms for $2.50 a night.

John is an avid hunter, so mounted trophies blend with Bavarian wainscoting, Black Forest clocks, and hand-thrown Czech pottery in the dining room and parlor. Czechoslovakian roast duck is a house specialty, served golden brown and lightly seasoned with caraway seeds. You will also enjoy venison, rabbit, pheasant, quail, and game hen among the dozens of entrées on the menu. All meals are accompanied by fried Czech potato dumplings, red cabbage in wine and spices, spaetzle, and more. There is also a "healthy-heart" menu that caters to guests on low-fat or low-sodium diets.

The guest rooms were originally named after the months of the year, though June and July have been incorporated into one large room. It features a European-style black elm ceiling and sky-blue furniture painted with wildflowers. The king-size bed is complemented by antique wall sconces. May has a high canopy bed painted with storybook scenes. The antique bed in December has been painted a soft black and overlaid with white ink. The room is decorated with hand-painted winter scenes, Santa figurines, ornate lace curtains, and Czech bath tiles. Every room has thick eiderdown comforters and pillows, and some have whirlpool baths.

The friendly pub, Big Cully's Bar, was named for John's father. Kathleen runs a gift shop that specializes in handmade gift items.

NORTHFIELD

The Archer House

212 Division Street
Northfield, MN 55057
507-645-5661
800-247-2235 in Minnesota
Fax: 507-645-4295

*A small-town
hotel for more
than a century*

Owner: Dallas Haas. **Accommodations:** 17 rooms, 19 suites. **Rates:** Rooms $40–$55, suites $90–$145. **Included:** All meals available. **Minimum stay:** No. **Added:** 9.5% tax. **Payment:** Major credit cards. **Children:** Yes. **Pets:** By arrangement. **Smoking:** Yes. **Open:** Year-round.

The Archer House has changed hands more than 30 times since it opened in 1877. But this French Second Empire structure, which anchors downtown Northfield, has always been a hotel. The downstairs now has shops, restaurants, and a bookstore next to a cluttered lobby with pressed-tin ceilings. During the day, tourists climb the open staircase to peek into the guest rooms. An elevator has also recently been added.

A stroll through Northfield eventually leads to the Northfield Historical Society Museum, in the former bank where Jesse James and his gang met their match. The town's special mix of agriculture, education, and small-town tranquility have resulted in the slogan, "Home of Cows, Colleges, and Contentment."

The rooms on the second floor are small but cozy. All are carpeted, with handmade quilts, stenciling, embroidered samplers, arrangements of dried flowers, and televisions. Four-poster beds and ceiling fans can be found in some rooms, while others have whirlpool tubs. The suites have mini-bars, sometimes in the center of the rooms.

Memories is a third-floor favorite in dark pines and plaids, with a checkered black and white bathroom floor and a red oval whirlpool bath. You'll find only one book in the Library, but it has a curved archway between the bedroom and sitting room, where a painted grandfather clock and writing desk are found. Many rooms have superb river views.

PRESTON

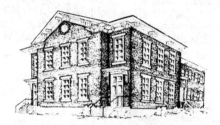

The Jail House Inn

109 Houston 3 N.W.
P.O. Box 422
Preston, MN 55965
507-765-2181

Spend a night behind bars in this well-appointed inn

Innkeepers: Marc and Jane Sather. **Accommodations:** 12 rooms, all with private bath. **Rates:** $58–$140 double on weekends; $40–$95 weekdays. **Included:** Full breakfast on weekends. **Minimum stay:** No. **Added:** 6.5% tax. **Payment:** MasterCard, Visa, Discover. **Children:** 12 years and over. **Pets:** No. **Smoking:** No. **Open:** Year-round.

Spending a night in jail is not most people's idea of a good time, but at the Jail House Inn, guests pay for the privilege. This is actually the Old Fillmore County Jail, built in Victorian Italianate style in 1869 and used to detain local lawbreakers until 1971. The new "wardens" spared no expense when they created a dozen rooms for overnight guests.

Of course, the most unusual room is the Cell Block, where the echo of steel-barred doors clanking shut behind you will send chills down your spine. Old cement bags are used for curtains. A far cry from spending a night in a dungeon, this spacious suite adjoins another cell with a sitting room. Its bathroom has a double whirlpool tub.

Other rooms, decorated in Victorian style, are named for the sheriffs who served here. The master bedroom, named for

> **Ask the innkeepers about the prisoners who tried to dig their way out with dinner spoons.**

H. C. Gullickson, features an eight-foot-high walnut bed, a fireplace, and a china tub weighing nearly 1,000 pounds. A copper tub can be found in the Amish-style B. C. Christenson Room, with an Amish doll and basket, access to a second-story porch, and a three-piece spoon-carved bedroom set.

RED WING

St. James Hotel

406 Main Street
Red Wing, MN 55066
612-388-2846
800-252-1875
Fax: 612-388-5226

> *The St. James still celebrates its thriving small town*

Manager: Eugene Foster. **Accommodations:** 60 rooms. **Rates:** $75–$145 double. **Included:** Beverage upon arrival. **Minimum stay:** No. **Added:** 6.5% tax. **Payment:** Major credit cards. **Children:** Yes. **Pets:** No. **Smoking:** Nonsmoking rooms. **Open:** Year-round.

The St. James Hotel, built in 1875, was the product of 11 proud businessmen who wanted to celebrate their town's success. Centennial celebrations showed what repairs the old place needed, so the Red Wing Shoe Company purchased the stone and brick building and began a two-year restoration project that resulted in a grand reopening of shops, offices, and historic lodgings in 1979.

> **The Port of Red Wing restaurant is on the lower level, which is sculpted from the rough limestone that lines Red Wing's bluffs.**

More than a decade later, the St. James has no fear of falling into disuse again. The hospitality offered by Clara Lillyblad (whose family owned the place for more than 70 years) is still alive and well in the helpful desk staff, who bend over backward to make sure your room is comfortable and that you have a bite to eat, even if you arrive late.

The hotel's rooms, in both the original structure and the addition, are all named after Mississippi riverboats. The hallways are lined with photographs of historic Red Wing, from tragic shipping accidents to stoic portraits of the original St. James investors. Some rooms have antique Victorian beds, but most offer comfortable reproductions in brass, iron, and fine woods. While the newer rooms don't have such high ceilings, they do offer clever details, like high rounded windows or quilts designed to match the wallpaper. Nearly half overlook the Mississippi. All offer air conditioning, cable TV, telephone, turndown service, morning newspaper, and wine or Catawba juice upon arrival.

The Verandah Café, in the rear of the shopping court, is open for all three meals. It is joined by bookstores and antiques and gift shops in an attractively designed shopping facility. Nine meeting and banquet rooms are also in the complex. Red Wing, meanwhile, is a bustling river town offering its own unique shops and restaurants.

ST. PAUL

The Saint Paul Hotel

350 Market Street
St. Paul, MN 55102
612-292-9292
800-292-9292
800-223-1588 National
  reservations
Fax: 612-228-9506
Telex: 297008

> *Still defining
> quality lodging
> in this half
> of the Twin Cities*

General manager: William Morrissey. **Accommodations:** 222 rooms, 32 suites. **Rates:** Rooms $134 single, $149 double; suites $159–$650; weekends $89 per room; packages available. **Included:** Daily paper, turndown service; all meals available. **Minimum stay:** No. **Added:** 12.5% tax. **Payment:** Major credit cards. **Children:** Yes. **Pets:** Yes. **Smoking:** Nonsmoking rooms available. **Open:** Year-round.

Built in 1910 by Reed and Stem, the designers of New York's Grand Central Station, The Saint Paul Hotel defines quality lodging in this half of the Twin Cities. Elegant and simple, it doesn't offer fancy fitness facilities or trendy room decor. But its old-fashioned service keeps it popular with no-nonsense business and vacation travelers.

> **The nightly turndown service includes a bottle of mineral water and a thoughtful card forecasting the weather. The concierge and chauffeur service here are extremely helpful.**

Limestone, white terra cotta, glazed tile, and Italianate cornices make up the exterior. The lobby, decorated in a gray-blue, salmon, and beige color scheme, is subtly lit by four chandeliers, three of them originals from the grand ballroom. There is usually a massive flower arrangement as its centerpiece.

The floral theme extends into the bedrooms as well, in the draperies, bedspreads, and dust ruffles. Suites offer private sitting rooms.

Two restaurants are available. The Café serves an informal

breakfast, lunch, and dinner. The St. Paul Grill, with a beautiful view of Rice Park, serves American fare, from sizzling steaks to chicken pot pies. It's not open for breakfast, but does serve brunch on Sunday. Look into the inexpensive weekend packages, most of which include dinner. Seven banquet and meeting facilities can accommodate groups from 25 to 500.

St. Paul's skyway system links the hotel with other commercial, business, retail, and entertainment establishments. There are no fitness facilities, though guests can have exercise equipment delivered to their rooms. They also have access to a nearby YMCA.

SANBORN

Sod House on the Prairie

Route 2, Box 75
Sanborn, MN 56083
507-723-5138

A little house on the prairie open to guests

Innkeepers: Virginia and Stan Mc-Cone. **Accommodations:** 1 sod house. **Rates:** $60 double; $100–$125 family. **Included:** Full breakfast. **Minimum stay:** No. **Added:** 6.5% tax. **Payment:** Cash, check only. **Children:** Yes. **Pets:** With approval. **Smoking:** Yes. **Open:** Year-round.

It doesn't have indoor plumbing or electricity, but the McCone Sod House has authentic historical touches you won't find at other Midwestern B&Bs. During an overnight here, oil lamps will be your lighting while an old-fashioned pitcher and bowl serve as the sink. The only running water is that which you run outside to retrieve and bring into the house. A sod outhouse lies nearby.

Stan McCone erected the 1880s-style structure with two-foot-thick sod walls in 1987 on a piece of virgin prairie. He said it sounded like "the ripping of a giant canvas" as the tightly-woven roots yielded to the cutter's blades. He estimates that 300,000 pounds of sod were used to built the house, which is fashioned of earthen blocks.

The interior is finished simply in the style of the pioneer homesteaders. Lumber salvaged from a 90-year-old Minneapolis flour mill became the roof, floor, window frames, and door. Century-old bricks were used for the chimney. Furnishings include two double beds, a fainting couch, a cook stove, and a pair of rocking chairs.

> **If you visit in colder months, the house will be heated by wood-burning stoves. The fire will be burning when you arrive. Wool blankets, quilts, and a buffalo skin robe keep you warm at night. Because of its thick walls, the home both maintains its heat in winter and stays cool in summer.**

A knock on the door in the morning means it's time for breakfast, which is served on the home's long wood table. The meal might include turnovers, peaches and cream streudel, and bacon and sausage.

This unique B&B is open for public tours, along with another home, the comparatively spartan "poor man's dugout," from May to Labor Day. A gift shop features handmade items by Native Americans, as well as pioneer items by local craftspeople. Area attractions include the Laura Ingalls Wilder Museum, 30 minutes away in Walnut Grove. Ancient Indian carvings are 15 minutes away at Jeffers Petroglyphs.

These ambitious innkeepers plan to open more guest accommodations in the log house they have moved here from northern Minnesota.

SHAFER

Country Bed and Breakfast

32030 Ranch Trail Road
Shafer, MN 55074
612-257-4773

A red brick farmhouse provides a true country haven

Innkeepers: Lois and Budd Barott.
Accommodations: 3 rooms, 2 with private bath. **Rates:** $55 single, $95 double. **Included:** Full breakfast; tax. **Minimum stay:** No. **Payment:** Checks, cash only. **Children:** 12 years and older. **Pets:** No. **Smoking:** No. **Open:** Year-round.

Lois Barott grew up in this 1870s farmhouse before she and her husband, Budd, purchased it and the surrounding 35 acres in 1965 to raise six children of their own. If the wake-up call of the rooster doesn't rouse you, the aroma of brewing coffee or sizzling bacon certainly will.

A cozy reading nook in the attic, the Carl Larsson Room, attracts guests during wet weather, when they can't relax on the wicker-filled front porch or back deck.

Lois is known for generous breakfasts, served near the warmth of the wood-burning stove. She whips up buttermilk pancakes, cuts fresh fruit into bowls, and brews her own recipe for Swedish egg coffee. Budd handles the ham, hashed browns, and mushroom and cheese omelettes. The eggs come from the farm's chicken coop — that is, if the pesky raccoons don't get them first.

The rooms are decorated with white wicker, flowered wallpaper, antique country furniture, and handmade comforters. The favorite is the Country Estates, with an antique double bed, wicker chairs, and a private bath with a clawfoot tub. The Little Room has a single bed and shares a bath.

Popularity has its price. The tariff has almost doubled in the past five years, but you'll hear few complaints from repeat guests. The inn is heavily booked during winter, when cross-country skiers enjoy the farm's acreage and nearby Taylors Falls. For dinner, the Barotts will probably suggest the short drive to Marine on St. Croix to sample Crabtree's Kitchen.

STILLWATER

The William Sauntry Mansion

626 North Fourth Street
Stillwater, MN 55082
612-430-2653

Much more than a typical midwestern Victorian inn

Innkeepers: Martha and Duane Hubbs. **Accommodations:** 5 rooms, all with private bath. **Rates:** $89–$119 double. **Included:** Full breakfast. **Minimum stay:** No. **Added:** 6.5% tax. **Payment:** Major credit cards. **Children:** Upon request. **Pets:** No. **Smoking:** No. **Open:** Year-round.

When Martha and Duane Hubbs set out to restore the William Sauntry Mansion to its former glory, they decided from the start not to cut any corners. As a result, this circa 1890 mansion is among the most splendid examples of late Victorian style in the Midwest.

The lumber baron William Sauntry was a logger and oxen driver who fought his way to the top. His home is a testament to his eccentricities and opulence, with examples of both Queen Anne and Eastlake styles. Four fireplaces, seven parquet floors, original chandeliers, painted canvas ceilings, cherry and oak woodwork, and stained glass windows all make the inn sparkle.

Moving here after completing successful restoration projects in Chicago and St. Louis, Martha and Duane were lucky enough to find several pieces of the home's original hardware in the basement, and they painstakingly replaced missing bits of oak, mahogany, maple, walnut, and birch in the floors. They are proud to have some of the home's original furniture, including a marble-topped table with

> **Stillwater offers antiques shops, skiing, hot-air ballooning, trolley tours, and golf. Evening activities include dining aboard train cars or in fine restaurants along the levee. Ask the innkeepers about it.**

a moon face carved upon it. The circa 1885 German clock is notable for the bullet hole in the number five on its face.

The guest rooms are named after Sauntry family members. The William Room has a king-size antique bed with a stained glass headboard and blue and gold decor. Eunice, named for his wife, reflects her soft-spoken nature in dusty rose, with a fireplace, antique double-poster bed, and parquet flooring. Beltram, which is a memorial to the Sauntrys' only son, faces south from the tower bay and overlooks the yard and gardens.

The Hubbses haven't added fancy baths because it would hurt the integrity of the restoration. Instead, they have used vintage plumbing, from pedestal sinks and clawfoot tubs to the home's original tin tub. Even the oak toilet tank is an antique. Because some of the private baths are down the hall, thick terrycloth bathrobes are provided.

All this attention to detail has paid off. Pictures of the home were entered in a wallpaper company contest and netted the innkeepers a $25,000 award. Much of it has already gone into the Brunswick Beltram Bed and Breakfast, a sister inn just six blocks away.

TAYLORS FALLS

The Old Jail Company Bed and Breakfast

100 Government Road
Box 203
Taylors Falls, MN 55084
612-465-3112

> *It's a pleasure to serve time in this former jail*

Innkeepers: Julie and Al Kunz. **Accommodations:** 3 suites, all with private bath. **Rates:** $90–$110. **Included:** Full breakfast. **Minimum stay:** No. **Added:** 6.5% tax. **Payment:** Personal checks, cash. **Children:** No. **Pets:** No. **Smoking:** Yes. **Open:** Year-round.

One of the suites here is in the old town jail, which was built in 1884. Don't expect a night behind bars, however. The innkeepers have added enough softer touches so that even on the coldest Minnesota nights, guests can relax in front of a pot-bellied stove in a spacious room with high ceilings, stenciled walls, and a full bath. A set of mint-condition Burma-Shave road signs line one wall. The loft bedroom has plaid sheets and soft down comforters. The only grim reminder of days past is the original iron-barred door, but even that is covered by a dainty, handmade curtain.

> **During your tour of Taylors Falls, make sure to visit Interstate Park with its ancient glacial "potholes" (one is 60 feet deep) and dramatic black basalt rock cliffs.**

The other suites are equally charming. Beer was once brewed in the Cave. This deeply set suite retains its exposed stone walls and arches, which keep it at a constant 72 degrees even on the hottest days of summer. It has a queen-size bed and a modern tile bath with a clawfoot tub in the middle of the cave. A stained glass window highlights the entrance. The third-floor Playhouse is reached by an outdoor wooden walkway and is decorated with antique toys; old-fashioned appliances highlight the kitchen. From here you can see Main Street, the St. Croix River, and the valley beyond.

Because the innkeepers feel privacy is the key here, breakfast is brought up the night before, and guests heat it up at their leisure in the morning. Fruit and homemade breads often precede the house specialty: potato pancakes served with sour cream, applesauce, and homemade sausage.

WABASHA

The Anderson House

333 North Main
Wabasha, MN 55981
612-565-4524
800-325-2270

A historic B&B brings new meaning to the term "cat house"

Owner: John Hall. **Accommodations:** 30 rooms, most with private bath. **Rates:** $42–$100. **Included:** Cats. **Minimum stay:** No. **Added:** 6.5% tax. **Payment:** MasterCard, Visa, Discover. **Children:** Yes. **Pets:** Yes. **Smoking:** Yes. **Open:** Closed for two weeks in January.

The 1856 Anderson House hasn't received all of its national attention because it is Minnesota's oldest operating hotel, nor because of its fine service and superb country cooking. What sets it apart are cats, a whole slew of them, that can be delivered to your room for an overnight stay. This extra-special amenity has become extremely popular with feline-loving travelers.

> **If you don't fancy having a cat curled up at the foot of your bed, the Anderson House will replace it with another turn-of-the-century tradition. On cold nights, you can have a hot brick delivered to your room in a quilted envelope. Nursing a cold? One of the staff will provide, with instructions, a fresh mustard plaster.**

The inn has recently undergone a $300,000 exterior restoration. The inside could still use some freshening, though some might argue that the squeaking floor boards, nicked woodwork, and sticky doors only add to the house's historic character. Miraculously, with the exception of the busy second-floor room where the cats spend their days, none of the usual cat odors are present. Aloysius, Buttons, Bess, Kitten, and their 11 other friends must be very well-mannered felines.

John, Gayla, and Jean Hall are the fourth generation to run the Anderson House. The spirit of Grandma Anderson is still very much present in the dining room, where her recipes are a mainstay. The chicken noodle soup, apple brandy pie, and Dutch oven steaks only scratch the surface of the choices available. Her recipes are compiled in *The Anderson House Cookbook,* which was picked up by a major publisher. There are several dining rooms here as well as the inviting grotto-style Lost Dutchman Lounge downstairs.

To work off all the delicious Anderson House cuisine, try a walking tour of historic Wabasha. Less than a block from the hotel are flea markets, antiques shops, and a farmers' market. Wabasha is also a stopping point for the *Mississippi Queen* and *Delta Queen* riverboats.

Missouri

Best Bed-and-Breakfast Inns

Hannibal
Garth Woodside Mansion
Hermann
The Captain Wohlt Inn
Pelze Nichol Haus
The William Klinger Inn
Kansas City
Doanleigh Wallagh
Southmoreland on the Plaza
Rocheport
School House Bed and Breakfast
Ste. Genevieve
The Southern Hotel
Springfield
The Mansion at Elfindale
Walnut Street Inn
Washington
Washington House

Best Full-Service Country Inn

St. Louis
Seven Gables Inn

Best Hotels

Kansas City
The Raphael
The Ritz-Carlton Kansas City
St. Louis
Adam's Mark Hotel
The Hotel Majestic
The Ritz-Carlton St. Louis

Best Lodges and Resorts

Excelsior Springs
The Elms

Lake Ozark
  The Lodge of Four Seasons
Ridgedale
  Big Cedar Lodge

Located at the confluence of the Mississippi and Missouri Rivers, **St. Louis** originally served as a center for the French fur trade. It's also noted as the starting point of westward expansion for the Lewis and Clark expedition. The respect for history here is most evident in the St. Louis Union Station. Once the busiest train station in the world, the Romanesque-style structure now houses shops, restaurants, entertainment, and lodging.

The dramatic downtown arch, built in the 1960s by Finnish architect Eero Saarinen, is still a St. Louis landmark. Beneath it, the Museum of Westward Expansion offers visitors some insight into life during the 1800s and also includes a dramatic film about the construction of the arch. Replicas of 19th-century steamboats offer narrated cruises and dining.

The town is known for fine Italian eateries, including Tony's, in the Italian community known as the Hill. Chinese, French, and German cuisine are also popular. St. Louis's riverfront also has the dubious distinction of having the world's first floating McDonald's, which is housed in a show-boat replica.

St. Louis's completely restored Fox Theater, built in 1929 in ornate "Siamese-Byzantine" style, stages musicals and concerts, and screens classic films. It's also open for tours. At the Anheuser-Busch Brewery, another popular attraction, visitors can learn about the brewing process and visit the world-famous Clydesdales.

A favorite part of the city is Forest Park, site of the 1904 World's Fair and St. Louis Exposition. The 1,300-acre park houses the St. Louis Zoo, Art Museum, and Planetarium. The 79-acre Missouri Botanical Garden, the oldest in the United States, features a Japanese Garden with raked sand gardens and a small lake with islands among the scenery.

Due west of St. Louis on Highway 94 is **Hermann,** a charming river town on the banks of the Missouri that, despite its popularity, has retained much of its historic personality. Hermann was settled in 1836 by the German Settlement Society of Philadelphia. The hills and valleys reminded them of their Rhine Valley homeland. Today, European-style homes, shops, and galleries sit close to the streets. The Stone Hill and Hermannhof Wineries offer tours and tastings. Book early for rooms during the popular Maifest and Oktoberfest weekends.

In the tourist mecca of **Hannibal,** the names of Huck Finn, Tom Sawyer, and their famous creator line everything from bumper boats to shopping malls. Still, there is plenty of authentic history at the Mark Twain Home and Museum, and you can tour caves featured in several of his books. While Mark Twain Cave is illuminated with dramatic colored lighting, Cameron Cave is a much more authentic cave where visitors are led through with only the light of lanterns to guide them.

A straight shot west of St. Louis on I-70, **Kansas City** anchors the opposite side of Missouri. It offers a sprawling downtown area highlighted by the Country Club Plaza. Built in 1922, the Plaza is the oldest American shopping center and features mosaics, statues, fountains, ornate ironwork, pastel-colored buildings, and red-tiled roofs.

Nearby is the Nelson-Atkins Museum of Art, renowned for its Oriental art holdings. The Museum is also home to a primo collection of works by Henry Moore, both inside and throughout the surrounding sculpture garden. The Kansas City Museum and the Toy and Miniature Museum also deserve a look.

Crown Center, about two miles north, is the headquarters of Hallmark Cards and includes restaurants, shops, and a visitors center illustrating the company's history and offering a surprisingly interesting look into greeting card production. Diners will want to sample authentic Kansas City barbecue at Arthur Bryant's, about a mile east of downtown.

Kansas City was once home to Count Basie, Charlie Parker, and Jay McShann. Jazz continues to thrive here in downtown clubs, especially during August, which the city has designated Jazz and Heritage Month. The free concerts of the Kansas City Jazz Festival draw some 100,000 fans annually.

EXCELSIOR SPRINGS

The Elms

Regent Street and Elms Boulevard
Excelsior Springs, MO 64024
816-329-4880 (in Kansas City)
816-637-2141
800-843-3567
Fax: 816-637-1222

*Missouri's
historic
luxury spa*

General manager: Doug Morrison. **Accommodations:** 97 rooms, 7 suites, 13 condominiums. **Rates:** Rooms $79 double, suites $95–$130 double, condominiums $150 double; packages available. **Included:** All meals available. **Minimum stay:** No. **Added:** 7% tax. **Payment:** Major credit cards. **Children:** Age 17 and under free. **Pets:** No. **Smoking:** Yes. **Open:** Year-round.

Like many historic luxury spas, the Elms has had ups and downs since its heyday in the first half of this century, when such luminaries as Jack Dempsey, John D. Rockefeller, and Harry Truman sampled the healing effects of its mineral springs. Built in 1888 and just a half hour from Kansas City, the limestone and brick resort hotel is on an upswing, with a slow but steady modernization of its rooms and recreation facilities.

Because of the building's design and the combining of smaller rooms into suites, the accommodations have unusual shapes that offset their generic hotel furnishings. The condominiums have Jacuzzis and kitchenettes. No fancy extras are offered, though a fruit and cheese tray or a bottle of champagne can be ordered for special occasions.

The marble staircase in the lobby leads to a balcony in front of a safe that survived a fire in 1910. Here also is the Meadowlark dining room, with seating below and along a railed balcony. Try the Italian or prime rib buffet or, better yet, plan your trip to coincide with the popular Sunday brunch.

The three-level New Leaf Spa is highlighted by six exotically decorated environmental rooms, which can simulate jungle rain and Arizona heat with the turn of a knob. There are also weight rooms with state-of-the-art rowing machines and Lifecycles and a European-style swim track, where you swim around the perimeter of the pool and take breathers on or between three center islands. Though their therapeutic qualities are often disputed, relaxing old-fashioned mineral baths can also be taken here. A cosmetologist is available by appointment.

Outdoor activities include shuffleboard, horseshoes, volleyball, badminton, tennis, and croquet, as well as swimming in a pool shaped like the Liberty Bell. A scenic bridge spans wildflowers and a trickling stream and leads to tennis courts on another section of the Elms' 23 wooded acres. There is also golf nearby. The game room, off the lobby, has a pool table and video machines and is a popular spot with children.

> **Harry Truman was staying at the Elms in 1948 when the famous "Dewey Defeats Truman" headline ran in the *Chicago Tribune*. He went to bed believing he had lost the election but awoke to learn he had been elected president of the United States.**

Business travelers and large groups will find several meeting rooms at their disposal, including a ballroom, which can hold up to 450 people. They will also appreciate the telephones, televisions, and desks in every guest room.

Many of Excelsior's downtown storefronts are boarded up, but you will still want to visit the art deco Hall of Waters, which now houses city offices. Here you can see a slide show about the mineral springs recalling the wild times at the Elms when Al Capone held all-night card parties with henchmen wielding machine guns standing by.

HANNIBAL

Garth Woodside Mansion

R.R. 1
Hannibal, MO 63401
314-221-2789

Mark Twain counted the home's original owners among his closest friends

Innkeepers: Irv and Diane Feinberg. **Accommodations:** 8 rooms, all with private bath. **Rates:** $58–$95 double. **Included:** Full breakfast. **Minimum stay:** No. **Added:** 5.225% tax. **Payment:** Major credit cards. **Children:** Over 12 years. **Pets:** No. **Smoking:** On the verandah. **Open:** Year-round.

Driving through Hannibal, you may think you've arrived at a shrine to Mark Twain. At every turn are billboards and landmarks indicating that Twain not only spent time here but still supports several tourist attractions. But beyond the Mark Twain Shopping Center and Tom and Huck's Bumper Boats and Go-Carts is the historic Garth Woodside Mansion. While this magnificent Second Empire inn is not overburdened with Twain memorabilia, it once welcomed the author himself, who counted the Garth family among his closest friends.

Irv and Diane Feinberg were lucky enough to acquire many of the home's original furnishings when they purchased it in 1988, and they continually add to the impressive collection of Second Empire bedroom and parlor furniture. As a result, the home is a veritable museum. On display in the upstairs corridors, for example, are vintage Victorian dresses, beaded purses, birth announcements, photographs, and other 19th-century accessories.

The John H. Garth Room is the most regal, with a 10½-foot-high Renaissance Revival headboard and white Carrara marble fireplace. The Rosewood Room features a walnut wardrobe and an 1840s half-tester Mitchell bed signed by the designer. Some baths have clawfoot tubs.

Breakfast is served in the formal dining room, but Diane keeps the atmosphere casual. The meal may include fresh fruit with lemon sauce, orange juice, apple muffins, and an entrée such as peach French toast.

> **The spacious guest rooms house massive armoires, elaborately carved headboards, dressers, settees, and old trunks, and the walls are papered in Victorian patterns.**

The Feinbergs encourage guests to use the furniture, relax in the two parlors, or rock the evening away in a vintage wicker rocker on the wraparound porch that overlooks the inn's 39 acres. Bring a fishing rod and try your luck Huck Finn style in the private pond.

HERMANN

The Captain Wohlt Inn

123 East Third Street
Hermann, MO 65041
314-486-3357

> *A riverboat captain's home*

Owners: Lee and Harry Sammons. **Accommodations:** 5 rooms, all with private bath, 3 suites. **Rates:** Rooms $55–$65 single or double, suites $85. **Included:** Full breakfast. **Minimum stay:** 2 nights on festival weekends. **Added:** 7.725% tax. **Payment:**

Personal checks, cash. **Children:** Yes. **Pets:** No. **Smoking:** No. **Open:** Year-round.

The Captain Wohlt Inn, a secluded clapboard house with deep green trim, sits high on a historic street. Built in 1886 by a German riverboat captain, its guest rooms have delicate floral wallpaper and antique quilts. A carpeted first-floor room has a four-poster queen-size bed and country accents. The upstairs rooms are similarly decorated, with crisp white coverlets, white wicker furniture, and excellent views of the town. The dormer rooms on the third floor aren't recommended for folks over five foot eleven. The owners haven't cluttered the rooms with valuable knickknacks, since they wanted to make sure that families feel comfortable here. Guests have limited kitchen privileges.

> In Hermann, guests can visit myriad specialty shops and antiques stores as well as wineries. There are special events each month, including Volksmarch and the Cajun Concert on the Hill in July. Reserve early for the popular Maifest and Oktoberfest weekends.

Rooms are also available in the carriage house next to the innkeepers' apartment. The spacious suites have beamed ceilings and queen-size beds, and one has a clawfoot tub. The Poechel Suite is especially nice for families, since it has a bedroom, a pull-out bed, and a nursery with a crib. It also opens onto a garden patio with tables and benches. All the guests gather in the main house for a hearty breakfast.

Pelze Nichol Haus

109 East Third
Hermann, MO 65041
314-486-3886

A year-round celebration of Christmas

Innkeepers: Jack and Chris Cady. **Accommodations:** 2 rooms, 1 cottage, all with private bath. **Rates:** Rooms $60–$65 single or double, cottage $75. **Included:** Full breakfast. **Minimum stay:** During Maifest. **Added:** 6.725%

tax. **Payment:** Cash, check only. **Children:** No. **Pets:** No. **Smoking:** No. **Open:** Year-round; only weekends in winter.

With many of Hermann's delightful bed-and-breakfasts either closing or for sale, it's a pleasure to find a new place that appears to be here to stay. Each of the three guest rooms is decorated in a Christmas theme, quite a relief when you arrive on a steamy Missouri afternoon.

> **Only the biggest Scrooge would be Santa'd out after a night here.**

The common rooms are set up as Christmas villages. A heavily bundled man in snowshoes and a witch with a raven on her shoulder are just two of the life-size personages that Chris creates out of papier-mâché and vintage clothing in her downstairs workshop. The decoration is tasteful, not tacky.

The guest rooms have their own delightful touches. Hand-thrown sinks grace the tiled bathroom in the upstairs Christmas Room, while the Tannenbaum Room uses dolls in the decoration. Make your first choice the Christmas Morning Cottage, which has a wooden folk art Christmas tree with an old toy tractor and other presents beneath it. It has a wooden bed high off the ground and an adjoining breakfast nook with twig furniture. Breakfast is served in the cottage or can be taken in the house.

Jack and Chris, both Kansas City educators, serve eggs Benedict and a dessert item, like custard French toast topped with rhubarb from their tiered garden off the back of the house. The innkeepers make good use of their small property; there's even a smokehouse used for drying flowers.

The William Klinger Inn

108 East Second Street
Hermann, MO 65014
314-486-5930

> *A homey base for exploring Hermann*

Innkeeper: Lauri Oliver. **Accommodations:** 7 rooms, all with private bath. **Rates:** $86.83–$121.37; 20% less on weekdays. **Included:** Full breakfast; tax. **Minimum stay:** 2 nights on festival weekends. **Payment:** Master-

Card, Visa. **Children:** No. **Pets:** No. **Smoking:** No. **Open:** Year-round.

This Victorian townhouse, built in 1878 by miller William Klinger, is the perfect base for exploring the wonders of Hermann.

A four-poster canopy queen-size bed highlights the Kallmeyer Room. The smaller Caroline Room has an antique dresser and some Victorian prints. Each floor has a little built-in refrigerator. Some of the private baths are across the hall. There's a sitting area and more guest rooms on the third floor, once the attic. The East Hill room here has a Tiffany-style lamp and a note on the bed philosophizing about travelers on life's journey.

> **The Klinger Room is the most impressive; it has a Victorian bedroom set with a carved grape design, woven rugs, antique clothes on the walls, and a decorative fireplace.**

Breakfast, served by the fireplace in the parlor or on the fenced brick patio, includes casseroles, homemade breads, and muffins. Bacon is rolled in cinnamon and brown sugar and then baked. The carriage house has been converted into a conference center that holds 10 to 12 people comfortably. Dinners can be arranged by reservation.

This a good spot from which to explore Hermann's justly famous specialty shops and German restaurants. The town celebrates special events throughout the year, including a Maifest and Oktoberfest.

KANSAS CITY

Doanleigh Wallagh

217 East 37th Street
Kansas City, MO 64111
816-753-2667
816-753-2408

> *Theatrical flair
> dominates
> at Doanleigh*

Innkeepers: Carolyn and Edward Litchfield. **Accommodations:** 5 rooms, all with private bath. **Rates:** $80–$110 single or double. **Included:** Full breakfast. **Minimum stay:** 2 nights on some holidays. **Added:** 6.5% tax. **Payment:** Major credit cards. **Children:** By prior arrangement. **Pets:** No. **Smoking:** Downstairs only. **Open:** Year-round.

The theatrical flair at Doanleigh Wallagh comes from Ed Litchfield, who once worked at Twentieth Century–Fox. Movie props, including a bust from *The Agony and the Ecstasy* and brass candlesticks from *Desirée*, highlight the common rooms. Ed and Carolyn proudly point out that Carol Channing rented this Georgian inn for a full week while performing in Kansas City.

The big-screen television in the solarium has a VCR and a collection of more than 100 classic films.

The red leather wingback chairs in front of the fireplace are from the old Muehlbach Hotel, a former Kansas City landmark. Before it was torn down, the Litchfields were able to purchase carpeting, beds, and other furnishings for their inn. There's also a grand piano and pump organ, used for small weddings.

A Mexican statue of St. Augustine greets you on the staircase leading to the guest rooms. The Hyde Park Room, originally the master bedroom, is the most lavish, with a wood-burning fireplace, queen-size four-poster bed, a large armoire that holds a television, and a desk made from a hundred-year-old grand piano. There is a tiny fridge in the closet. The Westport Room, with its own porch, is also the only room with both tub and shower.

The breakfast menu is similarly dramatic, from French toast topped with honey and an orange glaze to eggs Benedict with fresh fruit to Russian pancakes with sausage and bacon. Guests may have the meal in their rooms or at tables in the breakfast room. The innkeepers also keep a generous supply of cookies, candy bars, microwave popcorn, and soft drinks in the butler's pantry for their guests.

The Raphael

Country Club Plaza
Kansas City, MO 64112
816-756-3800
800-821-5343
Fax: 816-756-3800, ext. 2199

*A small hotel
with a
European flavor*

General manager: Maxine Hill. **Accommodations:** 123 rooms and suites. **Rates:** Rooms $91–$110 single, $111–$130 double; suites $120–$125 single, $140–$145 double. **Included:** Continental breakfast; all meals available. **Minimum stay:** No. **Added:** 12% tax. **Payment:** Major credit cards. **Children:** Yes. **Pets:** No. **Smoking:** Non-smoking rooms available. **Open:** Year-round.

Kansas City's Raphael successfully cultivates its image of a small private club rather than a city hotel. Repeat guests are usually known by name. The European touch is evident in the tapestries and reproduction oil paintings on the wainscoted lobby walls, including the hotel's trademark image, Raphael's *Count Castiglione*. A Chopin étude plays gently in the background — a welcome sound after the busy comings and goings in the driveway outside.

Built in 1927 and renovated several times since, the Raphael retains some of its historic character. Several original deep bathtubs remain, while modern conveniences like 24-hour room service, nightly turndown, mini-bars, and valet parking contribute to the hotel's reputation for excellent service.

Most of the rooms here are suites, many overlooking Country Club Plaza, an attractive shopping, dining, and entertainment district. The hotel restaurant keeps pace with the competition by providing a varied menu of beef, pasta, and seafood entrées.

The Ritz-Carlton, Kansas City

401 Ward Parkway
Kansas City, MO 64112
816-756-1500
800-241-3333
Fax: 816-756-1635

> *Kansas City's*
> *Ritz is smack in*
> *the heart of town*

General manager: Norm Howard.
Accommodations: 373 rooms, including 28 suites. **Rates:** Rooms $139–$179 single or double, suites $250–$1,000 single or double; packages available. **Minimum stay:** No. **Added:** 11.975% tax. **Payment:** Major credit cards. **Children:** Yes. **Pets:** No. **Smoking:** Nonsmoking rooms available. **Open:** Year-round.

Kansas City's Ritz-Carlton is located in the heart of the Country Club Plaza, Kansas City's prestigious and historic business, shopping, dining, and entertainment district. The 14-story hotel, with its waterfalls, sculptures, and wrought-iron balconies, reflects exquisitely the Moorish influence of the Plaza.

Guest rooms are decorated in traditional style, with marble-lined bathrooms, hair dryers, remote-control cable TV, honor bars, twice-daily maid service, terry robes, three telephones, in-room safes, and fancy toiletries among the amenities. The Ritz-Carlton Club, with guest

> **Key to the Ritz-Carlton's success is its location amid the courtyards, tree-lined walks, mosaics, sculptures, and fountains of the Plaza. Book early for the Plaza Art Fair in September and the Plaza Lighting Ceremony at Thanksgiving.**

rooms on two floors, has its own lounge and multilingual concierge staff, especially helpful when arranging airport transportation or securing restaurant reservations.

You may opt to dine in at the Ritz-Carlton's signature restaurant, the Grill, which serves a wonderful view of the Plaza along with its Continental and American cuisine. The Bar schedules live entertainment Wednesday through Saturday, and the Cafe remains a popular spot for breakfast. The Ritz-Carlton offers over 22,500 square feet of meeting and banquet space, including the Ballroom.

The hotel's fitness center provides state-of-the art treadmill, stair-climber, and biocycle machines as well as an outdoor pool. For joggers and tennis players, miles of jogging trails and lighted tennis courts are just two blocks away.

Southmoreland on the Plaza

116 East 46th Street
Kansas City, MO 64112
816-531-7979
Fax: 816-531-2407

> *Energetic innkeepers please everyone*

Innkeepers: Susan Moehl and Penni Johnson. **Accommodations:** 12 rooms, all with private bath. **Rates:** $95–$125 single; $10 per additional person. **Included:** Full breakfast. **Minimum stay:** No. **Added:** 8% tax. **Payment:** Major credit cards. **Children:** 13 years and older. **Pets:** No. **Smoking:** On verandah only. **Open:** Year-round.

Susan Moehl and Penni Johnson have worked hard to create an inn that's popular with business travelers while still providing the warm fuzzies that weekend guests want. And while it is impossible to be all things to all people, the high-powered innkeepers at Southmoreland on the Plaza come pretty close.

To begin with, they have a superb location. The 1913 Greek Revival home is just two blocks from Country Club Plaza and its more than 300 stores, restaurants, and theaters. Sculptures and fountains decorate the Plaza, and horse-drawn carriages clop by in the evenings. The famed Nelson-Atkins Museum of Art and Henry Moore Sculpture Garden are also nearby.

The staid light gray exterior, more New England than Midwest, doesn't even hint at the often whimsical decoration inside. The innkeepers have amassed a fine collection of antiques from the Midwest and abroad. As part of their restoration of the house, the staircase was rebuilt from original blueprints, while the addition required for more guest rooms maintains the home's integrity.

> **Afternoon wine and cheese are served in the white wicker solarium overlooking a croquet lawn shaded by century-old trees or in the dining room, with its wood-burning fireplace.**

Each room is named for a famous Kansas City native. Romantics will love the Russell Stover Room, with its pink and blue decor, heart-shaped Jacuzzi, and complimentary box of chocolates. The Leroy "Satchel" Paige Room, once a sleeping porch, now resembles a rustic cabin with vintage baseball posters and miniature bats lining the walls. The Victrola has Bessie Smith wailing on "Graveyard Dream Blues." Box seats for Kansas City Royals home games are included with this room.

Susan and Penni bend over backwards for business guests who check in after midnight or leave before dawn. They send them on their way with at least a portion of their elegant breakfast, which includes baked apples with raisins, blueberry muffins, and fancy egg ramekins stuffed with bacon and Lorraine Swiss. They even cater to vegetarian palates by using artichoke hearts instead of meat. A morning paper waits at the table for each guest.

Have a question about theater tickets, dinner reservations, or museum hours? If Susan and Penni don't know the answer, they will find out in a snap.

LAKE OZARK

The Lodge of Four Seasons

Box 215 Lake Road HH
Lake Ozark, MO 65049
800-THE-LAKE
314-365-3000
Fax: 314-365-8555

> *A lake resort
> to be enjoyed
> all year*

General manager: Mark Caney. **Accommodations:** 311 rooms, 100 condos. **Rates:** Rooms $99–$144 weekdays, $119–$164 weekends; condos $225–$299. **Included:** All meals available. **Minimum stay:** No. **Added:** 8.225% tax. **Payment:** Major credit cards. **Children:** Yes. **Pets:** No. **Smoking:** Nonsmoking rooms available. **Open:** Year-round.

About three hours from both St. Louis and Kansas City, the Lodge of Four Seasons spreads across 3,200 lush acres and 72 miles of Lake of the Ozarks shoreline. Harold Koplar opened the facility in 1964, and the family-run operation has since grown into a Midwest paradise for vacationers who enjoy the sporting life.

> **In winter, guests find plenty to do indoors. There are four bowling lanes, a billiard room, and live entertainment nightly at the Fifth Season Lounge. A 350-seat movie theater screens first-run family-oriented features.**

Power, pontoon, and sailing boats are available for rent from the 200-slip marina, along with a bass fishing guide. The Ship's Store, one of many shops at the resort, offers nautical apparel and accessories. Other outdoor activities include hiking, biking, skeet shooting, fishing, and riding. There are both indoor and outdoor swimming pools along with sauna, massage services, and aerobics classes.

Golfers at every level enjoy hitting the links on the resort's 27 holes, nine designed by Robert Trent Jones. You can brush up for the next day's game with indoor and outdoor driving ranges.

Tennis players will find 19 courts here, including indoor courts, clay courts, and a tournament stadium. The Tennis Institute, located in the Racquet Club, offers junior and adult clinics for all skill levels.

Seafood or pasta fans will want to try Toledo's, one of several dining options. HK's Steakhouse features sizzling steaks on an open grill and a splendid view of the golf course. Roseberry's offers family dining, while the Atrium Sidewalk Cafe has fresh baked goods and coffees for early risers.

If you spend any time in your room, you'll find contemporary furnishings in bright pastels and whites. Suites offer kitchenettes and bars, patios, balconies, and fireplaces. Two- or three-bedroom condominiums are popular with families.

RIDGEDALE

Big Cedar Lodge

612 Devil's Pool Road
Ridgedale, MO 65739
417-335-2777
Fax: 417-335-2340

*A fantasyland
for the serious
sportsperson*

General manager: Tony Shill. **Accommodations:** 60 rooms, 18 suites, 51 cabins and cottages. **Rates:** Valley View $115–$169 double, Spring View $115–$229, cottages $425–$749, cabins $119–$579; packages and off-season rates available. **Included:** All meals available. **Minimum stay:** 3 days over holidays. **Added:** 5.225% tax. **Payment:** Major credit cards. **Children:** Yes. **Pets:** No. **Smoking:** Yes. **Open:** Year-round.

Raccoon, deer, antelope, large-mouth bass — you name it, and it's probably mounted on a wall or perched on a beam somewhere at Big Cedar Lodge. This imaginatively decorated resort is a paradise for those who love the outdoors.

Before 1987, the lodge was the neglected Devil's Pool Ranch. Then Johnny Morris took charge. The entrepreneur owner of Bass Pro Shops, based in Springfield, wanted to create a resort where guests could indulge in luxury and rusticity at the same time.

The guest rooms, conference facilities, and common areas are decorated with antique rifle shell boxes, duck decoys, pipe tobacco tins, rods and reels, fancy lures, and a zoo full of stuffed and mounted animals. The contents of three museums were purchased to stock the place.

> The popularity of the lodge (with almost full occupancy from May through October) and its inevitable expansion have some regulars worried. It's like your favorite fishing hole, said one. You want everyone to know how great it is, but you don't want them to fish the place dry.

The property teems with well-heeled sportsmen wearing designer camouflage and driving late-model sport vehicles. Though the prices are too steep for many budgets, the lodge has remained genial and unpretentious.

Contemporary accommodations can be found in the native rock and log Valley View Lodge, where the rooms are tastefully decorated in deep forest greens. The lodge sits high on a bluff, and the more expensive rooms on the front offer views of Big Cedar's surrounding 800 acres.

Better yet, spring for a deluxe room at the Spring View Lodge down the hill. It takes the Banana Republic fantasy to the max, with carved wood or wicker beds, more animal heads, and exotic antiques. The baths have spacious Jacuzzis, and wildlife dioramas line the halls. Standard rooms are also found here.

The cabins, built between 1920 and 1940, have been renovated and modernized. Beds in the newer cabins may have headboards shaped like a tree, with wildlife perched in branches above the bed.

The historic Tudor Carriage House and beamed Truman Cottage, currently among Big Cedar's most expensive accommodations, are often booked for longer stays. Most impressive is the Governor's Suite, a 2,500-square-foot luxury apartment with four bedrooms, four Jacuzzis, and two spacious balconies. It took 14 years to carve the intricate bedroom set, which once belonged to the king of Norway.

Copper fish signs ("They were really bitin' yesterday") lead you through the winding roads between properties. Big Cedar Lodge is prettiest at night, when floodlights shine on myriad waterfalls and the towering main lodge.

The Devil's Pool Restaurant has an excellent menu, with

regional specialties including hillbilly meatloaf and smoked Ozark trout. Adventurous diners can try a chuck wagon dinner, where sizzling steak is cooked over a pit and java is poured from a big black coffeepot. Live entertainment is often part of the fun. The real Devil's Pool, by the way, is a mysterious spring on the property that is said to be bottomless. When the lake is low, you can get a glimpse of it in the clear water beneath the swinging bridge.

Family activities include miniature golf, tennis, horseback riding, and horseshoes. The outdoor pool and hot tub overlook the lake. A nearby golf course is accessible to guests. Of course, there's excellent fishing on Table Rock Lake, with top-of-the-line bass boats available for rent. The kitschy "country music capital" of Branson is just nine miles north.

ROCHEPORT

School House Bed and Breakfast

Third and Clark Streets
Rocheport, MO 65279
314-698-2022

Historic School House preserves an important part of childhood

Innkeepers: John and Vicki Ott. **Accommodations:** 9 rooms, most with private bath. **Rates:** $60–$105 double. **Included:** Full breakfast. **Minimum stay:** No. **Added:** 6.275% tax. **Payment:** MasterCard, Visa. **Children:** Yes. **Pets:** No. **Smoking:** No. **Open:** Year-round.

For John and Vicki Ott and their many guests, the School House Bed and Breakfast is more than just a creative commercial renovation of an old building. From its 13-foot ceilings and black slate chalkboard to the cast-iron school bell on the front lawn, the inn preserves an important part of childhood.

> A classroom feel still pervades the spacious upstairs common room, where Vicki writes guests' names on the slate chalkboard.

When the innkeepers bought the 1914 schoolhouse, it consisted of four large classrooms, which have since been renovated into the guest rooms. Vicki's favorite is the School Marm Room, with its clawfoot tub, pull-chain water closet, and antique pedestal sink. The School Master Room features an elegant four-poster rice plantation bed and a mahogany wardrobe. The Show 'n Tell Room offers Waverly fabrics and a heart-shaped Jacuzzi. The Otts make the undocumented claim that this room has the only bidet in the river town of Rocheport.

Among the common rooms are a reading room, a dining room, and a kitchen that guests share with the innkeepers. Breakfast often features an egg casserole, fresh fruit and juices, and homemade muffins. Tall windows provide a pleasant view of a neighbor's well-tended garden.

The entire town of Rocheport is listed on the National Register of Historic Places. You can tour antiques and pottery shops, walking and biking trails, a nearby winery, and historic Boone Cave. And though you should pay attention while exploring, this is one schoolhouse where you won't be given a pop quiz on your return.

SPRINGFIELD

The Mansion at Elfindale

1701 South Fort Street
Springfield, MO 65807
417-831-5400
Fax: 417-831-2965

*Spacious rooms
in a designers'
showcase*

Innkeeper: Jeff Gibson. **Accommodations:** 10 rooms, 3 suites, all with private bath. **Rates:** Rooms $70–$85 single or double, suites $85–$125 single or double. **Included:** Full breakfast. **Minimum stay:** No. **Added:** 7.975% tax. **Payment:** Major credit cards. **Children:** 12 years and older. **Pets:** No. **Smoking:** No. **Open:** Year-round.

When Alice and John O'Day were divorced in 1901, Alice obtained possession of their stately stone mansion. She changed its name from Park Place to Elfindale after imagining tiny elves playing in the dale in the early morning mist. From these fanciful origins comes a 13-room B&B, owned and run by the nondenominational Cornerstone Church next door.

Returning guests ask for the Tower Suite, where a cathedral-shaped arch separates the bedroom from the sitting room. A curved staircase leads to a third-floor observatory, complete with telescope.

The guest rooms are distinguished by their extreme spaciousness and their exquisite decor, done in a variety of styles as part of a Springfield decorators' showcase.

The Art Deco Suite is jade and coral, with a king-size brass bed beneath a cathedral ceiling and wood furniture painted a marbled blue. The Alice O'Day Suite mixes brass and wicker furnishings with rose and green accents. The John O'Day Suite is a bit wilder, with a canopy bed covered by a zebra-print spread and a six-foot clawfoot tub original to the house.

The formal dining room is now set up for meetings and Sunday school classes; the ballroom welcomes receptions. A full breakfast is served in the sunny tea room, with red iron chairs and marble-topped tables covered with crisp white tablecloths. The meal may include asparagus omelettes, crêpes or quiche, scrambled eggs and sausage, and always a fresh fruit bowl, coffee, and tea.

Walnut Street Inn

900 East Walnut Street
Springfield, MO 65806
417-864-6346
800-593-6346
Fax: 417-864-6184

A Queen Anne-style B&B where every room is a treat

Innkeeper: Karol Brown. **Accommodations:** 14 rooms, 3 cottage suites, all with private bath. **Rates:** Rooms $75–$120 double, suites $95–$120. **Included:** Full breakfast. **Minimum stay:** No. **Added:** 6% tax. **Payment:** Major credit cards. **Children:** Yes. **Pets:** No. **Smoking:** No. **Open:** Year-round.

Almost every bed-and-breakfast inn boasts individually decorated guest rooms, but the Walnut Street Inn has a special flair. Each of its rooms was decorated by a different designer as part of a Springfield Symphony benefit, and the rooms have since been reworked by the innkeepers. Some of the furnishings have been replaced and others switched, with outstanding results.

Hand-painted Corinthian columns frame the wide, airy verandah of the pale peach Queen Anne home. A beveled glass front door opens to hardwood floors in the downstairs common areas.

The living room takes up most of the first floor. Board games are set out, along with CDs and a wide range of travel guides. Many guests comment on the antique photographs that line the tables, bureaus, and 1862 square grand piano. Be sure to ask Karol about her great-grandfather, who invented a camera lens that was later sold to Kodak.

Choosing a guest room can be difficult. The Lilly Room is draped in yards of white Battenberg lace and has a tiny balcony. One of the attic rooms, the Treetop, named for the view from its third-floor balcony, has a clawfoot tub right in the room. The Loft is more contemporary, with painted boxcar siding and skylights. The many natural angles in this room create intriguing nooks and crannies.

> **The inn is on a major thoroughfare in a historic neighborhood just a block from Southwest Missouri State University. During a popular summer arts festival, booths are set up right in front of the inn, and the innkeepers decorate the place for the Christmas Festival of Lights.**

Karol Brown has taken over the innkeeping duties from her mother, Nancy, who runs the family's furniture store in Springfield. Both spend plenty of time at the inn. Karol announces breakfast with pleasant morning chimes. The full meal may include raspberry crêpes, country ham, persimmon and walnut muffins, and fresh fruit and juices.

The Browns also offer rooms in separate homes down the street. Collectively known as the Cottage Inn, the three spacious suites are good for business travelers, who often stay for weeks at a time. These suites offer Jacuzzis, fireplaces, private porches, fully stocked beverage bars, and European antiques. A carriage house recently opened with four additional guest rooms.

STE. GENEVIEVE

The Southern Hotel

146 South Third Street
Ste. Genevieve, MO 63670
314-883-3493
800-275-1412

*One of Missouri's
premier
B&B inns*

Innkeepers: Mike and Barbara Hankins. **Accommodations:** 8 rooms, all with private bath. **Rates:** $75–$105 double. **Included:** Full breakfast. **Minimum stay:** 2 nights on special weekends. **Added:** 6.725% tax. **Payment:** Major credit cards. **Children:** Limited. **Pets:** No. **Smoking:** No. **Open:** Year-round.

Their friends thought Mike and Barbara Hankins were crazy when the St. Louis restoration buffs bought a dilapidated hotel in Ste. Genevieve. That was in 1986. Today, the Hankins preside over one of the state's best bed-and-breakfast inns in a historic Federal building that, without them, most certainly would have been torn down.

The guest rooms display the Hankins' flair for decoration. Cabbage Rose, their High Victorian room, has a collection of fans over the fireplace and a painted clawfoot tub. Lulabelle is named for Barbara's favorite childhood doll. More than 20 handmade quilts decorate the Quilt Room, whose 19th-century bed is similar to one found in Lincoln's home. Folk art lovers opt for Wysocki's Room, with its country accents and hand-painted headboard fashioned into a three-dimensional Wysocki-style village. The Japonisme Room reflects the Victorian fascination with Oriental art.

A 1797 summer kitchen now houses a delightful antiques and craft shop. Items used at the inn — lamps, butter molds, garden products, coffee and coffee mugs, and handmade soaps — are all available here. Most popular are the Toad Abodes, hand-painted in the shop. They resemble decorated toadstools, with little gnome-like creatures perched on top. Barbara has populated her own splendid gardens with them.

> The common rooms have their own histories. The game room is dominated by a circa 1870 pool table, one of only two in existence. During its heyday as a luxury hotel, the Southern was the first public building in town to be granted a pool hall permit.

Barbara's elegant breakfast may include an entrée of mushroom quiche, artichoke heart strata, or French toast with Grand Marnier sauce. The entrée is usually accompanied by a croissant, a fruit dish, honey butter, juice, and coffee.

Ste. Genevieve, the oldest town west of the Mississippi and containing plenty of fine examples of historic preservation, waits just outside the door. St. Louis is an hour away. Before you leave, don't forget to add your name to the quilt in the parlor. The Hankins have filled at least nine of these unique guest registers.

ST. LOUIS

Adam's Mark Hotel

Fourth and Chestnut Street
St. Louis, MO 63102
314-241-7400
800-444-ADAM
Fax: 314-241-6618

> *Arch views and cosmopolitan flair*

General manager: Maurice Briquet.
Accommodations: 910 rooms, including 96 suites. **Rates:** Rooms $145–$175 single, $160–$190 double; suites $350–

$410 single or double; packages available. **Minimum stay:**
No. **Added:** 9.475% tax plus $2 occupancy per day. **Payment:**
Major credit cards. **Children:** Yes. **Pets:** No. **Smoking:** Non-
smoking rooms available. **Open:** Year-round.

In the shadow of the Gateway Arch, the Adam's Mark is the
largest hotel between Chicago and Atlanta. The hotel is situated on what was once part of the Pierce Building, a turn-of-
the-century office com-
plex. Extensive recon-
struction on the site led
to the creation of twin
towers designed to pro-
vide all guest rooms with
a sweeping view of the
Arch and the Mississippi
River.

> For convention groups, the
> Adam's Mark features the
> 20,000-square-foot St. Louis
> Ballroom, as well as
> 21 conference suites,
> 44 meeting rooms and three
> boardrooms. These are the
> largest facilities in town.

Many of the antique
fixtures were carefully
preserved, including ten
sets of bronze elevator
doors with enamel medal-
lions. The pair of lifelike bronze horses, nostrils flaring and
heads held high, were fashioned after 13th-century statues by
an Italian artist.

For dining, Faust's, the elegant formal dining room, serves
Continental and American cuisine. The Library is ideal for
special occasions. Chestnut's offers a more casual dining experience. A quartet of lounges join the hotel restaurants on
the first floor and create a pleasant, cosmopolitan atmosphere
in the evening, especially when there's live music.

The Adam's Mark fitness center includes a heated indoor
and glass-enclosed outdoor swimming pool, whirlpool, sauna,
two racquetball courts, and a fully equipped exercise room.
Other services include a gift shop, florist, barber/beauty shop,
shoe shine, and underground parking.

Standard rooms are nothing special but are more than func-
tional. For rooms with a view, ask for a room ending in 01, 02,
or 97. The 96 rooms on the hotel's Concorde Level have access to lounge areas with concierge services and special
amenities. Desks, phones, fax machines, copiers, and secre-
tarial service are all available.

The Hotel Majestic

1019 Pine Street
St. Louis, MO 63101
314-436-2355
800-451-2355
Fax: 314-436-2355
Reservations: 800-678-8946
    or 800-544-7570

> *Personal service abounds at this downtown hotel*

General manager: Randall H. Ross. **Accommodations:** 91 rooms including 3 suites. **Rates:** Rooms $155 double, suites $290–$850. **Included:** Continental breakfast; all meals available. **Minimum stay:** No. **Added:** 9.475% tax, $2 per room occupancy fee. **Payment:** Major credit cards. **Children:** Yes. **Pets:** No. **Smoking:** Nonsmoking rooms available. **Open:** Year-round.

This circa 1913 hotel, formerly the DeSoto, was refurbished in 1987, reducing its 200 accommodations to 91 spacious rooms and suites. The exterior renovation included restoring the wood windows, awnings, and terra cotta tile. Heavy brass doors lead to the small lobby's wainscoted walls and trim, chintz fabrics, and Italian marble floors covered by Oriental rugs. Fresh flowers and a bowl of red apples pose artfully on an antique side table.

> **There is no check-in desk here. Instead, arriving guests are seated with a concierge who personally arranges every aspect of their stay. The elegant touches only begin here, which is why the Majestic remains synonymous with luxury travel in downtown St. Louis.**

The guest rooms resemble small apartments, boasting turndown service with chocolates, a complimentary newspaper, overnight shoeshine, mini-bars, a fruit basket upon arrival, and morning coffee served on a silver tray, along with 24-hour concierge, valet, and room service. The bathrooms boast telephones, marble-topped vanities, and terrycloth robes.

The hotel's Just Jazz Restaurant is distinguished by its huge antique clock over a gleaming red oak and brass bar and

Toulouse-Lautrec mural variations against a back wall. The lengthy menu here includes beef, chicken, and seafood dishes. If they're available, try the grilled swordfish steak or Norwegian salmon, the latter poached in white wine and lemon and served with citrus beurre blanc and tomato fennel fondue. Visit the Just Jazz Bar and Lounge, which features local and nationally renowned musicians along with a house pianist and singer.

Another plus is the hotel's central location. The Majestic is within easy walking distance of the famed Gateway Arch, Busch Stadium, Union Station, and the St. Louis riverfront.

The Ritz-Carlton, St. Louis

1 Ritz-Carlton Drive
Clayton, MO 63105
314-863-6300
800-241-3333
Fax: 314-863-3525

> *The St. Louis Ritz
> defines luxury
> in the Midwest*

General manager: Hal Leonard. **Accommodations:** 301 rooms, including 33 suites. **Rates:** Rooms $140–$215 single or double, suites $350–$1,500 single or double; packages available. **Minimum stay:** No. **Added:** 12.975% tax. **Payment:** Major credit cards. **Children:** Yes. **Pets:** No. **Smoking:** Nonsmoking rooms. **Open:** Year-round.

Located in the fashionable St. Louis suburb of Clayton, this Ritz-Carlton opened in March 1990 and quickly moved into top position for a luxury stay in St. Louis. The entryway is flanked by greenery and fountains in a parklike setting. Arched windows and wrought-iron balconies distinguish the new brick and limestone facade.

Oversized, elegantly furnished rooms evoke the feeling of a country home, with mahogany beds, overstuffed club chairs and writing tables, private balconies, and marble bathrooms. Each room comes with the amenities you expect from a Ritz-Carlton: terry bathrobes, fancy toiletries, hair dryers, and a second telephone in the bathroom. Rooms on the front of the building offer the best views of Clayton, and some can even see the Gateway Arch rising in the distance.

The fitness center here offers a hot tub, a sun deck, personal trainers, and massages. The pool also has a touch of class, flanked by wrought-iron furniture and lit through several elegantly draped windows. The Ritz-Carlton Club is located on the 17th and 18th floors, offering complimentary food and beverage service and a private concierge.

For meetings, facilities include two boardrooms, six conference rooms, and a 201-seat amphiteater. The ballroom hosts up to 1,000 for receptions.

About 15 miles from downtown, Clayton plays host to the city's financial district and also its best

> **Inside, Italian marble floors, rich wood paneling, jewel-toned tapestries, and fresh flowers blend with a $5 million collection of 18th- and 19th-century art and antiques.**

eateries. The Ritz's own restaurant has richly enameled walls, crisp damask linens, and heavy silver. Meal options here include fresh Maine lobster, steaks, and specialties such as baked rabbit Lori with spinach and a mushroom mustard glaze.

Seven Gables Inn

26 North Meramec
Clayton, MO 63105
314-863-8400
800-433-6590
Fax: 314-863-8846
Reservations: 800-243-1166

> *A fine Tudor-style inn in the financial center*

General manager: Dennis Fennedy. **Accommodations:** 28 rooms, 4 suites. **Rates:** Rooms $85–$135 single or double, suites $155–$250. **Included:** Continental breakfast weekends only. **Minimum stay:** No. **Added:** 13% tax. **Payment:** Major credit cards. **Children:** Yes. **Pets:** Some, by prior arrangement. **Smoking:** Yes. **Open:** Year-round.

The Seven Gables Inn looks a bit out of place among the glass and concrete office towers of Clayton, the government and financial center of downtown St. Louis. The Tudor inn was built in 1926, inspired by the pen-and-ink sketches used to illustrate Hawthorne's *House of Seven Gables*.

Country French antiques are found in many rooms, and

cable television, desks, and dual phone lines for conference calls keep you in touch with the outside world.

Nice personal touches include the hand-milled French soap and thick terry robes found in each bathroom and the fine chocolate left on the bed at turndown. In the morning, room service brings coffee, juice, and breakfast pastries on fine country French china. There's also complimentary valet parking and passes to a nearby health club.

> **The small hotel caters primarily to business guests, but vacation travelers will also appreciate the well-decorated surroundings.**

The inn really shines in its dining rooms. Chez Louis, just off the lobby, is an award-winning French restaurant famous for its wine list; it was a fixture here before the inn opened. The menu changes daily, but seafood dishes with rich herb sauces are always recommended. For lighter fare, Bernard's boasts an informal turn-of-the century bistro and bar, decorated with framed posters.

In warmer months, lunch and dinner are served on the enclosed patio in the landscaped Garden Court, with umbrella-covered tables and window boxes filled with geraniums. Clayton is known for its excellent restaurants, so you may want to venture beyond the inn as well.

WASHINGTON

Washington House

3 Lafayette Street
Washington, MO 63090
314-239-2417
314-239-9834

> *A small-town inn with country primitive accents*

Innkeepers: Chuck and Kathy Davis. **Accommodations:** 3 rooms, all with private bath. **Rates:** $55 single, $65–$75 double. **Included:** Breakfast voucher for nearby restaurant. **Minimum**

stay: No. **Added:** 6.725% tax. **Payment:** Check, cash. **Children:** Yes. **Pets:** No. **Smoking:** No. **Open:** Year-round.

Chuck and Kathy Davis obviously had fun restoring Washington House to its country primitive origins. The 1837 home, first built as a haven for travelers and trappers along the Missouri River, has also served as a general store, riverboat captain's home, boarding house, fish market, speakeasy, restaurant, and apartment building.

> **All the guest rooms have wonderful views of the Missouri River.**

The only guest room on the main floor, the August Edouart Room, was so named because the French silhouettist's signature was found on the plaster during renovation. The Davises believe that he, like many itinerant 19th-century artists, traded his work for a place to stay. The circa 1860 bed and dresser here once belonged to a Union soldier. This is the only room with fancy Victorian wallpaper. The others' walls are painted in Williamsburg colors.

The inn offers several romantic touches. Some rooms have working fireplaces; candles can be used in the others. Wherever possible, exposed bricks or squares of stenciling show how the place looked before restoration. The Davises considered straightening the slanted window that had drooped in one corner from years of settling, but they got to like it. You will, too.

Complimentary wine and cheese greet guests on arrival. There's a coffeemaker in each room to brew some of the special Washington House coffee from the coffee shop downstairs.

No breakfast is served here. Instead, guests are given a voucher for breakfast at Cowan's Café, a block away, where they can order pancakes, French toast, or egg dishes from the menu. A side order of bacon and sausage may cost extra, however.

Kathy says that many of her guests are nine-to-fivers from St. Louis who want to relax on weekends in a small town with good restaurants and antiques shops. Interesting 19th-century architecture abounds, as do local wineries. Washington has a special claim to fame: it is the home of the only factory in the world that still produces corncob pipes.

Ohio

Best Bed-and-Breakfast Inns

Charm
 The Charm Countryview Inn
Circleville
 The Castle Inn
Cincinnati
 Prospect Hill B&B
Columbus
 50 Lincoln
Conesville
 Log House Bed and Breakfast
Kelley's Island
 Sweet Valley B&B
Loudonville
 The Blackfork Inn
Mount Vernon
 The Russell-Cooper House
Sagamore Hills
 The Inn at Brandywine Falls

Best Full-Service Country Inns

Chagrin Falls
 The Inn at Chagrin Falls
Cleveland
 The Baricelli Inn
 The Glidden House
Danville
 The White Oak Inn
Granville
 The Buxton Inn
Lebanon
 The Golden Lamb
Logan
 The Inn at Cedar Falls
Millersburg
 The Inn at Honey Run
Wooster
 The Wooster Inn

Best Hotels

Cincinnati
  The Cincinnatian Hotel
  Omni Netherland Plaza
Cleveland
  The Ritz-Carlton, Cleveland
Columbus
  The Great Southern Hotel
Coshocton
  Roscoe Village Inn
Worthington
  The Worthington Inn

Cincinnati, in the southwestern corner of the state and reached most directly by I-71, celebrated its bicentennial in 1988 and along with it a rebirth through new construction and the renovation of historic buildings downtown. Cincinnati's cultural life is concentrated at Eden Park, where you can find the Art Museum, the Krohn Conservatory, and Cincinnati Playhouse in the Park. To put the city in perspective, visit the observation deck on the 49th floor of Carew Tower or walk along the low-lying parks on the edge of the Ohio River, where the first settlers arrived. The Cincinnati Zoo, in nearby Clifton, puts you in the middle of the insect world through an incredible exhibition. Mason, 24 miles north of town, is the site of Kings Island theme park.

Cleveland, at the top of the state on the banks of Lake Erie, invested considerable money in developing its downtown during the 1980s. Although it retains its gritty industrial image, a number of cultural events attract visitors. Most of these are in the University Circle area, which includes the Cleveland Museum of Art, with its collection of 19th-century French and American impressionist paintings as well as a version of Rodin's *Thinker*. The Cleveland Museum of Natural History displays ancient evidence of both dinosaurs and humans, including the world's oldest, most complete fossil of a human ancestor.

You can drive south on I-71 for the easiest route to Columbus. Or take a zigzag route off the beaten path through Holmes County, considered the largest Amish community in the world. You may encounter **Millersburg, Danville, Granville,** and Zoar along the way. **Coshocton,** at the intersection of several rural roads, is the home of Roscoe Village. It has 25 restored brick and frame buildings, most of which are open for tours. Be sure to visit Steward's Antiques and Collectables and the Johnson-Humrickhouse Museum, with five galleries of Indian and Eskimo artifacts.

Columbus, the largest city in Ohio, lies roughly between Cleveland and Cincinnati off I-71. Amid the modern skyscrapers is the 1857 statehouse, a Greek Revival structure where the legislature still meets. And here is the largest college campus in North America, Ohio State University. Buckeye fans fill the famous horseshoe stadium to capacity during football season. In addition to an impressive permanent collection at the Columbus Museum of Art, the arts are always the focus of attention in the Short North gallery district.

A favorite among Ohio state parks is Hocking Hills, southeast of Columbus on Highway 33. This is the site of Old Man's Cave, Ash Cave, the Rock House, and thousands of acres of wooded hiking trails.

CHAGRIN FALLS

The Inn of Chagrin Falls

West Falls
Chagrin Falls, OH 44022
216-247-1200
Fax: 216-247-2122

A full-service country inn

Innkeeper: Mary Beth O'Donnell.
Accommodations: 12 rooms, 3 suites. **Rates:** Rooms $95–$155 single, $105–$165 double; suites $175 single, $185 double. **Included:** Continental breakfast. **Minimum stay:** No. **Added:** 11.5% tax. **Payment:** Major credit cards. **Children:** 8 years and older. **Pets:** No. **Smoking:** No. **Open:** Year-round.

Arthur Crane, inventor of LifeSavers candy, purchased a pair of cottages in 1927 on Western Reserve property, joined them with a 10,000-square-foot addition, and opened his famous Crane's Canary Cottage restaurant. Will Rogers, Charles Lindbergh, and the Rockefellers (not to mention Crane's own famous son, Hart) dined here over the next several decades. The inn is still canary-colored clapboard, but the property has undergone a dramatic change to romantic country inn that also caters to corporate guests.

The gathering room, with English-style furnishings and hunting prints, can accommodate up to 35. In winter, a fire is usually blazing as executives conduct business around a formal table or on plump sofas and chairs. The gracious staff will supply all audiovisual equipment. Meals are catered by the adjoining restaurant.

Summer finds guests supping on the outdoor patio under large market umbrellas. After-dinner strollers gravitate towards the bustling village of Chagrin Falls or its namesake waterfall, just steps from the front door via a wooden staircase.

Down comforters and gas fireplaces are just two of the special touches offered in the guest rooms. The Mill Room (the Chagrin Falls once powered a paper mill), has a draped canopy bed and antique Italian marble fireplaces. Reproduction antique armoires house remote-control color televisions. The three suites have Jacuzzis. Continental breakfast (including sour cream coffee cake) can be taken in the pine-paneled dining room or in the attached 150-seat restaurant, now called the Gamekeepers' Taverne. One of the original cottages, with maple and white oak floors, now houses a country gift shop and clothing boutique called Hearthside.

CHARM

The Charm Countryview Inn

State Route 557
P.O. Box 100
Charm, OH 44617
216-893-3003

> *An Amish inn in
> Holmes County*

Innkeepers: Paul and Naomi Miller. **Accommodations:** 15 rooms, all with private bath. **Rates:** $65–$92.50. **Included:** Full breakfast; Continental breakfast on Sundays. **Minimum stay:** No. **Added:** 9% tax. **Payment:** MasterCard, Visa. **Children:** By prior arrangement. **Pets:** No. **Smoking:** No. **Open:** Year-round.

The Charm Countryview Inn is about as close as you can get to a genuine Amish stay. From the glider on the wraparound porch , you can watch horse-drawn buggies pass by. That sort of traffic can get heavy here in the heart of Holmes County, which boasts the world's largest Amish community. The Mennonite innkeepers, Paul and Naomi Miller, live on the property owned by Paul's parents, Abe and Fannie Mast. The family built the inn in 1990.

There are no televisions in the guest rooms, which are all named for family members. Most rooms are decorated with handmade quilts; the solid oak furniture comes

> For sightseeing, you will want to visit the several good quilt shops that dot the town. There are also country craft shops, cheese factories, and livestock auctions along with plenty of winding scenic roads to explore. Even the hardware store sells crafts.

from the family's furniture store in Charm. Before breakfast, Paul will probably ask guests to share in a prayerful thought before digging into the generous meal of bran and rhubarb muffins followed by a bacon, egg, and cheese casserole. Continental breakfast is served on Sunday, which the innkeepers recognize as a day of rest. Within a 15-minute drive are fine restaurants offering Amish home cooking and Swiss cuisine.

CINCINNATI

The Cincinnatian Hotel

6th and Vine Streets
Cincinnati, OH 45202
513-381-3000
800-332-2020 in Ohio
800-942-9000 elsewhere
Fax: 513-651-0256
Reservations: 800-323-7500

Contemporary
touches in
a classic hotel

General manager: Denise Vandersall. **Accommodations:** 139 rooms, 8 suites. **Rates:** Rooms $160–$195, suites $250–$750; weekends $99; packages available. **Included:** All meals available. **Minimum stay:** No. **Added:** 10% tax. **Payment:** Major credit cards. **Children:** Yes. **Pets:** No. **Smoking:** Nonsmoking rooms available. **Open:** Year-round.

The Cincinnatian, built in 1882 and renovated in 1987 into a sleek contemporary hotel, lies just a short walk from business and tourist attractions in the heart of downtown Cincinnati.

The decor is decidedly modern in both the guest rooms and common areas. Tall ferns, comfortably stuffed art deco chairs, and touches of neon decorate the Crickets lounge, under an eight-story atrium. There are occasional reminders of the past, too, including the French Second Empire exterior. As you ascend the staircase to the second floor, notice how the marble steps have been worn from a century of use.

Afternoon tea is served in the Crickets lounge on weekdays. Patterned after similar presentations at the Dorchester Hotel in England, it includes finger sandwiches, scones, tea breads, and pastries. Reservations are advised for this popular event.

The rooms are decorated in shades of gray and black or peach tones. All have access to a complimentary overnight shoeshine and a full-time concierge. The weather forecast for the following day is reported during nightly turndown.

The Palace ranks among the city's finest restaurants, decorated in creams, burgundies, and periwinkle blues. The dishes have an artistic flair and are presented under glass domes. Chef Tim Anderson emphasizes American regional cuisine such as rack of lamb, swordfish, and beef tenderloin; each is prepared differently depending on the season. Try the Caesar salad, spiked with house-smoked salmon. The popular Sunday brunch and elegant picnic baskets prepared by the kitchen are also options here.

Business travelers fill the hotel during the week. International guests can easily exchange currency or order a traditional Japanese breakfast. Honeymoon and shopping packages help make the Cincinnatian appealing to weekend guests.

The Omni Netherland Plaza

35 West Fifth Street
Cincinnati, OH 45202
513-421-9100
Fax: 513-421-4291
Reservations:
Omni Hotels
800-THE-OMNI

> *A painstakingly restored art deco masterpiece*

General manager: Mark Kenney. **Accommodations:** 621 rooms, including 12 suites. **Rates:** Rooms $135–$145 single, $165–$175 double; suites $285–$800; packages available. **Minimum stay:** No. **Added:** 10% tax. **Payment:** Major credit cards. **Children:** Yes. **Pets:** No. **Smoking:** Nonsmoking rooms available. **Open:** Year-round.

When the Netherland Plaza Hotel opened in 1931, it was hailed as an art deco masterpiece, right up there with the Waldorf-Astoria in New York. Some even boasted that it "challenged the splendor of Solomon's Temple." Tastes changed over the years, leaving the hotel's elegance hidden beneath layers of paint and off-the-rack carpeting. A massive restoration and renovation effort in the early 1980s brought the hotel back to its original grandeur. A more recent updating in 1991 has added world-class facilities, creating an impressive blend of old and new.

The impressive foyer, fashioned of Roman marble, leads to a lobby lined in rare Brazilian rosewood. Herons are featured in the designs on the etched Benedict metal elevator doors. The breathtaking Hall of Mirrors ballroom is a two-story free-wheeling version of its namesake in Versailles. It seats 900 theater-style or 500 at a banquet amid gold-lined mirrored arches and peach-colored marble. The hotel's Hall of Nations, with its own impressive medley of decorating styles, offers 12 smaller conference rooms. Other meeting rooms on the property can accommodate meetings of from 10 to 1,200.

> **The Netherlands Plaza is true art deco, not Miami-style kitsch. A number of its bold patterns came directly from the famed Paris Exposition Internationale des Arts Décoratifs et Industriels Modernes in 1925.**

In its early years, the hotel welcomed countless presidents and entertainers. Winston Churchill, the story goes, was so enamored with his Netherland Plaza bathroom that he had it duplicated in his country home.

Now much less ornate, guest rooms include traditional wood furnishings and such niceties as individually controlled heating and air-conditioning units and personal computer and fax machine hookups.

Hotel guests also have access to a 13,000-square-foot health club. The Carew Tower Health and Fitness Center features high-tech weight training and cardiovascular equipment, an aerobics studio, plus a lap pool, whirlpool, steam room, and sauna.

For dining, the grand-scale Palm Court section of the hotel offers formal dining at Orchids or more casual fare at the Palm Court Cafe. Flourishes here include ceiling murals in Louis XV style and more rosewood paneling. At the dining room's entrance you'll find a fountain guarded by two handsome seahorses with lotus light crowns. Overhead is a mural of Apollo, the sun god, painted in Baroque style.

The hotel is linked with the Carew Tower Complex, an attractive shopping mall with restaurants and even a comedy club. On your way out, stop for breakfast at the deco-style Hathaway's Coffee Shop. Or drop by later for their justly famous milkshakes.

Prospect Hill B&B

408 Boal Street
Cincinnati, OH 45210
513-421-4408

*Hillside views
from
Cincinnati's
premier B&B*

Owners/innkeepers: Tony Jenkins and Gary Hackney. **Accommodations:** 3 rooms, 1 with private bath. **Rates:** $79–$99. **Included:** Continental breakfast. **Minimum stay:** No. **Added:** No tax. **Payment:** Visa, MasterCard. **Children:** 12 and over. **Pets:** No. **Smoking:** No. **Open:** Year-round.

Prospect Hill B&B perches high upon a hill overlooking downtown Cincinnati. In the foreground is the old section of town, reminiscent of a German village; beyond it are towering skyscrapers.

The gray Italianate townhouse with sandstone trim was built in 1867 for Jacob De-Boor, a flour and grain merchant. The houses in the area, once rundown, have been reclaimed in recent years. Gary Hackney and Tony Jenkins have been running Prospect Hill as a B&B since 1989.

The views, the fireplaces, and close proximity to just about anywhere downtown have placed Prospect Hill among the city's most popular urban inns.

The 1870s Room, in the home's original front parlor, is decorated in Victorian style with an Eastlake walnut bedroom set. The 1940s Room, decorated with traditional furnishings and lace curtains, has the best views. Both rooms have fireplaces. The Turn-of-the-Century Room has a three-piece walnut veneer bedroom set that came with the house. This is the only room with a private bath, with sparkling fixtures and a large Victorian clawfoot tub shower.

Breakfast, including homemade coffee cakes, muffins, and several varieties of fruit, is served buffet-style in the oak-lined dining room downstairs. Entrée items such as French toast, pancakes, waffles, or scrambled eggs are also set out.

A second-floor common room is outfitted with comfy wing chairs, antiques, and plenty of local menus and literature. A recent addition is a hot tub with a spectacular city view.

CIRCLEVILLE

The Castle Inn

610 South Court Street
Circleville, OH 43113
614-477-3986
800-477-1541

> *A Moorish-style castle is a highlight of a tiny town*

Innkeepers: Jim and Sue Maxwell. **Accommodations:** 4 rooms, all with private bath. **Rates:** $55–$75 single, $65–$85 double. **Included:** Full breakfast. **Minimum stay:** No. **Added:** Tax included. **Payment:** MasterCard, Visa. **Children:** Over 8 years. **Pets:** No. **Smoking:** No. **Open:** Year-round.

The Castle, as it has been known since its construction in 1899, features stately towers, Moorish arches, battlements, and flying buttresses. This unusual central Ohio home was an antiques shop before the Maxwells arrived in 1989.

The Round Tower guest room with its Rococo Revival decor is a honeymoon favorite; vintage valentines line shelves above a fireplace, and there's a pink marble bathroom. A homemade dollhouse is the centerpiece of the Garden Room, which has a lovely view of Sue's Shakespeare garden. The Tapestry Room, once the housekeepers' quarters, has an Eastlake-style bedroom set. The Square Tower Room offers an ornate turn-of-the-century four-poster bed and a large bathroom with clawfoot tub, shower, and marble sink.

Impressive touches are numerous downstairs as well, including the black and white checkered floor and brass and iron railing leading up the stairs. And what castle would be complete without a suit of armor standing guard in the front hall? He comes in especially handy during murder mystery weekends at the inn.

Breakfast features omelettes with fresh herbs or royal hash, a delectable concoction of corned beef and sour cream. A buffet is offered to full houses on Sundays. After breakfast, check out Circleville's historical museum, the genealogy library, and the Ted Lewis Museum.

> **Stained glass windows represent the four seasons, with cherubs cavorting through flowers, leaves, fruit, and snow. Even if it's not unsigned Tiffany, as the innkeepers suspect, it remains an amazing piece of craftsmanship.**

Nature preserves and Indian mounds are also found nearby.

You might want to ask about Hocking House, the country-style lodging the innkeepers opened in the Hocking Hills, about 15 miles away. It's a much different experience with quilts, handmade furnishings, and a wraparound front porch.

CLEVELAND

The Baricelli Inn

2203 Cornell Road
Cleveland, OH 44106
216-791-65009
Fax: 216-791-9131

> *Intimate lodgings in Little Italy*

Innkeeper: Gwynne Downing. **General manager:** Bridget Assing-Svoboda. **Accommodations:** 4 rooms, all with private bath, 3 suites. **Rates:** Rooms $100–$110, suites $125. **Included:** Continental breakfast. **Minimum stay:** No. **Added:** 10% tax. **Payment:** Major credit cards. **Children:** 12 years and older. **Pets:** No. **Smoking:** Yes. **Open:** Year-round.

The Baricelli Inn, a brownstone in the heart of Cleveland's Little Italy, was built in 1896 for Dutch architect John Grant, who lived here until 1913. In 1986, the Baricelli opened as an intimate country inn with sophisticated dining. It is owned by the Minnillo family, which is known in the area for top-quality restaurants such as the Greenhouse and Ninth Street Grill.

> While architectural touches like bay windows and cathedral ceilings give the feeling of an elegant residence, there are also modern details like fax machines, 24-hour desk service, and a lobby reminiscent of a small luxury hotel.

Paul Minnillo is the chef here. He combines French and Italian influences in popular duck and veal entrées. Lobster and crab ravioli, with a lemon butter and chive sauce, is a house specialty. A pastry chef attends to fresh breads, rolls, and desserts. The Continental breakfast includes croissants and brioches daily, along with fresh fruit, fresh juices, and Royal Kona coffee. It's served on the original glassed-in sun porch, which overlooks a private garden.

The guest rooms have 19th-century armoires, writing desks, and four-poster beds, accented by an array of chintz fabrics and subtle pastel color schemes. Each room has cable television, a telephone, and a hair dryer.

The lobby is the only common area available to guests, though in summer they can use the spacious patio area surrounded by gardens.

The inn lies on a quiet street surrounded by two-family homes. Little Italy's shops and restaurants are within walking distance, and the Cleveland Museum of Art and the Case Western Reserve University campus are less than a mile away.

The Glidden House

1901 Ford Drive
Cleveland, OH 44106
216-231-8900
Fax: 216-231-2130

Hotel amenities attract business guests to the university area

General manager: Sharon Chapman. **Accommodations:** 52 rooms, 8 suites. **Rates:** Rooms $99 single, $109 double; suites $140–$160. **Included:** Continental breakfast. **Minimum stay:** 2 nights on graduation weekend. **Added:** 13% tax. **Payment:** Major credit cards. **Children:** Yes. **Pets:** No. **Smoking:** Nonsmoking rooms available. **Open:** Year-round.

Built in 1910 for Francis Kavanaugh Glidden, this imposing French-style mansion remained in the paint-manufacturing family until 1953, when it was purchased by Case Western Reserve University. A new wing was added in 1988.

Ornate beamed ceilings with the original hand-painted filigree "G" and hand-carved woodwork act as a backdrop for turn-of-the-century Amerian antiques, Oriental rugs, and Victoriana found throughout the inn. The guest rooms and suites are done in soft pastels, with lace curtains and Laura Ashley wall coverings. Coffee and tea greet guests upon arrival, and each room has a

Glidden House mystery nights have become popular with both weekend and business guests.

telephone, cable television, and clock radio. One room has a wood-burning fireplace. A gazebo is surrounded by flowers.

A breakfast buffet includes bagels, homemade muffins, fresh fruit, and cereal. A new restaurant in the carriage house, Miracles, serves lunch and dinner. Try the special sandwiches, with roast beef or turkey wedged between potato cakes instead of bread.

Because it is right on campus, the inn is within walking distance of many cultural activities, including the Cleveland Museum of Art. It also borders Cleveland's Little Italy, with antiques shops, galleries, and more restaurants.

The Ritz-Carlton, Cleveland

1515 West Third Street
Cleveland, OH 44113
216-623-1300
Fax: 216-623-0515
Reservations:
Ritz-Carlton Hotels
800-241-3333

> *The Ritz has everything a business or pleasure traveler could want*

General manager: Cheryl O'Donnell. **Accommodations:** 208 rooms, including 19 suites. **Rates:** Rooms $160–$200, suites $235–$2,000; packages available. **Minimum stay:** No. **Added:** 13% tax. **Payment:** Major credit cards. **Children:** Yes. **Pets:** No. **Smoking:** Nonsmoking rooms available. **Open:** Year-round.

Cleveland's addition to the Ritz-Carlton family of hotels won't disappoint in its decor and service. Located in the heart of the city's bustling business and historic district, it has helped to fuel that city's renaissance.

The fineries here include crystal chandeliers and 18th- and 19th-century oils and antiques. Handwoven rugs grace marble floors. Guest rooms have marble baths with telephones, plush terry robes, and honor bars with refrigerators. There's round-the-clock room service and housekeeping twice daily. On the upper floor, the Ritz-Carlton Club offers elegantly appointed rooms and spacious suites with dramatic views of the Cuyahoga River and Lake Erie. The concierge staff will help coordinate dinner, theater, and travel reservations. Complimentary food and beverages are also offered here.

Dining options at the Ritz include the Restaurant, with a panoramic view, where Sunday brunch is especially popular. The Grill is richly appointed with mahogany and Italian marble for the look of an English club. The Cafe serves breakfast, lunch, dinner, and a spectacular Sunday brunch. A harpist accompanies afternoon tea in the Lobby Lounge.

> **On Sundays, there's a special children's tea with peanut butter and grape jelly pinwheels and mouse-shaped American cheese sandwiches.**

The fitness center, on the seventh floor, has an inviting indoor pool and spa beneath an atrium skylight. Business meetings are held in conference rooms, board rooms, and the elegant ballroom. The hotel also adjoins the over 120 shops at the Avenue at Tower City Center.

COLUMBUS

50 Lincoln

50 East Lincoln Street
Columbus, OH 43215
614-291-5056
Fax: 614-291-4924

> *Artistic flourishes and fancy breakfasts in funky Short North*

Innkeepers: Jeffrey and Kelly Wilson. **Accommodations:** 6 rooms, all with private bath, 2 suites. **Rates:** Rooms $99 single, $109 double; suites $109 single, $119 double. **Included:** Full breakfast. **Minimum stay:** No. **Added:** 15.75% tax. **Payment:** Major credit cards. **Children:** Yes. **Pets:** No. **Smoking:** Yes. **Open:** Year-round.

While you won't find fancy Victorian headboards and armoires at 50 Lincoln, you can be sure the queen-size mattresses are firm and comfortable. A telephone, cable television, and desk are found in each room. A brick chimney is the charming centerpiece of Room 8, a large suite under the sloping ceilings of the attic. The works of local artists are displayed in all the rooms, including gravestone etchings and hand-painted firescreens. Note, however, that most of the inn's seven marbleized fireplaces are just for show.

> The Wilsons have created the closest thing the Midwest offers to a well-run European *pensione,* with lots of art, eccentricity, and a darned good cup of morning coffee.

The fern-filled parlor is especially inviting, with wicker furniture and pink and peach hues. Next to it is the breakfast room, where guests enjoy a full breakfast prepared by innkeeper Jeffrey (a professional chef) that includes vegetable omelettes or heuvos ranchos. French toast made with homemade bread is also a favorite, as is the homemade granola.

Right outside the front door of the 1880s brick home is Columbus's Short North district, a once rundown area in the midst of revitalization that now houses ethnic restaurants, taverns, and artists' studios. You are centrally located, just a mile from both Ohio State University and downtown.

The Great Southern Hotel

310 South High Street
Columbus, OH 43215
614-228-3800
800-228-3789 in Ohio
800-328-2073 elsewhere
Fax: 614-228-7666

> *Restoration revives an impressive downtown hotel*

General Manager: Bill Neitzer. **Accommodations:** 186 rooms, 10 suites. **Rates:** Rooms $90–$110 single, $100–$120 double;

suites $110 single, $120 double; packages available. **Included:**
All meals available. **Minimum stay:** No. **Added:** 15.75% tax.
Payment: Major credit cards. **Children:** Yes. **Pets:** By prior
arrangement. **Smoking:** Nonsmoking rooms available. **Open:**
Year-round.

From the minute you step into the lobby of the Great
Southern Hotel, you'll understand the labor of love that went
into its restoration. The marble floors, polished brass, and
magnificent stained glass ceiling speak of turn-of-the-century
opulence, when the Great Southern Fireproof Building and
Opera House housed a theater, restaurants, shops, and residential space under its
roof.

The guest rooms could
use some tweaking, but
they hold to the antique
theme, with traditional
cherry furnishings, high
ceilings, and floral wallpaper. The Vintage Visit

> **The grand ballroom has
> stained glass windows and
> can accommodate wedding
> receptions of up to 500.**

and Southern Hospitality packages offer roses, champagne,
and a $15 voucher that can be used in the restaurant and
lounge or for room service.

The hotel restaurant, Chutney's, serves slow-roasted prime
rib and chicken Washington state topped with sun-dried cherries and a rich Marsala cream sauce. Sebastian's, an English
pub with a center island bar and wood-lined booths, offers
lighter meals and drinks. Thurber's, an elegant restaurant
decorated with illustrations by the humorist James Thurber,
has now become a meeting facility, one of seven on the
premises.

If you want a respite from the hustle-bustle of the cav-
ernous main lobby, try the cozy overstuffed chairs and
couches that line the mezzanine. While on the mezzanine,
note the exhibitions by local artists, which change monthly.
The building's link with the arts community goes back to the
1930s, when the Great Southern was the hub of Columbus's
cultural scene, welcoming Lillian Russell, John Barrymore,
and Sarah Bernhardt among its guests. Ask George Dill, a
local historian who runs the flower shop, to tell you more
about the hotel's history. He can also keep you updated on
the progress of the opera house restoration, still in need of financial backers.

CONESVILLE

Log House Bed and Breakfast

P.O. Box 30
Conesville, OH 43811
614-829-2757

A log cabin becomes an antiques lovers' dream

Innkeeper: Vicki and Dan Dennis. **Accommodations:** 3 rooms, 1 with private bath. **Rates:** $60–$65. **Included:** Full breakfast. **Minimum stay:** No. **Payment:** Visa, MasterCard. **Children:** Yes. **Pets:** No. **Smoking:** No. **Open:** Year-round.

They discovered the tiny log cabin, long abandoned, in an overgrown thicket near their central Ohio home. Board by board, log by log, Vicki and Dan Dennis moved the 1840s structure onto their property, about five miles south of historic Roscoe Village. After pouring a new foundation, rechinking the logs, and adding little niceties like plumbing and electricity, they were open for business. The Log House now joins other miniature log cabins on their property for an unforgettable primitive country getaway.

Through bright blue doors are the upstairs bedrooms, with odd-shaped wooden lamps, quilts made by Dan's great-great-grandmother, and Amish hats to remind you that you are in the heart of Holmes County Amish country.

The brick-lined walkway leading to the inn is surrounded by wildflowers, statuary, and birdhouses. A handmade bear climbs up a light post. Once on the porch, there is inviting willow furniture and countless potted plants. Inside, you'll find more unique touches — portraits and landscapes by folk artists, southwestern throw rugs, and mounted animal heads looking down over a comfortable couch. The well-preserved metal advertising signs in the kitchen, Vicki explains, are from Coshocton, which was once a sign-making capital.

Breakfast typically includes oven-baked French toast and

sausage apple rings, served on the brick patio or, in winter, by the fireplace.

Day-trippers will enjoy the area attractions, including Roscoe Village in Coshocton and Holmes County. The Longaberger Basket and Pottery Factory in Dresden is open for weekday tours. Or you can browse through Lock 147, Vicki's antique store on the property, which specializes in country and primitive pieces.

COSHOCTON

Roscoe Village Inn

200 North Whitewoman Street
Coshocton, OH 43812
614-622-2222
800-237-7397
Fax: 614-622-2222, ext. 218

> *Hotel amenities
> in historic
> Roscoe Village*

Manager: Don McIlroy. **Accommodations:** 51 rooms. **Rates:** $72; packages available. **Included:** All meals available. **Minimum stay:** No. **Added:** 6% tax. **Payment:** Major credit cards. **Children:** Yes. **Pets:** No. **Smoking:** Nonsmoking rooms available. **Open:** Year-round.

Roscoe Village Inn lies at the end of the main street in a restored 1830s canal town in central Ohio. Though the inn was built in 1984, its brick exterior blends well with the historic structures down the street. The hotel is clean, comfortable, and well designed, offering modern amenities in a relaxed atmosphere that should please lovers of country style.

Beamed ceilings and a brick-lined floor highlight the lobby. Amish craftsmen have succeeded in bringing an antique flavor

> **You can enjoy horse-drawn trolley rides, museum tours, antiques and craft shops galore, and a handful of restaurants.**

to the handmade country furnishings that are found throughout the inn. Four-poster beds, Windsor chairs, folk art reproductions, and occasional quilts on the walls decorate the rooms. Many of these pieces are sold in the shops of Roscoe Village, which exists today solely as a tourist attraction.

The inn's dining room offers chicken Marsala, gulf shrimp with bay scallops, and London broil among its standard American fare. King Charley's Tavern is popular for drinks and lighter meals. According to legend, this King Charley wasn't named after royalty. Charley Williams, the first white settler in Coshocton County, acquired his nickname after tossing a feisty nobleman out of his tavern in 1802. A painting of the scene hangs in the pub.

DANVILLE

The White Oak Inn

29683 Walhonding Road
Danville, OH 43014
614-599-6107

> Fabulous meals
> in "the middle of
> nowhere"

Innkeepers: Ian and Yvonne Martin. **Accommodations:** 10 rooms, all with private bath. **Rates:** $75–$135 double. **Included:** Full breakfast; dinner available by reservation. **Minimum stay:** 2 nights on peak season and holiday weekends. **Added:** 8.75% tax. **Payment:** Visa, MasterCard, check. **Children:** No. **Pets:** No. **Smoking:** No. **Open:** Year-round except Christmas and first two weeks in January.

The White Oak was appropriately named, since it showcases fine woods throughout. The downstairs features the original white oak woodwork and red oak floors, all timbered and milled on the inn's property between 1915 and 1918. Maple, cherry, poplar, walnut, and ash are all found in the guest rooms. The Oak Room is a favorite, with a four-poster bed and washstand original to the house, though you can also be easily lured by the bay windows in the Walnut Room. Country touches include rocking chairs and antique quilts. Additional rooms can be found in the former chicken house, with cedar paneling and exposed oak beams. Though newer in construction, they also have antique touches and antique reproduction bedsteads.

> **Outside, the inn's 14 acres offer horseshoes, badminton, croquet, and lush gardens. Hiking, fishing, canoeing, birdwatching, and bicycling are all available on the adjacent conservation land.**

Most guests take advantage of the dinners offered here by reservation. Unlike the traditional American dishes served by the previous innkeepers, Yvonne and Ian Martin add ethnic touches to peppered apricot pork loin, herb-stuffed chicken breasts, and beef rouladen. And don't forget dessert. You can usually choose from chocolate rocky road cake, sherry trifle, and Nanaimo bars.

Breakfasts include homemade muffins or scones, fresh fruit, and preserves. Guests often comment on the Amish-style peppered bacon, usually served with a main course such as herbed eggs or French toast. Ask about the White Oak Inn cookbook.

The downstairs parlor is a popular gathering place in the winter months, with a perpetual blaze in the fireplace and an antique square grand piano always in tune and ready to play. Two of the guesthouse rooms and one of the rooms in the main building also have wood-burning fireplaces.

Next to the main house, a screen house has tables and chairs, lights, and a ceiling fan that make it the perfect spot for a summer picnic, drink, or card game. A walking trail winds through the woods, with benches and picnic tables at the end of the journey, by a spring. Because of its location off the beaten path, the White Oak Inn has adopted a fitting slogan: "Escape to the middle of nowhere."

GRANVILLE

The Buxton Inn

313 East Broadway
Granville, OH 43023
614-587-0001
Fax: 614-587-1460

*A historic Ohio
inn conjures up
days long past*

Innkeepers: Orville and Audrey
Orr. **General Manager:** Cecil Snow.
Accommodations: 25 rooms, all with private bath, 7 suites.
Rates: Rooms $70–$75 double, suites $75–$90. **Included:**
Continental breakfast. **Minimum stay:** No. **Added:** 9% tax.
Payment: Major credit cards. **Children:** Yes. **Pets:** No. **Smoking:** Yes. **Open:** Year-round.

Should you be standing in front of the Buxton Inn on the
Fourth of July, you will see men with muskets, wearing the
garb of Civil War soldiers, stop to rest on the long wooden
verandah. They walk up the brick-lined path and pause at
tables made from old barrels. These soldiers are part of the
annual parade, but in this historic setting they conjure up
unforgettable images of days long past.

This is the same charm found throughout this well-known
inn, among the oldest continuously running lodgings in Ohio.
Built as a stagecoach stop in 1812, the Buxton Inn was transformed by Orville and Audrey Orr in 1972. The former educators turned the ramshackle old hotel into a retreat that blends
comfort and hospitality with an impressive collection of antiques.

Antique sleigh, spindle, and rope beds furnish the guest
rooms and suites, which are well worn but comfortable, papered and painted with documentary colors and patterns.
Four rooms are at the inn; others can be found in the 1815
Warner House down the street. The contrasting styles of the
simple brick main building and the Victorian frame addition
at Warner House are startling, but the rooms, named after
gemstones and colors, have attractive architectural details
like arched windows and skylights. There is also a brick-lined
courtyard in back.

A collection of unusual oil portraits and landscapes lines
the common areas, including a clean-shaven Abraham Lin-

coln, which the innkeepers believe the president actually sat for. Over the years, the inn has welcomed many famous guests, from Henry Ford and John Philip Sousa to Ann Miller and Joanne Woodward — Orville has saved the old guest registers.

There are rumors that the ghosts of Major Horton Buxton and Ethel Bounell, both former owners of the inn, roam these halls. Many guests and employees have spotted a mysterious lady in blue who disappears in a flash.

Granville, the home of Denison University, resembles a New England town, with shops, galleries, and historic sites. While the downtown has

> **Legend says that President William Henry Harrison once rode his horse up the inn's stairs to a second-floor ballroom.**

many excellent restaurants, you might choose to have dinner in one of the inn's seven dining rooms. The specialties include shrimp, scallops, and crab served on seashells and topped with a Mornay sauce. Louisiana chicken is a breaded breast of chicken with mushrooms, artichoke hearts, and toasted almonds. For dessert, triple chocolate mousse cake is prepared by Orville's mother, who is called "Grandma" by the staff.

There are also a pair of pubs here, one with its original "burglar step": in the old stagecoach days, travelers would sleep in this room, where one step was built higher than the others to trip thieves in the night. Also note the sign in front. Its prominent cat symbol was a guide for 19th-century travelers who never learned to read.

KELLEY'S ISLAND

Sweet Valley Inn

715 Division Street
P.O. Box 733
Kelley's Island, OH 43438
419-746-2750

> *A Victorian
> time capsule on
> a Lake Erie island*

Innkeepers: Paul and Beverly Johnson. **Accommodations:** 4 rooms sharing 2 baths. **Rates:** $75 single, $85 double; packages available. **Included:** Full breakfast. **Minimum stay:** 2 nights on weekends. **Added:** 7% tax. **Payment:** Visa, MasterCard. **Children:** Over 12 years. **Pets:** No. **Smoking:** No. **Open:** Year-round.

Ohio's Lake Erie Islands welcome tourists every year, but their ferry-only access keeps them off the beaten path. When visiting Kelley's Island, leave your car on the mainland and make the rounds on foot or by bike or golf cart.

> **Breakfast is served on fancy china, on the inviting screened porch overlooking the gardens.**

A short walk or drive from the hustle and bustle of main street, the Sweet Valley Inn can't help but catch your eye. An old-fashioned surrey with fringe on top is parked in front of a bright yellow Victorian farmhouse with white-painted accents. Outside you might find innkeeper Beverly Johnson picking flowers in preparation for a house tour. The home was built in 1892, she explains, by the original owners of the Sweet Valley Wine Company, and remained in the family for 90 years. You can still see vestiges of the dilapidated winery next door.

Inside, you'll find well-preserved touches. The kitchen, for instance, has old utensils on display, such as a rug whacker and an old cistern, which still collects rainwater and feeds it directly to the wood-burning cook stove for heating. There's even an old outhouse on the property.

A favorite guest room has robin's-egg blue walls and original millwork untouched by paint after all these years. Beautifully finished floors and stained glass accent the other guest rooms, which are attractively decorated in pinks, blues, and soft greens. Four of the original fireplaces are for guest use.

You'll want to kick back in the hammock or rent one of the bikes from the barn ($5 for the weekend). The innkeepers will be glad to tell you about favorite trails or schedule a complimentary evening ride on their surrey, which you mount from the property's original carriage stone.

LEBANON

The Golden Lamb

27 South Broadway
Lebanon, OH 45036
513-932-5065
Fax: 513-621-8373, ext. 21

From stagecoach stop to award-winning country inn

Innkeeper: Jackson Reynolds. **Accommodations:** 17 rooms, 1 suite. **Rates:** Rooms $52 single, $67–$85 double; suite $100. **Included:** Continental breakfast; lunch and dinner available. **Minimum stay:** No. **Added:** 11% tax. **Payment:** Major credit cards. **Children:** Yes. **Pets:** No. **Smoking:** Yes. **Open:** Year-round.

The Shakers arrived in southwest Ohio in the 19th century. They sold their Union Village more than 50 years ago, but their influence remains in the furnishings and especially the cooking at the Golden Lamb. Erwin Pfeil, the chef, has worked here for more than two decades, offering his own special twists on such Shaker specialties as lemon pie, chicken spinach pudding, and Sister Lizzie's Shaker sugar pie.

The four-story Federal brick building with white balconies was built as a stagecoach stop at a busy intersection; travelers who couldn't read were told to look for the image of the lamb on the lodging sign. A number of notable guests have visited since, including several presidents, Henry Clay, Mark Twain, and Charles Dickens, who enjoyed his stay until he discovered he couldn't get a drink here.

These guests are remembered in the rooms named for them. The Dickens Room has a replica of a Lincoln bed as a centerpiece, along with a marble-topped dresser with a mirror and several Victorian chairs. The William McKinley Room has a four-poster canopy bed, wing chairs, an antique secretary and a nice view of the main street below.

> Dickens would be pleased that the Golden Lamb now has a pub called the Black Horse Tavern. It, too, is decorated with Shaker antiques. Be sure to see the museum-quality Shaker pieces displayed on the fourth floor.

The four main dining rooms and additional private ones divide the inn's mealtime crowds into intimate groups. The fresh turkey served here is raised on a nearby farm. Other menu regulars include roast duck with orange gravy and a lamb selection. For breakfast, guests will find complimentary coffee, tea, juices, and coffee cake in the Henry Clay Room.

LOGAN

The Inn at Cedar Falls

21190 State Route 374
Logan, OH 43138
614-385-7489

> Log cabins
> in Hocking Hills
> State Park

Innkeeper: Ellen Grinsfelder. **Accommodations:** 9 rooms, all with private bath, 3 log cabins. **Rates:** $55–$70 single, $65–$145 double. **Included:** Full breakfast; dinner available. **Minimum stay:** 2 nights on weekends. **Added:** 9% tax. **Payment:** MasterCard, Visa. **Children:** Limited. **Pets:** No. **Smoking:** Nonsmoking rooms available. **Open:** Year-round.

Anne Castle had a vision. The former business consultant wanted not only to live in a log cabin but to share the experience with others. Anne has since passed away, but her Inn at Cedar Falls, a deceptively rustic country inn in Hocking Hills

State Park, perpetuates her dream of helping guests commune with nature.

Two 1840s log cabins (one here originally, the other reconstructed on the property) are fashioned of 18-inch-thick logs. The chinking between the logs is dyed the appropriate hue to match Hocking Hills dirt. The cabins are separated by a country kitchen.

> **The inn's elaborate herb and vegetable gardens provide the basis for seasonal meals. The menu is constantly fine-tuned by Ellen Grinsfelder and her kitchen staff.**

The guest rooms, in a barnlike outbuilding, are simply decorated, with furnishings that include a rocking chair, desk, and usually a Shaker antique bed on wide-planked floors. All the rooms overlook 80 acres of wildflower-filled parkland. One room in this building has been set aside as a common area, with board games, books, magazines, and a refrigerator full of juices and soft drinks, which guests purchase on the honor system. There are no telephones or televisions.

In summer, meals are served on the deck, with a view of the sloping gardens. In cooler months, diners gather in the beamed dining room. Entrées might include grilled shrimp scampi, apple-smoked pork loin, or chicken stuffed with oranges and leeks. Celebrity chefs often stay here and prepare their specialties.

The inn is only minutes away from park attractions like Ash Cave, Old Man's Cave, Cantwell Cliffs, and the Rock House. The inn also sponsors activities, including wine-tasting weekends, antiques seminars, arts and crafts displays, and nature hikes.

Many guests prefer simply relaxing in the cozy places provided by the inn. It's a rare evening that you won't find a couple enjoying the rustic side porch of the log cabin or gently rocking in the hammock beneath a shady tree.

LOUDONVILLE

The Blackfork Inn

P.O. Box 149
303 North Water Street
Loudonville, OH 44842
419-994-3252

*A Victorian inn
with Amish
overtones*

Innkeepers: Sue and Al Gorisek.
Accommodations: Six rooms, all
with private bath. **Rates:** $43 single on weekdays, $65–$75
double on weekends. **Included:** Full breakfast. **Minimum
stay:** No. **Added:** 6% tax. **Payment:** MasterCard, Visa. **Children:** Negotiable. **Pets:** Negotiable. **Smoking:** No. **Open:** Year-
round.

Though Victorian in both demeanor and decor, the Blackfork
Inn lies on the outskirts of Amish country. Cheese made by
the Amish highlights the breakfast here, which typically
includes omelettes, crois-
sants, and fruit with
frozen yogurt. The library
is filled with books about
Ohio history and the
Amish, a good primer,
Sue Gorisek says, before
exploring the surrounding
countryside.

> **Quilts, cabinets, clocks,
> and dolls, not to mention
> down-home cooking, are all
> easily found at Amish
> cottage industries within a
> half hour of the inn.**

Sue and her husband,
Al, heard that the 1865
Italianate home was on the auction block in 1988. Considerable time and money had already gone into renovating it as an
inn, so the journalists from Cleveland decided to take the
plunge. Al still goes to work during the week, and Sue has
taken on the innkeeping duties while enjoying an active life
as a writer.

The inn has two Victorian parlors, and its guest rooms are
named after family members of the original owner, Philip
Black. The Josephine has botanical print wallpaper and tall
windows. The whimsical Margaret has a turn-of-the-century
wardrobe painted with exotic figures and a mosquito-netted
bed. The unusual collections throughout the inn include a set

of drinking glasses made in the 1880s to commemorate President Garfield. Some of the more ornate carved pieces came from demolished Cleveland mansions. The framed fashion illustrations were done by Sue's grandmother in the flapper era.

Nearby are two state parks, Mohican and Malabar, as well as hiking, biking, golfing, and canoeing.

MILLERSBURG

The Inn at Honey Run

6920 County Road 203
Millersburg, OH 44654
216-674-0011
800-468-6639 (in Ohio)

Handcrafted furniture and earth-sheltered lodgings

Innkeeper: Marge Stock. **Accommodations:** 24 rooms, 12 Honeycomb units. **Rates:** Rooms $79–$150, Honeycomb units $120–$145; call for winter rates. **Included:** Continental breakfast; dinner available. **Minimum stay:** 2 nights on weekends. **Added:** 6.25% tax. **Payment:** Major credit cards. **Children:** Not allowed in Honeycombs. **Pets:** No. **Smoking:** Nonsmoking rooms available. **Open:** All year except 2 weeks in January.

This fine country inn will appeal to travelers who don't require Victorian beds and Laura Ashley wallpaper. The Inn at Honey Run showcases the talents of nearby furniture makers and craftspeople.

Marge Stock wanted to create a place that fit naturally into the wooded landscape. She has succeeded most impressively in the Honeycomb rooms. Literally dug into the side of a hill, these may be the only earth-sheltered lodgings in the country. But don't expect rustic cave dwellings. Honeycombs offer stone patios and fireplaces as well as modern amenities like televisions and whirlpool baths.

> The surrounding beauty of Holmes County invites hiking on the inn's 60 wooded acres, which are populated by sheep and ducks as well as the resident cats and dogs.

The guest rooms in the main building have reproduction Shaker and Empire furnishings using native red oak and pine. A number feature quilts both on the walls and on the beds. All have clock radios with cassette players (classical tapes are available in the lobby). Televisions are tucked into armoires or hidden beneath specially made cozies. Marge has made sure that the maple, ash, oak, and black walnut trees lining her property butt right up to the windows, providing ample entertainment from the bird feeders outside.

The dining room uses fresh local ingredients. A number of the cooks are Amish and bring their time-honored flair to homemade apple nut and zucchini muffins and entrées of sesame baked chicken or pan-fried trout. Chocolate silk pie is the favorite dessert.

Continental breakfast includes fresh orange juice, followed by melon, coffee cake, and a choice of cereals, including granola. Honeycomb rooms have breakfast delivered. For an added charge, guests in the main building can have French toast or pancakes added to their meals.There is an exercise room and a downstairs lounge with bumper pool, Ping-Pong, and a large-screen television with a VCR and movies. Golf and canoeing are a short drive away. The inn can serve up to 70 people in its conference facilities. The walnut-paneled Executive Room has its own fireplace and deck.

Special touches are added daily by the ever-inventive Marge. Ask her about the trout and fruit farm she is cultivating on 160 acres of adjoining property.

MOUNT VERNON

The Russell-Cooper House

115 East Gambier Street
Mount Vernon, OH 43050
614-397-8638

*A grand home
that embraces its
own historic past*

Innkeepers: Maureen and Tim Tyler. **Accommodations:** 6 rooms, all with private bath. **Rates:** $75 double, $55 single Monday–Thursday. **Included:** Full breakfast. **Minimum stay:** No. **Added:** 3% tax. **Payment:** Master-Card, Visa, American Express. **Children:** 13 years and older. **Pets:** No. **Smoking:** Allowed on first floor only. **Open:** Year-round.

The Russell-Cooper House is the former home of two prominent Ohioans. Dr. John Russell was the first American to employ a female physician in 1852. His son-in-law, Colonel William Cooper, enjoyed a distinguished career as an attorney and U.S. congressman. Built in 1829 in the Federal style, the house underwent several changes over the years to reach its current High Victorian status. The exterior colors come from nature, with carefully chosen grays, greens, reds, and creams.

Tim and Maureen Tyler, former New Yorkers who yearned for small-town life, have stocked the home with memorabilia relating to both men. The items include ornate buttons from a Civil War uniform, antique medical devices, rare books, even old dance cards. Colonel Cooper's field desk is used to check in guests. High embossed ceilings, rich woods, etched and stained glass windows, and fireplaces all add to the opulence. Even the carpeting dates back a century.

Since the inn caters to both vacationers and a steady corporate clientele, all the rooms have central air conditioning and cable TV, and telephones are available. The Grand Ballroom is available for parties, meetings, and seminars.

The intricately scrolled bed in the Colonel Cooper Room once belonged to the Cooper family. With its wide-plank pine floors, Eastlake dresser, Oriental rug, and Bradbury and Bradbury wallpaper, this is the most outstanding guest room.

The restoration continues. The ceiling in a dining room remains to be done, and an artist's apartment will eventually be vacated to create more guest rooms. Still, the Russell-Cooper House is chock full of unusual artifacts and history.

SAGAMORE HILLS

The Inn at Brandywine Falls

8230 Brandywine Road
Sagamore Hills, OH 44067
216-467-1812
216-650-4965

*Fine family meals
by the waterfall*

Innkeepers: George and Katie Hoy.
Accommodations: 3 rooms, 3 suites. **Rates:** Rooms $85–$125 double, $200 weekends; suites $110–$175 double, $240–$295 weekends. **Included:** Full breakfast. **Minimum stay:** 2 nights on weekends. **Added:** 6.25% tax. **Payment:** MasterCard, Visa, Discover. **Children:** Yes. **Pets:** No. **Smoking:** No. **Open:** Year-round.

Sunday morning is a special time at the Inn at Brandywine Falls. By then, weekend guests who arrived as strangers have become old friends as they gather in the formal dining room for the bountiful Sunday brunch. George and Katie Hoy not only plan and prepare the feasts, they also sit down and enjoy them with guests. The meal starts with George's famous raisin pumpernickel bread followed by a heaping bowl of fruit. A salad and green beans are passed around and then placed within easy reach

> For a private spot and the best view of the falls, try Anna Hale's Garret, a spacious suite beneath the eaves. Antique quilts cover the double cannonball beds and even the bathroom shower curtain.

on a lazy Susan. A delectable chicken with currant sauce serves as the main course.

The family atmosphere is strong at this gracious home in the Cuyahoga Valley National Recreation Area. The 67-foot Brandywine Falls are just steps away. The falling water was used to power a sawmill and gristmill owned by James Wallace, who built his Greek Revival farmhouse here in 1848.

A portrait of the white-bearded Wallace hangs in the dining room. He also has his own room on the main floor, the James Wallace Parlour, with a double sleigh bed on Axminster carpeting. Adeline's Retreat, on the second level, has a stenciled floor and Greek key-tiled bathroom with a clawfoot tub. A silver pitcher for ice water is set on a side table.

All the rooms have cotton sheets on firm mattresses. The innkeepers thoughtfully leave buckeyes (rich chocolate and peanut butter balls) on bedside tables. For a clever folk art touch, George has painted scenes of the nearby landscape on the window shades, as was done in 1848.

A converted granary now uses chicken wire and the original structure's planking to decorate two bi-level suites. King-size or twin beds are found here in cozy sleeping lofts. A headboard in one was made from a well-used wooden workbench. These rustic touches are offset by a small refrigerator and microwave, which make these units comfortable for longer stays. Towering windows on either side overlook a hemlock grove.

Breakfast on most mornings includes juices, fruited oat-

meal soup, homemade breads, fresh fruit, granola, and omelettes loaded with fresh spinach and Black Diamond cheddar.
In the granary rooms, you can enjoy your morning meal in the
main house or take advantage of what George calls the Greta
Garbo "I vant to be alone" plan and have it brought to your
room.

WOOSTER

The Wooster Inn

801 East Wayne Avenue
Wooster, OH 44691
216-264-2341
Fax: 216-264-9951

*Comfortable
lodgings at the
College of Wooster*

Innkeeper: A.R. Lazar. **Accommodations:** 16 rooms, all with private
bath. **Rates:** Rooms $55–$70 single, $70–$95 double; suites
$100–$115. **Included:** Full breakfast. **Minimum stay:** 2 nights
on special weekends. **Added:** 8.5% tax. **Payment:** Major credit
cards. **Children:** Yes. **Pets:** Yes. **Smoking:** Yes. **Open:** Year-
round.

When a major benefactor planned a visit to the College of
Wooster and insisted on staying in a hotel, then-President
Holden was in a quandary. Overnight lodgings in the central
Ohio college town left something to be desired, so the presi-

dent found the biggest dorm room he could and redecorated it thoroughly. That was in 1910. It wasn't until 1959 that the Wooster Inn opened to offer guests and alumni a comfortable place to stay right on campus.

The Georgian Colonial lodging, owned by the college, fits well with the older buildings on campus. Rooms are decorated comfortably with reproduction antiques, wing chairs, and plants. Many offer views of expansive lawns and surrounding trees. From the bay windows in the colonial dining room, you can see the college golf course, which is open to guests.

> **During the school year, guests can attend the lectures, concerts, and other events offered on campus. Especially popular are the Ohio Light Opera performances in the Freedlander Theater, about a 10-minute walk.**

The meals here include American fare such as beef tenderloin au poivre, veal Marsala, locally raised trout, and even a vegetarian entrée. Homemade cheesecake is a must for dessert. For breakfast, you can order anything on the menu, from buttermilk pancakes with Ohio maple syrup to mushroom and cheddar omelettes.

WORTHINGTON

The Worthington Inn

649 High Street
Worthington, OH 43085
614-885-2600

A former stage-coach stop in a historic village

General manager: Aarne Seck. **Accommodations:** 26 rooms, 4 suites, all with private bath. **Rates:** Rooms $105, suites $120–$160. **Included:** Continental breakfast. **Minimum stay:** No. **Added:** 11.75% tax. **Payment:** Major credit cards. **Children:** Yes. **Pets:** No. **Smoking:** Nonsmoking rooms available. **Open:** Year-round.

Established as a stagecoach stop in 1831, the Worthington Inn was added on to several times before the most recent renovation in 1983. The brick inn now boasts a handsome mansard roof and romantic balconies. While offering the service and decorative touches of the finest bed-and-breakfasts, the Inn caters best to wedding parties and business travelers who enjoy the relative peace and quiet of this historic village just 15 minutes from downtown Columbus.

The Continental breakfast is served in one of the four dining rooms. Fresh seafood and exotic salads are the specialties at dinner. Three second-floor meeting rooms cater to family gatherings or small corporate meetings while the third-floor Van Loon Ballroom boasts a huge Czechoslovakian chandelier suspended from a cathedral ceiling. This is a popular spot for weddings and banquets.

Though motel-like in design, the rooms have early American and heavy Victorian motifs. Antique and quality reproduction beds almost reach the eight-foot ceilings. One room has a pair of rope beds with mattresses raised high off the floor. Hand-done stenciling includes a stagecoach silhouette, in honor of the inn's origins. They all have telephones, televisions, wet bars, and desks.

Four additional suites are in the 1817 Snow House down the street. While some of the historic charm has been renovated out of the Worthington, these rooms have retained their 19th-century character with slightly off-kilter brick walls and staircases, the product of almost 175 years of settling. They also have queen-size antique oak and walnut bedsteads.

> **The Worthington Inn is in a tiny historic village full of New England–style craft and antiques shops and stately homes and churches. Golfing, fishing, and boating are nearby, and Ohio State University is about five miles away.**

Wisconsin

Northern Wisconsin and Door County

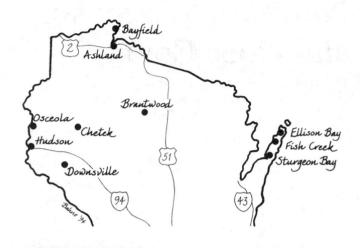

Best Bed-and-Breakfast Inns

Bayfield
   Cooper Hill House
   Le Chateau Boutin
Brantwood
   Palmquist's "The Farm"
Ellison Bay
   The Griffin Inn
Fish Creek
   Thorp House Inn and Cottages
Hudson
   Boyden House
   1884 Phipps Inn
   Jefferson-Day House
Osceola
   St. Croix River Inn
Sturgeon Bay
   The Scofield House
   White Lace Inn

Best Full-Service Country Inns

Bayfield
   Old Rittenhouse Inn
Chetek
   The Lodge at Canoe Bay
Downsville
   The Creamery
Fish Creek
   The White Gull Inn
Sturgeon Bay
   The Inn at Cedar Crossing

Best Hotel

Ashland
   Hotel Chequamegon

Best Spa

Osceola
Aveda Spa

Door County, a 40-mile long peninsula stretching north into Lake Michigan, is often called the "Cape Cod of the Midwest." It's an exceedingly popular and often pricey summer place. It includes five state parks, 250 miles of shoreline, and eight inland lakes. Painters, sculptors, and other artists have long been attracted to Door County, as evidenced by the studios and galleries that thrive here.

Sturgeon Bay is the region's largest community and the gateway to Door County. The displays at the Door County Historic Museum include an antique fire truck and a reconstructed turn-of-the-century street scene. The Miller Art Center, in the public library, regularly displays works by local artists. For a closer look at the Great Lakes freighters, commercial fishing boats, and luxury yachts that are built here, take a ride out to the shipyards at Sunset Park. A trip to the Sturgeon Bay Maritime Museum puts it all in historical perspective.

Highways 42 and 57 head north to delightful lakefront communities. **Fish Creek** holds a popular fish boil at the White Gull Inn. It's also home to the venerable Peninsula Players Summer Theater. At Bailey's Harbor, you'll find an 800-acre nature and wildlife preserve. Wisconsin cherries are also a tradition, best enjoyed at roadside stands in July and early August.

Bayfield, a Lake Superior fishing community and popular summer retreat, is much closer to Duluth, Minnesota, than anyplace of note in Wisconsin. Some 50 buildings here are on the National Register of Historic Places. This is also the gateway to the Apostle Islands National Lakeshore, with cruise boats visiting lighthouses, seacaves, and a restored fishing camp. Some even include a fish boil on one of the islands. Many folks choose to focus on an afternoon ferry trip to Madeline Island, which has its own historical museum, Indian cemetery, and state park.

Tiny towns line the edges of the St. Croix River, trailing down the northwestern edge of Wisconsin. Check out the Hoffman Hills State Recreation Area, just nine miles north of Menominee.

ASHLAND

Hotel Chequamegon

101 Lake Shore Drive West
Ashland, WI 54806
715-682-9095
800-946-5555
Fax: 715-682-9410

*New lodgings
recall grand old
Lake Superior
resort hotels*

General manager: Andrea Fischer.
Accommodations: 46 rooms, 16 suites. **Rates:** Rooms $74–$84 summer, $50–$60 winter; suites $90–$140 summer, $70–$110 winter; packages available. **Included:** All meals available. **Minimum stay:** No. **Added:** 8.5% tax. **Payment:** Major credit cards. **Children:** Yes. **Pets:** No. **Smoking:** Nonsmoking rooms available. **Open:** Year-round.

Hotel Chequamegon resembles the rambling turn-of-the-century resort hotels that once dotted Lake Superior's shores, which is just how the owners like it. The hotel opened in 1985 near the site of a grand hotel with the same name that was damaged by fire twice before its demise in the 1950s. Working with photographs of the old Chequamegon, the designers of the new hotel have created an attractive homage, with a long white clapboard front, a low-angled green roof, and Victorian cupolas flanking the side.

Ashland's prosperous lumbering days are recalled in the oak woodwork that lines the lobby. It was salvaged from nearby ore docks. Overstuffed floral couches and fluted glass chandeliers welcome guests at check-in. The antique registration desk and bar downstairs came from an old hotel in Iowa.

The guest rooms are cleanly decorated and sunny, thanks to the many windows. While the double beds in lakeside rooms are popular with family travelers, cityside rooms with a single bed cater to people on business. Kitchenette suites have microwaves and queen-size brass beds; Jacuzzi suites in the turrets have whirlpool baths and lake views.

> **Nearby Cooper Falls State Park has hiking trails and a swimming beach, along with the natural beauty of canyons, streams, and waterfalls.**

Two restaurants are on the property. Fifield's offers an elegant breakfast and dinner with planked whitefish, chicken parmigiana, and pasta specialties. Molly Cooper's cultivates a Victorian pub atmosphere, with sandwiches and beer on tap. You can also enjoy cocktails in the Northland Parlor, just off the lobby behind the front desk. The Hall of History is a meeting and banquet facility serving as many as 200.

The indoor pool is surrounded by more white clapboard. The bandshell next door features summer concerts. Just around the corner is Ashland's historic district, with brick and brownstone buildings that are on the National Register of Historic Places. Bayfield, a popular summer place, and several downhill ski areas are within a half hour's drive.

BAYFIELD

Cooper Hill House

33 South Sixth Street
P.O. Box 5
Bayfield, WI 54814
715-779-5060

> *Family treasures*
> *are at home*
> *in a cozy B&B*

Innkeepers: Larry and Julie Mac-Donald. **Accommodations:** 4 rooms with private bath. **Rates:** $62–$80. **Included:** Continental breakfast. **Minimum stay:** 2 nights on holiday weekends. **Added:** 8.5% tax. **Payment:** MasterCard, Visa. **Children:** By prior arrangement. **Pets:** No. **Smoking:** Permitted on front porch only. **Open:** Year-round.

Family antiques fill the common rooms of Bayfield's Cooper Hill House. Larry's rustic first pair of skis lean against a living room wall; a cabinet holds Julie's doll collection. The spinning wheel belonged to Larry's great-grandmother, and the mining pan was used by his great-grandfather during the Alaska Gold Rush. Larry says it's all the prospector brought home.

> **The bathroom sinks come from the old Curtis Hotel in Minneapolis. You can tell where they once belonged by checking the room number on the bottom of each one.**

The MacDonalds, former Twin Cities residents, purchased the inn in 1989 and have added their own touches. The bedrooms include the Cottage Room, with a Scandinavian boat line poster and a spool collection on a shelf. The Country Room features quilts and stenciling. Note the painting here of the farm where Julie grew up.

A memorable Continental breakfast is highlighted by Julie's homemade bran raisin nut or Bayfield blueberry muffins. You can enjoy the meal with wild birds, visible through a clever glass birdhouse on the side of the inn. Ferries and boat excursions tour the Apostle Islands. Big Top Chautauqua, with lectures, music, and programs, lies only a few miles away.

Le Chateau Boutin

7 Rice Avenue
Bayfield, WI 54814
715-779-5111

*The sister lodging
of Bayfield's
Old Rittenhouse has
charms of its own*

Innkeepers: Jerry and Mary Phillips. **Accommodations:** 5 rooms, all with private bath, 2 suites. **Rates:** Rooms $99–$119, suites $129. **Included:** Continental breakfast. **Minimum stay:** 2 nights on weekends. **Added:** 10.5% tax. **Payment:** MasterCard, Visa. **Children:** Yes. **Pets:** No. **Smoking:** Yes. **Open:** Year-round.

Frank Boutin was a lumber baron who built his grand Queen Anne mansion as a year-round residence. The heavily turreted and gabled home, with stained and leaded glass ornamenting an exotic wood interior, was also the first house in Bayfield wired for electricity. Boutin's wife, perhaps frustrated by the rough Wisconsin winters, disliked Bayfield so much that, after only five years, they sold the place and moved to California.

> **In the ballroom (actually half of the home's original ballroom), a mirror replaces the window where children once stood and watched parties; they weren't allowed inside.**

After numerous owners and uses (including a period as a convent), the home was sold to Jerry and Mary Phillips, owners of the renowned Old Rittenhouse Inn, who have added it to a growing collection of historic Bayfield properties. They have retained some of the original furnishings, including the lion-clawfoot cherry table in the dining room.

The Master Suite has the original brick fireplace and king-size brass bed and a stained glass window in the sitting area. The North East Room has a black walnut bed whose carved angels are meant to guard sleepers. It also has a brick fireplace and a splendid view of the sunrise.

Let your imagination wander to the time when the fountain and rosebed were just part of an elaborate landscape of gardens. The sloping property today has been parceled off, but it's still big enough for guests to stage impromptu croquet tournaments. Weddings are also held here. As part of a long list of projects, the Phillipses plan to restore the inn's carriage house.

Old Rittenhouse Inn

301 Rittenhouse Avenue
P.O. Box 584
Bayfield, WI 54814
715-779-5111

Bayfield's best-loved establishment

Innkeepers: Jerry and Mary Phillips. **Accommodations:** 9 rooms, all with private bath, 1 suite. **Rates:** Rooms $99–$149, suite $189. **Included:** Continental breakfast; add $5 for full breakfast; dinner available. **Minimum stay:** 2 nights on weekends. **Added:** 10.5% tax. **Payment:** MasterCard, Visa. **Children:** Yes. **Pets:** No. **Smoking:** Not in dining rooms. **Open:** Year-round.

A self-assured grin plays across the face of the tuxedoed waiter as he describes the menu selections for the night. We're not just talking about a brief outline. He rhapsodizes about the "succulent" entrées for at least 10 minutes before he leaves you to ponder the tempting choices. Pretentious? A little, but it's all part of the unusual multicourse meal at Bayfield's Old Rittenhouse Inn, arguably the finest dining experience at a midwestern inn.

This tradition of reciting the menu started in 1976, when the restaurant opened and the menus weren't yet back from the printer. The guests enjoyed the oral description so much that the idea stuck. Mary Phillips had had no formal training when she and Jerry began. Since then, she has perfected some incredible dishes. One of her specialties is lightly spiced fruit soup, made with the seasonal bounty of raspberries, strawberries, cherries, and blueberries. Wild fruit also figures prominently in the preparation of glazes for pork and breast of chicken dishes. Other favorites include the fresh Lake Superior whitefish and trout, probably poached with champagne. Mary is an accommodating cook and will make a vegetarian entrée if it's not already on the menu.

> There's plenty to see in Bayfield, the headquarters of the Apostle Islands National Lakeshore. Ferries to the islands, along with restaurants and shops, are just a few blocks from the inn. In the summer, you'll find lectures, music, and other cultural programs at the nearby Big Top Chautauqua.

Be prepared for the dessert descriptions. The waiter will tempt you with the "bold but not overpowering" qualities of the lemon chess pie or triple chocolate cheesecake.

Oak and maple antique tables furnish the three dining rooms, one of which has heavy green embossed Victorian wallpaper. A stained glass image of a fish highlights a corner in another, along with fine antiques displayed in cabinets. Yet the Phillipses haven't gone for out-and-out luxury. Dining room chairs might not match, but that's all part of the charm.

The rooms are cleverly decorated. Room 7 has a king-size bed, whirlpool bath, fireplace, and a splendid lake view. Room 2 has wood floors, a tile fireplace, and a Persian rug. Note the drawer by the mantel where turn-of-the-century boot polishes were kept warm and supple. Room 10, formerly the 500-square-foot ballroom, is perhaps the inn's highlight, with wicker accents and narrow tongue-and-groove fir paneling. The fireplace here is central to the room and can be seen from the sitting area, the raised whirlpool, and the brass king-size bed. Mary calls it the inn's rainy-day Jacuzzi room.

Though a Continental breakfast is included, pay the extra $5 to enjoy the full meal. The menu litany is considerably shorter. You may choose from French toast with homemade cinnamon bread, three-egg omelettes, or Arctic scrambled eggs with a dollop of sour cream, green peppers, onions, and dill. Cleansing cranberry-orange juice or apple cider comes with the meal.

BRANTWOOD

Palmquist's "The Farm"

N51 36 River Road
Brantwood, WI 54513
715-564-2558

Farm life without the chores

Hosts: Jim and Helen Palmquist.
Accommodations: 4 rooms with shared bath, 4 cabins, Log Cabin Inn with 4 suites. **Rates:** $52.25–$62.25 per person MAP, $65 double with breakfast only in spring, summer, and fall. **Included:** All meals. **Minimum stay:** 2 nights, December through March. **Added:** 5.5% tax. **Payment:** MasterCard, Visa, Discover. **Children:** Yes. **Pets:** Yes. **Smoking:** Limited. **Open:** Year-round.

Winter is the busiest season at "the Farm," when cross-country skiers flock here for 30 kilometers of well-groomed trails. After gliding through tunnels of snow-covered balsam forests, they are welcomed home by the Palmquist family at their 70-year-old farmhouse. Bed-and-breakfast guests have been staying here since 1949.

The guest rooms in the main farmhouse and four cabins all have antique and heirloom furnishings. These are fairly rustic accommodations, with woodburning stoves providing most of the heat for the paneled cabins. The largest cabin has four bedrooms and a loft. Another spacious cabin, the White Pine Inn, has four suites with private baths.

Three meals come with most stays at "the Farm." The

breakfast buffet is loaded with scrambled eggs, homemade yogurt with raspberries, granola, hot cereals, orange and grapefruit slices, and cinnamon rolls. Pancakes are topped with pure maple syrup from the Palmquists' own sugar house.

> **Chickens, dogs, and a pair of Belgian draft horses are among the animals on this working timber and cattle farm of 800 acres.**

Soups and sandwiches are served for lunch; dinner brings Finnish and American favorites such as roast beef, baked chicken, or ham, again served buffet style. On weekends, the innkeepers stage a lumberjack show and a sing-along in the recreation hall, which has a large stone fireplace and player piano.

Activities are plentiful in all seasons. In summer, guests hike and bike, take hay rides, and make ice cream. In winter, skis can be rented in the recreation hall. There is also a Finnish sauna here, where some crazy guests bake themselves lobster red and then cool off by rolling in the snow.

CHETEK

The Lodge at Canoe Bay

W16065 Hogback Road
Chetek, WI 54728
715-924-4594
800-568-1995
Fax: 715-924-2078

> *A secluded,*
> *artful retreat*

Innkeepers: Dan and Lisa Dobrowolski. **Accommodations:** 3 rooms, all with private bath, 1 suite. **Rates:** Rooms $89–$139, suites $129–$159. **Included:** Full breakfast. **Minimum stay:** No. **Added:** 5.5% tax. **Payment:** Major credit cards. **Children:** No. **Pets:** No. **Smoking:** No. **Open:** Year-round.

They call it the Monet Bridge for good reason. With lily pads beneath and the muted colors of wildflowers behind, the wooden foot brige extending over a private lake really does look like an impressionist painter's dream. This is just one of several artful touches at the Lodge at Canoe Bay, which mixes luxury accommodations and simple sophistication.

Innkeeper Dan Dobrowolski isn't shy when it comes to trumpeting the great things about his inn. The former Chicago weatherman and his wife Lisa chucked high-powered careers in New York and Chicago to develop a piece of property long close to Dan's heart. He grew up on a farm just behind the property and he, like his father and grandfather before him, used to hang out on the banks of the secluded lake.

> **Beaver, ducks, heron, minx, and even bears are often spotted on the surrounding acreage, which offers two miles of nature trails.**

The property was first developed in 1960 by the Seventh Day Adventists, who built the A-frame-style lodge as a site for spiritual retreats. Small rooms flanked either side of the great room, where a massive 30-foot-tall fieldstone fireplace served as the dramatic centerpiece. Dan says each of the stones comes from the surrounding 280 acres.

The fireplace is still there, but the rooms — now down to a select four — have gotten larger and fancier. All have whirlpool baths. The Sheridan Suite has a private audio/video room with a large-screen television and mini-fridge, a lake view, and Shaker/Mission furnishings. A stack of CDs, from Streisand to *West Side Story*, are provided for guest use. The suite boasts oil paintings by Lisa's mother, Nancy Bush Sheridan, a nationally known artist who was among the finalists selected to paint the official portrait of President Clinton.

Breakfast is delivered in a basket to your door. Swathed in napkins, it might include a little ramekin of egg strata, with a croissant, orange juice, fruit, and coffee. Guests can enjoy it in the great room, on the outside patio, or in the privacy of their rooms. The innkeepers, put off by the communal breakfast at other inns, want their guests to have options. Dinner for guests only is now available upon special request.

While many innkeepers' libraries are stocked with *Readers Digest* condensed editions, the Dobrowolskis offer an intelligent selection of current bestsellers and classics, from John Grisham's latest to an anthology by Kurt Vonnegut, a favorite of Dan's. The same is true of the videotape collection, with a discriminating selection of independent and foreign films.

And how many inns can you name that have their own

wildlife preserve? Ask Dan to introduce you to Snout, the inn's deer mascot, who lives in a large fenced area out back.

Guests may take full advantage of the private lake, which has canoes and rowboats for their use. Dan offers a rod and reel should you want to try your luck. When asked how the fishing is, he takes guests down to the dock, scatters a few small pieces of bread on top of the glassy water's surface, and waits for the feeding frenzy. He calls this his own private aquarium.

DOWNSVILLE

The Creamery

P.O. Box 22
Downsville, WI 54735
715-664-8354

> *Rooms with views and meals made with care*

Owners/innkeepers: The Thomas family. **Accommodations:** 4 rooms, all with private bath. **Rates:** Rooms $75–$90, suites $105. **Included:** Continental breakfast. **Minimum stay:** No. **Added:** 5.5% tax. **Payment:** No credit cards. **Children:** Yes. **Pets:** By arrangement. **Open:** April–December.

The buildings that now house the Creamery inn and restaurant were once the site of a major butter-making operation, founded in 1904. The Thomas family arrived in 1987 and their new operation blends well with the tiny Wisconsin farming community of Downsville, population 175.

Guests flock here for dinner, which the staff calls "simple food prepared with care." Favorites include sage-stuffed pork loin with homemade applesauce or grilled lamb chops with fresh mint and raspberry sauce, and chicken grisez. Five different greens go into the salad, and many of the vegetables come straight from the inn's garden, which the Thomases cultivate with horses. The dining rooms (including the sunny patio) seat 65, while an L-shaped bar remains cozy and inviting, with old glass milk bottles lining high shelves. Weddings are often held on the property, which is lined with spectacular gardens.

Upstairs, the Creamery offers three spacious rooms, spartanly decorated but cozy with white stucco walls and cherry trim. The spacious rooms offer sweeping views of the Red Cedar and Chippewa river valleys and the hills beyond. Room 1 is the biggest, with a bedroom, a living room, and a bathroom with a double-sized tub. Each room is furnished with a loveseat, an overstuffed chair, solid walnut furniture, and a queen-size bed. TVs are housed in wood armoires.

The Continental breakfast always includes fresh baked goods from the

> **Off the property, the Chippewa River lures canoeists and fishermen while the 40-mile-long Red Cedar State Park Trail offers year-round pleasures for hikers, bikers and skiers. It passes within a third of a mile of the Creamery.**

Creamery kitchen and a selection of juices. For an additional fee, larger breakfasts can be requested.

Stop into Dunn County Potters, adjacent to the Creamery. This is the showroom for John Thomas, who creates handmade stoneware, earthenware, and porcelain pottery. He is responsible for much of the tile in the guest bathrooms along with many of the dishes in the dining room. He also displays work for sale by local artists.

ELLISON BAY

The Griffin Inn

11976 Mink River Road
Ellison Bay, WI 54210
414-854-4306

> *Cross-country trails lure skiers to the tip of Door County*

Innkeepers: Jim and Laurie Roberts. **Accommodations:** 10 rooms sharing 2½ baths, 4 cottages. **Rates:** Rooms $71 single, $75 double; cottages $77 double. **Included:** Full breakfast in main lodge; Continental in cottages; dinner available. **Minimum stay:** 2 nights during summer and fall weekends. **Added:** 5.5% tax. **Payment:** Personal checks, cash. **Children:** Welcome in cottages; 5 years or older at inn. **Pets:** No. **Smoking:** No. **Open:** Year-round; cottages open May–October.

Most folks think of Door County as a summer playground, with art shows, boating, and fish boils among the main attractions. Winter lures another breed of traveler: cross-country skiers who take full advantage of the diminished crowds and yards of virgin snow. The Griffin Inn, a 1910 Dutch reform–style house on five tranquil acres, is about as far north up the Door County peninsula as you can get without skiing off the tip.

The guest rooms in this white clapboard inn are on the second floor, each with an antique double bed and a handmade quilt. The decor picks up the colors from the quilt. Two of the rooms have an additional twin bed, and baths are at the end of the hall. Four additional rooms are found in two cottages. Each has a beamed ceiling and rough cedar walls as well as its own bath with shower. Guests often congregate at the fireplace in the spacious living room.

Guests in the main house enjoy a full breakfast that might include quiche, poppyseed pancakes, or cherry-stuffed French toast. Cottage guests pick up a breakfast basket filled with baked goods, coffee, and juice, or they can sit in on the full meal for an additional charge. Winter weekend packages also include an elegant five-course dinner on Saturdays. The entrée can be a boneless chicken breast in puff pastry with orange wild rice and Door County cherry sauce. Ask the Robertses to show you the cookbooks they published.

> **The county's cross-country ski and snowmobile trail runs through the inn's backyard, though the best ski and hiking trails are at Newport State Park, about five miles away.**

Ellison Bay is full of year-round galleries, gift and antiques shops, and excellent restaurants. Summer guests like to sit on the inn's long front porch or take naps on the wicker furniture in the gazebo. Here you are within walking distance of sandy Green Bay beach. During the winter, you can still head 20 minutes south for a traditional fish boil on Wednesdays and Saturdays at the White Gull Inn (see listing under Fish Creek below).

FISH CREEK

Thorp House Inn and Cottages

4135 Bluff Road
P.O. Box 490
Fish Creek, WI 54212
414-868-2444

> *Subtle romance*
> *at an*
> *unpretentious inn*

Innkeepers: Christine and Sverre Falck-Pedersen. **Accommodations:** 4 rooms, all with private bath, 7 cottages. **Rates:** Rooms $70–$130 double; cottages $70–$125 nightly, $395–$645 week. **Included:** Continental breakfast. **Minimum stay:** 2 nights with reservations; 3 nights on weekends July through October and holidays. **Added:** 5.5% tax. **Payment:** Cash, personal checks. **Children:** Welcome only in cottages. **Pets:** No. **Smoking:** In cottages only. **Open:** Cottages, year-round; inn, July–October and weekends year-round.

The Thorp House Inn has been serving guests in one way or another for almost 90 years, yet it remains for the most part an undiscovered treasure. The romance of this turn-of-the-century white clapboard home is not all hearts and flowers. Sverre Falck-Pedersen calls it a more subtle, sturdy, mature type of romance for people who don't necessarily want to spend all their time in the bedroom. It's a place for hopping on a bike (supplied by the inn) or taking long, leisurely country strolls.

Thorp House is classic Door County in the tiny Wisconsin village of Fish Creek, whose year-round residents number fewer than 200. A small enclave of gift shops keeps busy with summer trade during the day. For dinner, guests usually go a couple of blocks to the popular fish boils at the White Gull Inn.

The intimate guest rooms are charmingly decorated in Victorian and English country styles. They all take their names from female family relatives of Asa Thorp, the home's original owner. The most enchanting room is the Lillian, with flowered pink William Morris wallpaper meeting a simple border

> **Stenciled borders, ceiling fans, lace curtains, and embroidered sheets and pillows are all part of the decor.**

and a double bed with a headboard set into an arched alcove.

The tiny living room with a granite fireplace is one of two cozy common areas in the main house. The upstairs library has a collection of antique porcelain bathing beauties and framed postcards along with a number of fascinating books, one of which has a special significance to the inn. A best-selling romance, *Bittersweet*, was inspired by Jessie Thorp, the original innkeeper, who took in boarders out of necessity when her husband died in a shipping accident in 1905. The book's author, LaVyrle Spencer, has visited here frequently.

Sverre and his wife, Christine, live on the first floor but try to stay out of sight, making guests feel completely at home. The couple is available, however, for directions, day-trip suggestions, and certainly during breakfast, when they serve a Continental breakfast that includes fresh scones.

The cottages range in fanciness and price. Six have decks, five have fireplaces, one has a whirlpool, and each has a fully equipped kitchen. Each is decorated in Scandinavian or country antiques. Nostalgia pervades right down to the old refrigerators and kitchen fixtures. Newlyweds will think they are honeymooning in the 1950s.

The White Gull Inn

P.O. Box 160
Fish Creek, WI 54212
414-868-3517
Fax: 414-868-2367

A historic site for a Door County fish boil

Innkeepers: Jan and Andy Coulson.
Accommodations: 9 inn rooms, 4 with private bath; 4 in Cliff House, all with private bath; 5 homes. **Rates:** Inn rooms $50–$98, Cliff House rooms $112–$120, homes $135–$225; winter packages available; all meals available on European plan. **Included:** All meals available. **Minimum stay:** 2 nights on weekends; 3 nights in homes in July and August. **Added:** 5.5% tax. **Payment:** Major credit cards. **Children:** Yes. **Pets:** No. **Smoking:** No. **Open:** Year-round.

There's still a friendly controversy over where the first Door County fish boil was held. In the version offered at the White Gull Inn, diners gather at patio tables to watch master boiler Russ Ostrand demonstrate his culinary art. Whitefish, potatoes, and some secret ingredients are assembled in a huge pot over a wood fire, highlighted by the dramatic flare-up, or "overboil," at the end. Inside, Russ entertains with his accordion while the meal is served with coleslaw, fresh bread, and cherry pie for dessert.

Fish boils are held here on Wednesdays and weekends during the summer and on Wednesdays and Saturdays only in the winter. Candlelight meals featuring beef Wellington, broiled whitefish, shrimp and artichoke Romano, and duck are served from the regular menu. Though it isn't included in the rate, breakfast is a treat, with eggs Benedict, corned beef hash, and cherry-stuffed French toast.

The homey accommodations in the main building have plank floors, floral curtains, and wrought-iron and carved wood beds. Most share men's and women's bathrooms, but thick terrycloth robes are provided. The rooms in the deluxe Cliff House, across the yard, have private sitting areas. Other homes are available nearby, including some quaint cottages and the newer Olson House, a housekeeping facility with two bedrooms, a kitchen, and a utility room with washer and dryer. The innkeepers also own the Whistling Swan, just a block away.

> **The inn's history stretches back to 1896, when Dr. Welcker built the main house as a lodging for wealthy German immigrants who arrived by steamer at Fish Creek. Some of the antiques at the White Gull belonged to the original owner.**

HUDSON

Boyden House

727 Third Street
Hudson, WI 54016
715-386-7435

> *Innkeepers make beautiful music at this B&B*

Innkeepers: Carl Nashan and Julie Ayer. **Accommodations:** 2 rooms with shared bath, 1 suite. **Rates:** $75–$100. **Included:** Full breakfast. **Minimum stay:** No. **Added:** 8.5% tax. **Payment:** Personal checks, cash. **Children:** Over 12 years old. **Pets:** No. **Smoking:** No. **Open:** Spring–fall.

Carl Nashan and Julie Ayer are violinists with the Minnesota Orchestra, and their love of music is obvious at Boyden House, which they opened as a retirement project. A 1926 Steinway grand piano, antique pump organ, and Edison cylinder phonograph are found in the guest parlors. Carl makes stained glass, and many examples of his craft are displayed throughout the house.

> **Hudson, on the St. Croix River, offers plenty of diversions. Lakefront Park, the Octagon House, and the Phipps Center for the Performing Arts are all within walking distance of the inn.**

More than simply providing musical decoration, the Boyden House also offers regular concerts called Sunday Soirées. The monthly program regularly includes poets and performers from the University of Minnesota, the Minnesota Orchestra, and the St. Paul Chamber Orchestra. The large sliding doors of the inn's twin parlors open to admit an audience of 30 music lovers, primarily from the Twin Cities area.

Boyden House's guest rooms are somewhat less impressive than those found in nearby inns, but they are comfortable and filled with period antiques. Only the Boyden Suite has a private bath with a shower. It also has a Renaissance Revival bedroom set, a marble-topped dresser (original to the house), and a small sitting room with a daybed. An old trunk overflows with quilts. A refrigerator in the upstairs hall is for guests' use.

Breakfast here may include blintzes, German pancakes, casseroles, or vegetarian quiche along with fresh fruit. Morning coffee is available at 8 A.M. on the upper level.

1884 Phipps Inn

1005 Third Street
Hudson, WI 54016
715-386-0800

A historic home has been lovingly restored

Innkeepers: Cyndi and John Berglund. **Accommodations:** 6 rooms, all with private bath. **Rates:** $95–$159. **Included:** Full breakfast. **Minimum stay:** No. **Added:** 8.5% tax. **Payment:** MasterCard, Visa. **Children:** By arrangement. **Pets:** No. **Smoking:** No. **Open:** Year-round.

According to local historians, turn-of-the-century horse races were commonplace on Third Street. From the turret of his Queen Anne home, the respected William Henry Phipps watched these competitions, knowing that the owner of the

Octagon House, across the street, was doing the same. Their detailed hand motions to each other signaled which animal they thought would win. Stories like this abound at the antique-filled 1884 Phipps Inn.

The Master Bedroom remains most popular with return guests at this gracious inn. It features a pine four-poster canopy bed, an Italian ceramic fireplace, and a large double whirlpool bath. The Bridal Suite has a lovely sitting area in a turret, a private fireplace, and a half-tester mahogany bed. Most cozy are the redwood-lined accommodations in the original third-floor ballroom.

> **The Peacock Room and Willow Chamber can be rented separately or together. Each is outfitted with queen-size beds, hardwood floors, and double whirlpools.**

A 1920s baby grand player piano serenades guests during breakfast, which is served on fine china with silver settings. Afternoon coffee, lemonade, and iced tea are usually set out in the downstairs parlor, which has both a fireplace and a pump organ. Phipps was a philanthropist, so you will probably hear his name around town, especially at the Phipps Center for the Performing Arts. The Octagon House is now a museum and contains several Phipps family heirlooms.

Jefferson-Day House

1109 Third Street
Hudson, WI 54016
715-386-7111

Retired teachers make this a popular retreat

Innkeepers: Wally and Sharon Miller. **Accommodations:** 3 rooms, all with private bath, 1 suite. **Rates:** $89–$119 double on weekdays, $119–$159 double on weekends. **Included:** Continental breakfast on weekdays; full breakfast on weekends. **Minimum stay:** No. **Added:** 8.5% tax. **Payment:** Personal checks, cash. **Children:** Over 9 years old. **Pets:** No. **Smoking:** No. **Open:** Year-round.

A favorite room at the Jefferson-Day House is the downstairs library. During the Civil War, this was the home of the Ladies' Literary Society, a group of the town's most prominent women who met to discuss books and regularly scanned the "missing in action" list for the names of their loved ones. The room is still a popular gathering spot, with Brown and Bigelow calendar girls and the innkeepers' collection of Roseville pottery on display. Hors d'oeuvres are served here in the late afternoon, and guests often return later to watch a videotape supplied by the inn.

The St. Croix riverfront is always a big draw; the Millers recommend Mama Maria's for dinner. For concerts and plays, there's the Phipps Center.

The Captain's Room, with its antique brass bed and ten-foot ceiling, has a nautical theme: a navy, white, and rose decor and ship pictures and models throughout. The Hudson Suite has a queen-size oak bed covered with an antique quilt. Most spectacular is the St. Croix Suite, with an entry room and a fireplace set so that you can see it from both the bed and whirlpool. A small doll collection is here, along with a pair of wedding dresses.

Sharon and Wally Miller, retired teachers, serve Continental breakfast for guests during the week. On the weekend, they add an egg dish to the usual assortment of fruit, muffins, granola, coffee cake, juice, and coffee.

The inn is on a quiet residential street of restored homes, including the Octagon House, now open as a museum.

OSCEOLA

Aveda Spa

1015 Cascade Street
Route 3, Box 72
Osceola, WI 54020
715-294-4465
800-283-3202
Fax: 715-294-2196

> *A full service,*
> *luxurious spa*

General manager: Horst Rechelbacher. **Accommodations:** 10 rooms, all with private bath. **Rates:** One night $340 single, $600 double; weekend $640 single, $1,210 double; packages available. **Included:** All meals; some treatments and facilities. **Minimum stay:** No. **Added:** 5.5% tax. **Payment:** Major credit cards. **Children:** No. **Pets:** No. **Smoking:** No. **Open:** Year-round.

Everything at Aveda Spa has a common goal: to create a soothing environment where guests will feel more relaxed than ever before. This is accomplished through the almost mystical quality in the guest rooms, the meals, and the health facilities.

It's easy to drive past the spa unless you keep your eyes open for the two peacocks perched on the columns at the front gates. The circa 1908 Prairie mansion is painted a creamy yellow, set on a hill overlooking 60 acres of forest and the St. Croix River. Horst Rechelbacher, the Austrian hairdresser and cosmetic manufacturer who established the Aveda Corporation in 1978, intended to live here but instead created the Spa.

An open oak staircase leads to guest rooms with polished wood floors, exotic carpets, and feather mattresses on antique bedsteads. French doors lead into the beamed dining room and then the sunny Restaurant Organica. The wait staff describes the menu selections in a near whisper

> **Flower and plant essences play a vital part in the spa treatments, according to Aveda's founder, whose theory of aromatherapy states that certain natural fragrances can affect both your mood and your health.**

against a background of New Age music. The choices on one night: endive and nasturtium salad, wild mushroom sauté with steamed vegetable and Wehani rice pilaf, hazelnut-crusted rainbow trout with lemon basil pesto.

As with restaurant items, spa facilities are offered à la carte. You can come for a day, a weekend, even a full week of body massages, face and scalp treatments, yoga instruction, and haircuts and styling.

St. Croix River Inn

305 River Street
Osceola, WI 54020
715-294-4248

> *Romantic flourishes and river views*

Innkeeper: Bev Johnson. **Accommodations:** 7 rooms, all with private bath. **Rates:** $100–$200. **Included:** Full breakfast. **Minimum stay:** No. **Added:** 5.5% tax. **Payment:** Major credit cards. **Children:** Yes. **Pets:** No. **Smoking:** Yes. **Open:** Year-round.

High on a wooded bluff overlooking the river, the St. Croix River Inn offers spacious, comfortably decorated rooms named for steamboats built in Osceola. The inn boasts truly outstanding views from five of its guest rooms.

Cheese and crackers, tea, and coffee greet you at the front

desk even when the innkeeper doesn't. In fact, guests have the place pretty much to themselves. The sleeping quarters all have double baths and reproduction antiques. The Jennie

> **The full breakfast of banana French toast or omelettes is delivered to your room.**

Hays room has floor-to-ceiling Palladian windows and its own balcony. Another room has white-painted brick walls and an oversize tub placed so that you can look out over the river during a luxurious soak.

The upstairs sitting room, nicknamed "the crow's nest," is papered with another river scene. It has a round table for games and a miniature Pepsi machine. Osceola offers downtown shops and restaurants as well as the celebrated Aveda Spa. In nearby Taylors Falls, Minnesota, you'll find historic home tours and paddleboat cruises.

STURGEON BAY

The Inn at Cedar Crossing

336 Louisiana Street
Sturgeon Bay, WI 54235
414-743-4200

> *Local artists added unique touches to a popular inn*

Owner/innkeeper: Terry Wulf. **Accommodations:** 9 rooms, all with private bath. **Rates:** $78–$128. **Included:** Continental breakfast. **Minimum stay:** 2 nights most weekends; 3 nights on holidays. **Added:** 5.5% tax. **Payment:** Discover, MasterCard, Visa.

Children: Yes. **Pets:** No. **Smoking:** Nonsmoking rooms available. **Open:** Year-round.

The elaborate stenciling here was created by Carol Williams, who owns a decorating shop down the street. Dick Meyer, a Sturgeon Bay furniture maker, crafted many of the beds. To decorate her inn, Terry Wulf called on local artists and craftspeople, including her mother, who made the handsome curtains, pillow cases, and dust ruffles.

> Terry pays tribute to local artisans each December with a Country Folk Art Fair, when furniture makers, painters, and craftspeople display their wares in the guest rooms.

The 1884 building once held Sturgeon Bay storefronts with apartments above. Over the years it served as a tailor's shop, an apothecary, a soda fountain, and doctors' offices.

The inn retains some of the original brick walls both in its restaurant and guest rooms. Room 1 has a pine four-poster bed trimmed in white Battenberg lace linens and Border of Buds stenciling in rose and green. An antique stained glass window is on the wall separating the bedroom from the bathroom, where the muted colors spill onto a two-person Jacuzzi. The country Victorian Room 3 has a brass canopy bed, ivory lace, and a cedar-lined window box. An old-fashioned cabbage rose design is splashed on the wallpaper and large wool rugs. Room 6 is a woodworker's delight, with a hand-carved archway and golden oak furniture.

Downstairs is a spacious restaurant that serves breakfast, lunch, and dinner beneath original tin ceilings. A specialty of the house is stuffed pork loin topped with a pungent cherry chutney. More than 2,000 pounds of Door County cherries are used by the restaurant each year. Stenciled geranium vines use detailing that recalls the exposed brick. Another section of the restaurant has a dried herb look with mauves, salmons, and sage greens. A mahogany and brass bar has been added to create a pub area along one side.

Breakfast is served in a separate guest dining room with a woodburning fireplace and country primitive tables. The bakery provides most of the Continental repast, with muffins and scones accompanied by fresh fruit in season. Works for sale by local artists decorate the walls.

The Scofield House B&B

908 Michigan Street
P.O. Box 761
Sturgeon Bay, WI 54235
414-743-7727

Where there's a story behind every antique

Innkeeper: Fran and Bill Cecil. **Accommodations:** 6 rooms, all with private bath, 3 suites. **Rates:** $69–$180. **Included:** Full breakfast. **Minimum stay:** 2 nights with reservations; 3 nights on holidays and fall color weekends. **Added:** 5.5% tax. **Payment:** Personal checks and cash. **Children:** 14 years and older. **Pets:** No. **Smoking:** No. **Open:** Year-round.

Clutter. That's what comes to mind when you enter the Scofield House. Not messy clutter, but wonderful Victorian clutter. You can stay here a week before noticing the portrait of Queen Victoria peering out from a parlor wall.

This Queen Anne home was the grandest residence in Sturgeon Bay when it was built in 1902. It may still be. Bill and Fran Cecil have decorated this late Victorian painted lady with more than a bit of whimsy. Bowing to the demand for increased amenities, they have added fireplaces, whirlpool baths, and VCRs and televisions (with a movie library available) to many of the guest rooms.

The Rose Room is a romantic hideaway where floral patterns abound on the lace-trimmed comforter and pillows that cover the Renaissance Revival bed. The maple floor has an intricate inlaid border and a wool Axminster rug. A bath with a cathedral ceiling offers a double whirlpool tub and separate shower.

In the Turret Suite, the Eastlake influence can be found in

the antique burled walnut bed and marble-topped washstand and dresser. A connecting sitting room features a private balcony with oak porch furniture, and the adjoining turret bath has a double shower and pedestal sink. Note the elaborate crazy quilt that dominates a wall of the sitting room. Bill's baby quilt, made by his grandmother in 1935, is a favorite conversation piece in the Blue Room.

> **If you're not stirring by 9:00 in the morning, Bill gives a few quick blows on the trombone to announce breakfast. Some guests linger in bed just to hear him do it.**

Unveiled in early 1992, the 800-square-foot Room at the Top, tucked beneath the third-floor gables, has an 1860 Eastlake walnut bedroom set, a Jacuzzi, and a hundred-year-old solid cherry mantle over the fireplace. The Cecils also offer a cottage and ranch-style home about 21 miles away, with a third lodging, an 1860 log house reconstructed on Lake Michigan available for romantic escapes.

Fran and Bill say guests especially enjoy afternoon tea on the porch swing or in the garden. Or perhaps they admire (or, better yet, play) the antique musical instruments that share wall and cabinet space with other bric-a-brac in the downstairs parlors. A circa 1863 piano, handmade dulcimer, concertina, auto harp, guitars, and a ukulele are all on display.

The elaborate breakfast may include eggs Benedict, apple cinnamon French toast with fresh pears, or baked apple crisp with vanilla ice cream on top. Hot chocolate, fancy teas, and a well-stocked cookie jar are always available for guests.

In a quiet residential section near downtown Sturgeon Bay, the Scofield House is also within walking distance of the Miller Art Center, Door County Museum, and the Maritime Museum, along with fine restaurants and the water. Potawatomi State Park is just a short drive away, offering hiking and cross-country ski trails.

White Lace Inn

16 North 5th Avenue
Sturgeon Bay, WI 54235
414-743-1105

*Romantic rooms
in several
beautiful homes*

Innkeepers: Dennis and Bonnie Statz. **Accommodations:** 14 rooms and 1 suite in 3 buildings, all with private bath. **Rates:** Rooms $58–$118 single, $65–$125 double; suite $143 single, $150 double. **Included:** Continental breakfast. **Minimum stay:** 2 nights on weekends; 3 nights on holidays. **Added:** 5.5% tax. **Payment:** MasterCard, Visa. **Children:** 12 years and older. **Pets:** No. **Smoking:** Nonsmoking rooms available. **Open:** Year-round.

The White Lace Inn wasn't always so romantic. When Dennis and Bonnie Statz discovered the 1903 Queen Anne home in 1982, it had served for years as a Knights of Columbus meeting hall. Heavy green drapes allowed little light to enter the golden oak and maple interior. The opening of the main house, now with a crisp coat of ivory paint and surrounded by a white picket fence, was the start of a decade-long project that now finds a total of three neighboring buildings open for guests.

All the rooms offer thick towels, designer linens, handmade comforters, extra pillows, antique furnishings, and bedside reading lights. Special touches abound, such as white pitchers filled with dried lavender on mantels and oodles of namesake white lace on beds, walls, and around windows. Paths connect the buildings and pass by a gazebo and garden beds that grow more elaborate each year.

A favorite with repeat guests in the main house, the Door County Orchard Room recalls a summer picnic, with Laura Ashley fabrics in red and green trimming all six windows. A white wicker couch faces the 1880s four-poster canopy bed swagged in white lace. A bathroom with a double whirlpool is in the adjoining tower room.

> **Most popular during the summer, the White Lace is also a good base for cross-country skiing; guests return happily to their private whirlpool or fireplace (sometimes both) after a day on the trails.**

Each room in the Garden House has its own fireplace. Here, Vintage Rose invites you to snuggle in an 1830s half-tester bed with side curtains. The walls are covered in a rose-on-burgundy paper and complemented by Ralph Lauren fabrics in forest green with bold bouquets of roses. Casual Victorian defines the atmosphere of an English squire's study, with flamestitch wallpaper in rich burgundy, ivory, and green. A walnut bed with hand-turned spindles and posts from the 1850s is tucked beneath the eaves while an Eastlake parlor set faces the fireplace.

The Washburn House, the newest addition, has three rooms and one suite. The Victorian Suite is the star here, where the two-sided fireplace warms both the bedroom and sitting room. Rich shades of peach, rose, and aqua fabric complement the magnificent walnut Eastlake Victorian bed.

Breakfast here features homemade muffins and Scandinavian fruit soup, served hot or cold depending on the season. The White Lace is in a quiet residential neighborhood just a block or two from downtown Sturgeon Bay and the Door County Historical Museum. Swimming, tennis, and horseback riding are never far away from this gateway to the Wisconsin Peninsula. Whitefish Dunes and Potawatomi State Park are also nearby.

There are no telephones or televisions in the guest rooms, only reproduction antique radios. A television and VCR are available in the sitting room of the main house, however.

Southern
Wisconsin

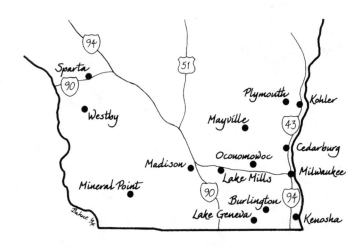

Best Bed-and-Breakfast Inns

Burlington
  Hillcrest Inn and Carriage House
Cedarburg
  The Stagecoach Inn
  Washington House Inn
Kenosha
  The Manor House
Lake Mills
  Fargo Mansion Inn
Madison
  The Canterbury Inn
  The Collins House
  Mansion Hill Inn
Oconomowoc
  Inn at Pine Terrace
Sparta
  Just-N-Trails Bed and Breakfast

Best Full-Service Country Inns

Lake Geneva
  The Geneva Inn
Mayville
  The Audubon Inn
Mineral Point
  Chesterfield Inn
Plymouth
  52 Stafford
Westby
  Westby House

Best Hotel

Milwaukee
  The Pfister

Best Resort

Kohler
  The American Club

Milwaukee's downtown is hardly a bustling metropolis, but it has excellent shopping options at Grand Avenue Mall, which extends along four city blocks on Wisconsin Avenue. The Milwaukee Antique Center has 75 dealers on three floors. The Domes at Mitchell Park Conservatory are three glass enclosures with distinct horticultural environments. The Milwaukee County Zoo houses about 4,000 wild animals and birds, including a number of endangered species. The Milwaukee Art Musuem, housed in the lakefront War Memorial, was designed by Eero Saarinen and David Kahler and includes an eclectic permanent collection ranging from Toulouse-Lautrec to Warhol. Several breweries, including Pabst and Miller, offer tours and tastings. Among local theatre groups, the Milwaukee Repertory Theater remains the best. It's across from the Performing Arts Center, which schedules symphony, ballet, opera, and choral performances.

Day trips from Milwaukee lead to Wisconsin small towns. **Cedarburg,** north of town on Highway 57, first attracted German and Irish immigrants, who created dams and mills along its creek. The entire downtown of cream-colored buildings has been preserved as a historic landmark, while the Cedar Creek Settlement is a historic village of shops in an old woolen mill. It has more than 35 businesses, including restaurants, antique and specialty shops, and art galleries. Wisconsin's last remaining historic covered bridge, built in 1876, crosses Cedar Creek three miles north of town.

If you're heading north to Door County along Lake Michigan, stop for an hour or two in **Kohler.** Corporate headquarters, factories, and employee-owned homes are all part of this planned community. You can tour the complex as well as a showroom with state-of-the-art fixtures. Stop for lunch or dinner in one of several restaurants at the famed American Club.

In **Madison,** due west of Milwaukee on I-94, activity revolves around the 45,000-student University of Wisconsin and its numerous athletic, musical, and dramatic events. The Oscar Mayer Theater and Madison Art Center are located in the Madison Civic Center. The State Historic Museum on Capitol Square focuses on the area's Native American heritage while The Elvehjem Museum of Art displays fine art on five floors of galleries. For dining, the university area offers a number of inexpensive ethnic eateries. Madison's top attraction remains the Wisconsin State Capitol, with free tours of the domed Roman Renaissance structure offered daily.

Take a day trip to the Blue Mounds State Park. It has picnic areas and hiking trails with markers identifying the best spots for viewing certain types of birds. Visit Cave of the Mounds, where the diverse mineral formations are pointed out during the guided tour.

BURLINGTON

Hillcrest Inn and Carriage House

540 Storle Avenue
Burlington, WI 53105
414-763-4706

A neighborhood inn in a world of its own

Innkeeper: Karen and Dick Granholm. **Accommodations:** 6 rooms, 2 sharing a bath. **Rates:** $60–$140. **Included:** Full breakfast. **Minimum stay:** No. **Added:** 5% tax. **Payment:** MasterCard, Visa. **Children:** Over 12 years old. **Pets:** No. **Smoking:** No. **Open:** Year-round.

The approach to this bed-and-breakfast, past rows of ranch homes, is far from spectacular. You need to drive past the fieldstone gates and head around back to realize that the stately Edwardian mansion sits at the end of a cliff with an incredible view. It creates its own world, both inside and out.

The house was built in 1908 for a prominent New York radiologist and his wife. Now the Granholms are beginning to restore the formal gardens that once graced the property's four acres. Wildflowers cover the slope that leads down to the scenic river.

Three rooms are offered in the original home. The Cambridge Room has a country French decor in

Burlington is best known for its Nestlé plant, whose aroma reaches the inn when the winds are right. An annual Chocolate Festival draws sweet tooths from all over.

navy and rose colors, with a queen-size carved walnut bed and its own bath. The Avondale and the Brittany rooms share a bath. Quilts, lace curtains, and antique furnishing evoke a country feel. Three more rooms are now housed in the carriage house, with fireplaces, queen-size beds and double whirlpool baths. The Windemere Suite is a favorite of many guests. It has an English garden theme and occupies the entire second floor.

Guests often gather in the kitchen before breakfast, which includes Karen's favorite recipe of scrambled eggs with croissant pastry.

CEDARBURG

The Stagecoach Inn

W61 N520 Washington Avenue
Cedarburg, WI 53012
414-375-0208

Guests check in at the pub of this restored stagecoach stop

Owners and operators: Liz and Brook Brown. **Accommodations:** 13 rooms, all with private bath, 5 whirlpool suites. **Rates:** Rooms $55 single, $65 double; suites $85 single, $95 double. **Included:** Continental breakfast. **Minimum stay:** No. **Added:** 5.5% tax. **Payment:** Major credit cards. **Children:** Over 10 years. **Pets:** No. **Smoking:** No. **Open:** Year-round.

The Stagecoach Inn looks and feels much as it did when 19th-century visitors stopped here during horse-drawn trips along the Lake Michigan shoreline. Guests check in at the pub room downstairs. The wood planking is rough-hewn and creaks beneath their feet as they head to their rooms upstairs.

Only a few sticks of reproduction furniture can be found among the inn's brass, four-poster, and sleigh beds. The innkeepers haven't sacrificed comfort for historical authenticity, however. They now provide air-conditioning, televisions (on request), and whirlpool baths set in raised wood bases for a more rustic feel. A first-floor suite features an 1820s Empire four-poster bed and a blue and white quilt on the wall. It also has a separate sitting room and a private entrance. The 1847 Weber Haus annex, across the street, has three rooms, similarly decorated and considerably more private with its own garden/sitting area.

The Stagecoach Pub, the inn's sole common area, has a liquor license but serves no meals. Breakfast is served here or on the deck and includes croissants, muffins, coffee, juice, and herbal teas. Also on the first floor is Beerntsen's candy shop; the aroma of hand-dipped chocolates wafts through the inn.

> **The Browns can recommend excellent restaurants, such as Victor's, Mortons, Barth's, and the Settlers' Inn, all a few blocks away in the historic district.**

The little town of Cedarburg is full of surprises, including mid-1800s stone buildings and mills and the last original covered bridge in Wisconsin. Ozaukee Pioneer Village has restored homes, barns, and a blacksmith's shop.

The Washington House Inn

W62 N573 Washington Avenue
Cedarburg, WI 53012
414-375-3550
800-554-4717

> *English accents brighten a stagecoach hotel*

Manager: Wendy Porterfield. **Accommodations:** 29 rooms. **Rates:** $59–$159. **Included:** Continental breakfast. **Minimum stay:** No. **Added:** 5% tax. **Payment:** Major credit cards. **Children:** Yes. **Pets:** No. **Smoking:** Yes. **Open:** Year-round.

The Washington House Inn, one of a number of "cream city" brick buildings found in Cedarburg, was constructed in 1886 on the stagecoach line between Green Bay and Chicago. The renovations here include private bathrooms with chin-deep whirlpools, telephones, cable televisions tucked into wardrobe cabinets, and firm, queen-size beds.

> Cedarburg, just 15 miles from Milwaukee, is a historic woolen mill town where the Cedar Creek Settlement and Winery, Pioneer Village, and Ozaukee Covered Bridge are all open for tours.

Above the wainscoting in the halls throughout the inn is an English embossed tissue wallpaper that simulates tin. Bradbury and Bradbury borders are in the common areas, while handmade quilts and Laura Ashley and Schumacher fabrics and wallpapers decorate the rooms, all named after prominent residents from Cedarburg's history. Some rooms are furnished in a Victorian style while others resemble a cozy English cottage, with beamed ceilings, rough-hewn rock walls, shuttered windows, and four-poster beds with gingham ruffles. Some bedrooms are reached by red metal spiral staircases, remnants of the Pabst Brewery.

The Continental breakfast buffet serves turn-of-the-century recipes, from Winterfest fruit soup to chocolate zucchini bread. There is also fresh fruit, cereal, and fresh juice.

KENOSHA

The Manor House

6536 Third Avenue
Kenosha, WI 53143
414-658-0014

> *The largest house in town is now open to guests*

Innkeepers: Dr. C.E. Peterson. **Accommodations:** 4 rooms, all with private bath. **Rates:** $100–$140 double. **Included:** Continental breakfast. **Minimum stay:** No. **Added:** 11.5% tax. **Payment:** Major credit cards. **Children:** Over 12 years. **Pets:** No. **Smoking:** Permitted only in common rooms. **Open:** Year-round.

The Manor House lives up to the grandeur you'd expect from the largest house in town. The 20-room brick Georgian mansion, in the heart of the Lakeshore Historical District, was built in the 1920s for James T. Wilson, a vice-president and son-in-law of the founder and president of Nash Motor Company. It was made to last, with 16-inch-thick walls and a sturdy slate roof.

Listed on the National Register, the home served as a school before Dr. Clifton Peterson welcomed his first guests in 1986. He traveled extensively in search of unusual antiques to decorate the place. Some are from the Rothschild's Mentmore Manor in Buckinghamshire, England.

The largest guest room is the Purple Room, originally the master bedroom, with a fireplace (one of seven in the inn) at the foot of a queen-size Victorian bed. A separate nurse's bed dating from the Crimean War and two dressing rooms are also found here. The Rose Room overlooks the gardens and, with its circa 1780 Sheraton four-poster bed, has become a favorite with wedding and anniversary guests.

Plenty of common areas, including a cherry-paneled library, offer privacy. A favorite spot is the third-floor ballroom, now a den where guests can play cards or admire the bird's-eye view of Lake Michigan. A balcony here allows a closer look.

> **The grounds include a lily pool with a fountain, a rose garden, a gazebo, and 40 varieties of trees.**

Breakfast, which includes fresh fruit, muffins, coffee cake, and cereal, is taken in the elegant dining room. A basement reception room, the original handball court, is now used primarily for small weddings.

The Manor House is in a quiet residential area on the Lake Michigan shoreline. It's also across the street from Kemper Center, an 11-acre historical and recreational park containing tennis courts, an art gallery, and a fishing pier. Downtown Kenosha is within easy walking distance.

KOHLER

The American Club

Highland Drive
Kohler, WI 53044
414-457-8000
800-344-2838 or 800-344-2838
Fax: 414-457-0299
Reservations: 800-323-7500,
    800-678-8946, 800-GOLFERS

> *The resort that Kohler built*

General manager: Alice Hubbard. **Accommodations:** 236 rooms, all with whirlpool baths. **Rates:** May–October $109–

$292 single, $134–$338 double; November–April $88–$239 single, $112–$280 double; packages available. **Included:** All meals available. **Minimum stay:** 2 nights, July through Labor Day and special weekends. **Added:** 7% tax. **Payment:** Major credit cards. **Children:** Yes. **Pets:** No. **Smoking:** Nonsmoking rooms available. **Open:** Year-round.

The Tudor-style American Club was built in 1918 by the Kohler Company to house its immigrant workers. At its dedication, Walter J. Kohler expressed his belief that workers should be given "roses as well as wages." Today, the resort offers outstanding restaurants, shopping, sports facilities, and lodgings on a 600-acre nature preserve.

To carry on the star-spangled theme, the guest rooms are named for famous Americans, from Mary Pickford to Lou Gehrig, represented in photographs or bits of memorabilia. Most rooms have four-poster or brass beds with down comforters. In some, the firm mattresses are lit subtly from beneath the bedframe for a most unusual nightlight. You don't stumble on your way to the exquisite bathrooms. Of course, Kohler fixtures are used throughout.

> **The fanciest baths offer the Kohler Habitat, a space-age environmental enclosure that allows you to dial up summer rain, desert heat, or tropical steam.**

The rooms that once served as a laundry now make up the elegant Immigrant Restaurant, where each of the six dining rooms pays tribute to the varied European ethnic groups that once populated the club. The Dutch Room, for instance, has an abundance of Delft tiles and terra cotta. Antique walnut furnishings grace the French Room, while the German Hunt Room represents its theme with elaborate woodcarvings, mounted antlers, and duck decoys.

Other restaurants (nine at last count) include the Wisconsin Room, where the workers once ate, now highlighted by commissioned tapestries and leaded windows. Soup, salad, and appetizers are offered at the Horse and Plow, the most casual restaurant. A favorite spot for ice cream and tea is the Greenhouse, once part of an English solarium, which was dismantled and meticulously reconstructed on the property. Light through the stained glass windows now shines on marble-topped ice cream tables and countless plants.

Guests have free access to the pool and weight room at the neighboring Sports Core building and can also enjoy other facilities à la carte, including tennis and racquetball courts, massages, and aerobics classes. The pool area opens to a deck overlooking Wood Lake. Blackwolf Run, also on the property, offers 36 holes of championship golf designed by Pete Dye. The River Course follows the meandering Sheboygan River; the Meadow Valleys Course has a forest and lake backdrop.

The resort also features well-appointed meeting rooms and conference facilities, conveniently placed below the main lodge. These carry on the comfort and traditional furnishings, from the royal blue velvet chairs, large oval table, and fireplace in the Washington Room to deep leather sofas and Oriental rugs in the library.

If you have time, rent a bike and tour the streets of Kohler, which was built according to a company plan in 1925 with curving avenues and brick Tudor houses. Residents take pride in keeping their properties picture-perfect. The Kohler Design Center is worth a stop; it pays tribute to the company's past while showcasing its state-of-the-art products.

All of this doesn't come cheap, but the American Club makes no apologies. After a night or two, you'll understand that it's hard to put a price on lodging in a class by itself.

LAKE GENEVA

The Geneva Inn

N2009 State Road 120
Lake Geneva, WI 53147
414-248-5680
800-441-5881
Fax: 414-248-5685

> *Lake Geneva's only inn on the water offers fine dining*

General manager: Richard Treptow. **Accommodations:** 33 rooms, all with private bath, 4 suites. **Rates:** Rooms $145–$235, suites $350; packages available. **Included:** Continental breakfast. **Minimum stay:** No. **Added:** 5.5% tax. **Payment:** Major credit cards. **Children:** Yes. **Pets:** No. **Smoking:** Nonsmoking rooms available. **Open:** Year-round.

The Geneva Inn prides itself as the only lakeside inn on popular Lake Geneva. It has nine unique room styles with Waverly wall coverings and reproduction antique furnishings. Most rooms offer oversize double whirlpool baths and balconies overlooking the lake. Guests also have their own private wet bar and well-stocked fridge (on a pay-as-you-go basis, of course). Honeymoon and anniversary stays in the deluxe rooms or suites come with a complementary bottle of champagne and hors d'oeuvres. The morning newspaper is delivered free.

> **Thick bathrobes add to the fancy touches here, along with cognac and cookies left on a pewter tray at bedtime.**

Continental breakfast starts with coffee and tea and is usually highlighted by fresh fruit, baked goods, smoked duck and cheeses set out buffet-style. Proper dress (ties are optional, jeans out of the question) is required at the aptly named Grandview Restaurant, which finds a patio sloping to the water's edge for a spectacular view at sunset. Specialties of the house include the fish specials, which on a typical night include broiled salmon, shrimp and pasta, and South African lobster tail. A pianist plays standards and current pop tunes during dinner. There's also an inn lounge and a bar set-up on the dock.

Guests can leave their car in the underground parking lot and take the courtesy van to and from busy downtown Lake Geneva. The popular resort town, halfway between Milwaukee and Chicago and just a couple miles from the inn, teems with visitors in the summer. The Geneva Inn has found similar popularity since opening in 1993.

LAKE MILLS

Fargo Mansion Inn

406 Mulberry Street
Lake Mills, WI 53551
4144-648-3654

> *Gregarious inn-*
> *keepers create a*
> *memorable stay*

Innkeepers: Tom Boycks and Barry Luce. **Accommodations:** 4 rooms, all with private bath, 4 suites. **Rates:** $68–$95, suite $145–$185. **Included:** Full breakfast. **Minimum stay:** Over major holidays. **Added:** 5.5% tax. **Payment:** MasterCard, Visa. **Children:** Yes. **Pets:** No. **Smoking:** No. **Open:** Year-round.

The Fargo Mansion was once the social center of Lake Mills. Its owner, Enoch Fargo, a descendant of the stagecoach Fargos, held many lavish turn-of-the-century soirées. Tom Boycks and Barry Luce, who opened the home to bed-and-breakfast guests in 1987, revel in the house's eccentric history. They're eccentrics themselves who thoroughly enjoy returning the Queen Anne mansion to its original splendor, though they admit they still have a long way to go.

They have restored many major and minor details, such as the molding, stove doors, and massive carved newel posts. The dark wood staircase winds to the guest rooms, decorated with Victorian pieces picked up at estate sales. Some of the original fixtures and ornamentation have been returned to the home by thoughtful neighbors.

The bright Master Bedroom is most spacious and luxurious, with an ornate Victorian headboard on a queen-size bed. A hinged bookcase opens to reveal a secret bathroom, with white Italian marble and a whirlpool bath for two. The Elijah Harvey Suite, in earth tones with Oriental rugs and a marble-topped bedroom set, has a separate sitting room for reading.

The full breakfast features baked apple crêpes, egg casseroles, quiches, muffins, and beverages served in the dining room. Afterward, you can hike or cross-country ski at Aztalan State Park, about two miles away, while bikers can ride the Glacial

> The house once boasted a walk-in freezer, an extensive wine cellar, and a marble fountain in the dining room. There was even a pit on the property where the original owner kept two pet bears.

Drumlin Bike Trail. It's only five blocks to Rock Lake, with beaches, boat rental, and fishing.

Tom and Barry have made their mark on tiny Lake Mills. They run both Opera Hall Antiques and the Fargo Mercantile and Ice Cream Parlor downtown.

MADISON

The Canterbury Inn

315 W. Gorham at State
Madison, WI 53703
608-258-8899
Fax: 608-283-2541

> *A literary hide-away in a busy college town*

Manager: Jennifer Sanderfoot. **Accommodations:** 6 rooms, all with private bath. **Rates:** $80–$200 single; $100–$220 double. **Included:** Full breakfast. **Minimum stay:** 2 nights on special weekends. **Added:** 12.5% tax. **Payment:** Major credit cards. **Children:** Yes. **Pets:** No. **Smoking:** No. **Open:** Year-round.

Anglophiles stepping inside downtown Madison's Canterbury Book Store and Coffee House will marvel at the beauty of its book presentation, not to mention the excellent espresso and baked goods. Owner Trudy Barasch uses wall murals and forest greens to create an atmosphere of browsing beneath a canopy of trees in the English countryside. Amazingly, you're just steps away from the professors and neo-hippies strolling downtown Madison, a quintessential midwestern college town.

> **On any given day there will be entertainment, from afternoon tea to evening jazz to authors' readings in the coffee house.**
> **For the true book lover, the Canterbury Inn offers everything your heart might desire.**

The Canterbury Inn, perched above the bookstore and visible through the upper windows of a glass atrium, continues this aesthetic beautifully. This isn't just a couple of hastily decorated rooms; it's a world all its own, newly designed and highlighted by murals by Madison artist Nancy Lee depicting scenes from Chaucer's randy *Canterbury Tales*. The entrance door sports a picture of a tale's teller; behind each bed, in an arched alcove, a depiction of the story they relate.

The Merchant's Room shows young May reaching into the tree that hides her lover from her blind and cuckolded husband January. The Wife of Bath's Room remains a favorite, with the lusty knight forced to choose between an old hag and a beautiful woman. The Clerk's Room, the smallest, shows the long-suffering Griselda as she watches the wedding procession marking her ex-husband's marriage to the woman she doesn't realize is her daughter.

The literary motif continues through the wall hangings, including attractive publishers' advertisements and broadsides. A selection of new books from downstairs line the wooden shelves, while a copy of Chaucer's medieval masterpiece graces the night table. The inn offers each guest a $10 gift certificate, which can be used in the coffee shop or bookstore.

An admittedly pricey stay for a college town, the Canterbury Inn offers special amenities that make a knight's, er night's, stay well worthwhile. Sodas, juices, cookie plate, wine and cheese are typically left out in the upstairs parlor. All rooms have fresh flowers, elaborately carved chess boards, window seats, and TV/CD players tucked into attractive wooden cabinets. More than half the rooms have whirlpools in fancy tiled baths. Colorful Vietri china, just like they use in the coffee house downstairs, stocks the kitchenettes found in five of the rooms. The sandalwood soap comes from the Soap Opera, one of many unusual State Street shops.

Breakfast here can be served in the room, in the upstairs parlor, or downstairs at the coffee house and includes any item on the menu. This might include assorted pastries, scones with jam, orange or grapefruit juice, granola with seasonal fruit, and a French baguette with jam, butter, or Brie. Coffee comes either hot or iced.

The Collins House

704 East Gorham Street
Madison, WI 53703
608-255-4230

Prairie School architecture distinguishes a college stop

Innkeepers: Barb and Mike Pratzel. **Accommodations:** 5 rooms, all with private bath. **Rates:** $59–$119 single; $65–$125 double. **Included:** Full breakfast. **Minimum stay:** No. **Added:** 12.5% tax. **Payment:** MasterCard, Visa. **Children:** Yes. **Pets:** By arrangement. **Smoking:** No. **Open:** Year-round.

The Collins House overlooks Lake Mendota, the largest lake in the college town of Madison, Wisconsin. Built in 1911 for lumber executive William H. Collins, the inn is a distinctive example of the Prairie style of Midwestern architecture popularized by Frank Lloyd Wright. Though the home had served as an office building, innkeepers Barb and Mike Pratzel brought the place back to its former glory. Many of the architectural touches remain — the oak and red maple floors, oak and mahogany beamed ceilings, and the dining room's oak wainscoting — while the innkeepers have filled it with coveted examples of Mission-style furniture. Wright-style stencils were uncovered and reproduced downstairs.

Upstairs, the Claude and Starck Room, large enough to be a suite, pays tribute to the home's architects with original leaded glass windows, an arched entry, and a cast-iron firestove. The sitting room and bedroom are painted a rich Wedgwood blue. Note the pictures of other historic Madison homes. This is one of two rooms with double whirlpool baths.

> The inn's curio-filled common areas, including a reception area, dining room, and plant-filled sun porch, are large enough to host weddings and other special occasions.

The other also has a private balcony.

Breakfast is typically served downstairs on the Mission-style table and includes gourmet selections such as Swedish oatmeal pancakes, Italian potato frittata, or eggs topped with sautéed leeks, mushrooms, and peppers. A fruit bowl is usually complemented by decadent pastries such as streusel muffins and chocolate cream cheese danish. Coffee is served in handmade pottery mugs.

One word of warning: Though you'll be treated cordially by the innkeepers, don't expect pampering. Cobwebby windows and occasionally dusty corners could use some attention, but overall the Collins House gives you the feeling you might expect in the home of an eccentric history professor.

Mansion Hill Inn

424 North Pinckney Street
Madison, WI 53703
608-255-3999
800-798-9070
Fax: 608-255-2217

> *A luxurious inn in eclectic downtown Madison*

Managing innkeeper: Polly Elder.
Accommodations: 5 rooms, all with private bath, 6 suites.
Rates: Rooms $100–$200 single, $120–$220 double; suites $200–$230 single, $220–$250 double. **Included:** Continental breakfast. **Minimum stay:** No. **Added:** 12.5% tax. **Payment:**

Major credit cards. **Children:** 12 years and older. **Pets:** No. **Smoking:** Yes. **Open:** Year-round.

Mansion Hill Inn is the rich kid on the block, for it's surrounded by student housing in a residential area near downtown Madison. A belvedere crowns the gabled roof of this 1858 Romanesque Revival house, where wrought-iron railings encircle the carved sandstone facade. It offers a luxurious stay within sight of the capitol.

> **During the $1.5 million restoration, artisans worked on gold-leaf cornices, ceiling medallions, and Carrara marble. A staircase spirals four stories to the belvedere, where round arched windows provide a complete view of the horizon.**

The amenities here are in keeping with those of the most luxurious small hotel. A doorman in a tuxedo greets you upon arrival. Each guest room has a stereo system with a collection of tapes, remote-control cable television, a mini-bar, and 24-hour valet service and parking. Most rooms have whirlpool tubs, and some offer fireplaces.

A favorite is the Sarah Fairchild Conover Suite, named for Governor Fairchild's sister, who became a leader of Madison society in the 1880s. It has floor-to-ceiling bookcases with editions of Shakespeare and Dickens, a hand-carved Carrara marble fireplace, and an Eastlake bedframe. The bathroom is behind a hidden panel in the bookcase. The whirlpool bath is surrounded by round arched windows, classic columns, marble, and tile.

The Turkish Nook represents the Victorian love of the exotic, with a sultan's bed tented in tapestries and silk. In the Craftsman's Suite, the look is more understated, with a brick fireplace and fabrics in rich earth tones creating a warm background for its comparatively simple oak furnishings. Quarry tile and parquet flooring decorate the arched-ceiling bath with a whirlpool.

The morning newspaper and breakfast are delivered to your room. You use a checklist the night before to select cereal, fruit, and fresh bakery items, along with the time of delivery. You will want to explore Madison, a funky college town with varied ethnic restaurants, shopping, and cultural activities.

MAYVILLE

The Audubon Inn

5 North Main Street
Mayville, WI 53050
414-387-5858
800-421-INNS

*You don't have
to love birds to
flock to this
small-town hotel*

Innkeeper: Rip O'Dwanny. **Accommodations:** 13 rooms, all with private bath, 4 suites. **Rates:** Rooms $69 weekdays, $89 weekends; suites $79 weekdays, $99 weekends. **Included:** Continental breakfast on weekdays; full breakfast on weekends. **Minimum stay:** No. **Added:** 5% tax. **Payment:** Major credit cards. **Children:** Yes. **Pets:** Yes. **Smoking:** Nonsmoking rooms available. **Open:** Year-round.

Opened in 1896 as the Beaumont, the hotel that anchors downtown Mayville has been resurrected as the Audubon Inn. It joins three other historic properties reopened by Rip O'Dwanny, the Irish innkeeper and preservationist from 52 Stafford in Plymouth (see listing). A huge glass storefront window brightens the lobby, which has English carpeting and original millwork. The grand staircase is highlighted by an intricately carved newel post.

A friendly bar area is lit from above by an etched glass ceiling depicting geese in flight. More stained and etched glass shows Audubon birds and an 18th-century after-the-hunt scene.

The guest rooms open onto an atrium that rises the full three stories of the hotel. When decorating, Rip chose a simple country decor in keeping with the theme of John James Audubon, who never visited Mayville but would certainly feel comfortable here. There are no antiques in the rooms, but their four-poster Shaker beds were designed for the inn and are dressed with handmade comforters. O'Dwanny's trademark palette of deep burgundies and greens make up the color scheme, carried out in the lightly embossed wallpaper. All the large bathrooms have double whirlpool baths.

The dining room's menu changes monthly, but you can usually count on fresh fish, pheasant, and rack of lamb.

A 50-minute drive north of Milwaukee, Mayville is called the gateway to the Horicon Marsh, a 35,000-acre wildlife refuge that may have suggested the Audubon theme. The town itself is small and historic, with plenty of antiques shops and local characters. A golf course lies nearby.

MILWAUKEE

The Pfister

424 East Wisconsin Avenue
Milwaukee, WI 53202
414-273-8222
800-558-8222
Fax: 414-273-0747

> *The century-old Pfister is still Milwaukee's premier hotel*

General manager: Rosemary Steinfest. **Accommodations:** 250 rooms, 57 suites. **Rates:** Rooms $155 single, $175 double; suites $175–$650 single, $195–$650 double. **Included:** All meals available. **Minimum stay:** No. **Added:** 12.5% tax. **Payment:** Major credit cards. **Children:** Yes. **Pets:** No. **Smoking:** Nonsmoking rooms available. **Open:** Year-round.

When Charles Pfister unveiled his namesake hotel in 1893, he wanted it to become "the Grand Hotel of the Midwest." He would be proud to know that his creation, recently polished to its original grandeur, has reestablished itself as Milwaukee's premier historic hotel. The lobby alone is worth a visit, with its marble-topped front desk, cherry paneling, and oodles of gold leaf. Bronze lions guard the grand stairway, which ascends to a series of brass-railed landings. Greetings on the wall read *Salve,* Latin for "welcome."

> You pay a high tariff for all these extras, from the concierge in high collar and tails to the shoeshine man, asleep in the corner with a cigar dangling out of his mouth. But as one employee proudly put it, anyone who's anyone stays at the Pfister.

The hotel comprises the main building and the 23-floor Tower, built in 1966. The top floor of the Tower houses a pool, a health club, and La Playa lounge, with a panoramic view of the city and Lake Michigan. Leslie Uggams, David Brenner, and Joan Rivers are among the entertainers who have performed here.

Though the accommodations aren't necessarily luxurious, they all have nice touches such as live plants, wet bars, and hair dryers in modern, marble-lined bathrooms. The cabbage rose carpeting and paneled halls create a nostalgic atmosphere leading to the original Pfister rooms, which have Victorian wallpapers and flame-stitched chairs. Note the ornate doorknobs and knockers, also part of the restoration.

One of the country's most extensive wine cellars can be enjoyed through the English Room, the main dining room; the Café Rouge and the Café at the Pfister offer lighter fare, with the former especially popular for Sunday brunch. The massive parlor fireplace, originally a fixture in the lobby, now highlights the Lobby Lounge. The corridors and galleries here are lined with an impressive collection of 19th-century artwork.

MINERAL POINT

Chesterfield Inn

20 Commerce Street
Mineral Point, WI 53565
608-987-3682

> *A former
> stagecoach stop
> with rustic appeal*

General manager: Debra Ehr. **Accommodations:** 6 rooms, some with private bath, 2 suites. **Rates:** Rooms $55–$70; suites $70–$85. **Included:** Full breakfast; lunch and dinner available. **Minimum stay:** No. **Added:** 5.5% tax. **Payment:** Major credit cards. **Children:** Yes. **Pets:** No. **Smoking:** Yes. **Open:** May–October.

Perhaps the most interesting historical feature at the Chesterfield Inn is its "badger hole." Desperate workers carved these crude shelters into the limestone bluffs during Mineral Point's heyday as a mining town. The one next to the inn's restaurant is one of the few remaining "holes" around.

> **Among the attractions here are the artists who have set up shop and sell their wares from galleries and homes in the historic settlement.**

While the accommodations at the inn are considerably more luxurious today, you will have to share baths in the main building. Built as a stagecoach stop, the Cornish brick building retains its rustic appeal with low ceilings and wide-plank floors. Room 4 is the largest, with a flowered bedspread on a four-poster bed and a sitting area with a couch. The suites are in a building on Shake Rag Street, several blocks away. This section of Mineral Point is said to be named for a Cornish wife's habit of shaking a dishrag to signal her man at the mine when dinner was ready.

The inn's restaurant, which serves three meals daily, is best known for its Cornish pasty. The meat and potato dish is served in pie pastry and topped with midwestern chili sauce. Pastry crust also figures prominently in "figgyhobbin," a delicious jelly roll packed with brown sugar, cinnamon, nuts, and raisins and topped with caramel sauce. A full breakfast is served to guests in the dining room. Note the exquisite circa 1830 quilt, decorated with a Texas star.

OCONOMOWOC

Inn at Pine Terrace

351 Lisbon Road
Oconomowoc, WI 53066
414-567-7463

A Victorian mansion that has hosted five presidents

Innkeeper: Mary Morrison-Quissek. **Accommodations:** 13 rooms, all with private bath. **Rates:** $60–$120. **Included:** Continental breakfast. **Minimum stay:** No. **Added:** 10% tax. **Payment:** Major credit cards. **Children:** Yes. **Pets:** No. **Smoking:** Nonsmoking rooms available. **Open:** Year-round.

This three-story brick and stone mansion was built in 1884 by the Schuttler family, wagonmakers from Chicago, and their family S can still be seen in the ornate carved bookcases that line the library. The stately "summer cottage" has welcomed no fewer than five presidents as well as Mark Twain.

In the 1950s, much of the Victorian detailing was removed. Happily, all this and more has been restored by current owner

> **Rip O'Dwanny has recreated turrets and balustrades and the original high, narrow windows with stone lintels.**

Rip O'Dwanny, who also owns four other historic Wisconsin lodgings, including 52 Stafford in Plymouth (see below).

Common rooms, including a reception area, smoking room, breakfast room, and library, are on the first floor, along with a pair of guest rooms. Honeymooner's Paradise, on the third floor, is the most breathtaking, with its sunken tub and whirlpool tucked into the tower. The Eastlake-style pieces in the guest rooms are impressive reproductions; Bradbury and Bradbury wallpapers, Schumacher fabrics, and Kohler bathroom fixtures add a designer touch.

A swimming pool and a meeting room on the property are shared with a neighboring condominium development. Oconomowoc, a suburb of Milwaukee between Fowler Lake and Lac La Belle, offers plenty of activities year-round, including boating, fishing, sailing, and ice skating.

PLYMOUTH

52 Stafford

52 Stafford Street
P.O. Box 565
Plymouth, WI 53073
414-893-0552
800-421-INNS
Fax: 414-893-1800

> *Rip O'Dwanny*
> *brings a*
> *bit of Ireland*
> *to Plymouth*

Innkeeper: Rip and Christine O'D-wanny. **Accommodations:** 19 rooms, all with private bath. **Rates:** $69.50–$99.50. **Included:** Full breakfast on weekends, Continental weekdays. **Minimum stay:** No. **Added:** 9% tax. **Payment:** Major credit cards. **Children:** Yes. **Pets:** Yes. **Smoking:** Nonsmoking rooms available. **Open:** Year-round.

52 Stafford is one of four historic lodgings renovated across the state by Cary "Rip" O'Dwanny; in this one he has given his Irish imagination free rein. The theme begins downstairs, where cherry floors are joined by stained glass windows depicting the four green fields of Ireland. The carpeting is imported from England, while the silk in the parlor chairs is Chinese.

> **Guinness flows freely on tap in the pub, where Irish folk bands sometimes appear. The glass is all beveled and etched, displaying Celtic emblems from the 4th through the 10th centuries.**

By comparison, the guest rooms are understated but still extremely comfortable and quite well equipped. All the rooms have queen-size four-poster beds, handmade comforters, remote-control cable television, and writing desks as well as modern conveniences such as air conditioning, television, and telephones. Hunting and Irish prints line the walls. Seventeen rooms offer whirlpool baths, supplied with (of course) Irish Spring soap.

The restaurant menu changes monthly, but perennial favorites are corned beef and cabbage and Guinness brisket with Calconnan potatoes. The full breakfast can be ordered from the menu. Try the corned beef, baked for twelve hours and served with potatoes and corn mixed in.

Should you find yourself here on St. Patrick's Day, you may be part of an Irishman's Walk through town. It ends at the hotel, where participants receive their first shot of Irish whiskey on the house. The revelry lasts for four days, presided over by Rip, who will initiate at least one Irish ballad. There is also a German Fest here in fall and seasonal events at Christmas and Easter.

SPARTA

Just-N-Trails Bed and Breakfast

Route 1, Box 274
Sparta, WI 54656
608-269-4522

Guests can pitch in with the chores at this dairy farm

Innkeepers: Donna and Don Justin. **Accommodations:** 5 rooms, 3 with private bath, 3 cottages. **Rates:** Rooms $65–$95, cottage $145–$195. **Included:** Full breakfast. **Minimum stay:** 2 nights on holiday weekends. **Added:** 5.5% tax. **Payment:** MasterCard, Visa. **Children:** Yes. **Pets:** No. **Smoking:** No. **Open:** Year-round.

Early risers can follow Donna Justin out to the barn for the morning milking ritual. Her husband, Don, welcomes children of all ages to ride along with him on the tractor and "help" with the chores. Just-N-Trails, in the heart of Wisconsin's dairy country, offers these bucolic pleasures along with splendidly decorated guest rooms.

The rooms in the main house have antique country furnishings and Laura Ashley coverlets. The Maple Room, on the second floor, features a bird's-eye maple sleigh bed and a green, pink, and white floral color scheme. The other rooms are decorated similarly, all with king- or queen-size beds and whimsical touches like teddy bears and cow memorabilia. Only the first-floor Queen Room shares a bath with the innkeepers. Two other buildings offer overnight accommodations, including Little House on the Prairie, a Scandinavian-style log house with a loft bedroom. A log cottage, with two bedrooms, fireplace, large whirlpool, and a common area, was recently added.

> The "trails" in the Just-N-Trails name refer to cross-country skiing: 12 miles of well-groomed paths wind through neighboring hills. There is also an ice skating pond.

Early risers, typically woken by the gentle mooing of Donna's 50 head of Holstein cows, gather for breakfast in the main house. Donna serves a hearty breakfast of French toast, homemade applesauce, and freshly ground coffee. The television set has long been broken, according to the innkeepers, so guests often peck out a tune on the main house piano or play cards at the Amish tables and chairs on the front porch.

The farm has been in the Justin family since the turn of the century. A glance at the enchanting countryside, with no fewer than five rivers nearby, will help you understand why Don's grandfather never left.

WESTBY

Westby House

200 West State Street
Westby, WI 54667
608-634-4112

> *Dinner is the big draw at this popular Queen Anne inn*

Innkeeper: Patricia Benjamin Smith. **Accommodations:** 5 rooms, 2 with private bath, 1 suite. **Rates:** Rooms $60–$80 double, $5 less for single (weekdays only); suite $130. **Included:** Continental breakfast on weekdays; full breakfast on weekends; lunch and dinner available. **Minimum stay:** No. **Added:** 5% tax. **Payment:** MasterCard, Visa. **Children:** Yes. **Pets:** No. **Smoking:** Restricted. **Open:** Year-round.

The Westby House has had only three owners since it was built in 1892. No paint had touched the fine oak woodwork when Patricia Benjamin Smith arrived in 1984 and turned the Queen Anne home into a popular inn and restaurant. A no-nonsense dinner menu offers American favorites such as shrimp, filet mignon, and rib-eye steak. The three dining rooms are decorated with country antiques, many of which are for sale. During warm weather, desserts and drinks are served on the verandah.

Many of the furnishings are also for sale in the upstairs guest rooms, which are comfortably outfitted if not necessarily luxurious. The Anniversary Room has its own bath with a tub and shower. It has a queen-size brass bed with a love seat and a wingback chair. The peach and mauve-toned Tower Suite has its brass bed tucked under the curved glass of the tower. The heavy crown molding is mahogany. The second room, the Fireplace Room, has a comfortable rocking chair as well as a fireplace and can be rented without the tower room. The Greenbriar has green floral wallpaper and a pair of double beds, one a white iron model covered with an antique quilt. All rooms have televisions.

> **Guests can start their antiques and craft hunting in the gift shop, which has an assortment of Norwegian craft items.**

A Continental breakfast with homemade muffins is served during the week. On weekends, guests order from the menu. The restaurant is open for lunch daily and for dinner on Friday and Saturday nights in the winter and Wednesday through Saturday in the summer. Cross-country ski trails attract winter travelers while biking and canoeing are popular during warm weather.

What's What

The lodgings in this book offer a variety of amenities, from full-service restaurants to bicycle rental. Here's just a sample.

Restaurants

Illinois
   DeSoto House Hotel, 17
   The Drake, 6
   Eagle Ridge Inn and Resort, 18
   Four Seasons Hotel, 8
   Hotel Inter-Continental, 9
   Hotel Nauvoo, 27
   Hotel Nikko, 11
   Ohio House Hotel, 12
   Pere Marquette Lodge, 24
   The Ritz-Carlton Chicago, 14
   Starved Rock Lodge and Conference Center, 28
Indiana
   Abe Martin Lodge, 65
   Brown County Inn, 68
   Canterbury Hotel, 60
   The Checkerberry Inn, 37
   The Columbus Inn, 54
   Essenhaus Country Inn, 40
   Holiday Inn at Union Station, 61
   Larry Bird's Boston Connection, 74
   The New Harmony Inn, 70
   The Patchwork Quilt Country Inn, 42
   Potawatomi Inn, 36
   Spring Mill Inn, 64
   Story Inn, 72
   Turkey Run Inn, 63
   Walden Inn, 57
Iowa
   Jumer's Castle Lodge, 83
   La Corsette Maison Inn, 102
   Strawtown Inn, 103

Conference Facilities

Fitness Centers

Swimming Pools

Golf Courses

Tennis Courts

Horseback Riding

Lakeside Location

Canoeing

Bicycles Rented

Recommended Reading

General References

**The Complete Guide to Bed and Breakfasts, Inns &
Guesthouses.** Pamela Lanier, Ten Speed Press, 1993, $16.95.
Pamela Lanier's book has long been considered the best ency-
clopedic listing of bed-and-breakfasts in the United States.
Sentence-long descriptions only give you a taste of a property's character, though basic information about rates, children
policies, and price prove extremely helpful. A majority of inns
are simply listed with address and phone number. Don't use
this as a selective guide, since featured innkeepers pay to be
included.   .

    Country Inns and Back Roads. Norman T. Simpson (re-
vised by Jerry Levitin), Harper Perennial, 1992–1993, $12.95.
Norman Simpson passed away several years ago, but you'd
never know it from the latest edition of his guidebook. Jerry
Levitin parrots Simpson's folksy style in revised first-person
accounts of overnight stays in 200 inns while including much
more practical information.

    The Innkeepers' Register. Independent Innkeepers' Associ-
ation, 1993–1994, $6.95. Though essentially a directory of
more than 250 Independent Innkeepers Association member
lodgings, it is also marketed to specialty bookstores nation-
wide. The IIA has tough standards for membership, so you
can rest assured that featured inns are well worth a visit.

    **The National Trust Guide to Historic Bed and Breakfasts,
Inns, and Small Hotels.** Suzanne G. Dane, the Preservation
Press, 1992, $13.95. The lodgings in this edition must be at
least 50 years old and have retained their architectural integrity — no "remuddling." The various states show off their
regional styles, so of course you'll find lots of prize Victorians
in the Midwest, along with some oddball places like the Arts-
and-Crafts Pebble House in Michigan.

The Midwest and the Great Lakes

America's Wonderful Little Hotels and Inns — The Midwest.
Edited by Sandra Soule. St. Martin's Press, $12.95. This book

works on a unique premise: Traveling correspondents relate experiences at over 200 hotels and inns. Sandra Soule credits their insights after introducing the basic services offered at each lodging. The writing is extremely detailed and the personal insights uncommonly clever. Midwestern states in this book also include Kansas, Nebraska, and the Dakotas.

Fodor's Bed and Breakfasts, Country Inns, and Other Weekend Pleasures. Edited by Caroline Haberfield (with various regional writers). Fodor's Travel Publications, Inc., 1993, $15. With typical completeness, the folks at Fodor's have given the concise lowdown on top hotels, resorts, and campgrounds in the midwestern states. Because of the number of contributors (at least seven from as many states) the quality of writing is not always consistent nor are the standards for inclusion. Still, this is a worthwhile source.

Northern Retreats — A Guide to Unique Lodging in the Upper Midwest. Jeff Hagen, Heartland Press, 1991, $14.95. Artist Jeff Hagen has spent the past several years enjoying the hospitality of Midwest bed-and-breakfast inns. He has returned the favor with this illustrated love letter to his favorite lodgings. Hagen's whimsical color drawings and first-person descriptions result in a unique and heartfelt guide.

State Parks of the Midwest. Vici DeHaan, Johnson Printing Company, 1993, $16.95. From the author of *State Parks of the West* comes a survey of 470 state parks throughout America's heartland described in terms of location, interesting features of the park, facilities, and actvities. There are few pictures in the book, just lots of good nuts-and-bolts information to guide you to some of the best vacation deals in the Midwest.

Illinois

Chicago's Museums. Victor J. Danilow, Chicago Review Press, 1991, $11.95. The author, a president emeritus from the Museum of Science and Industry, has a good handle on the special museums in the Windy City. Aside from the usual information about the Field Museum and the Art Institute of Chicago, Danilow also spends plenty of time at lesser-known museums like the Blackberry Historical Farm Village and the Morton B. Weiss Museum of Judaica. Black-and-white photographs, most supplied by the museums, give a decent feel for the places, though the quality sometimes wavers.

Frommer's Chicago '93–'94. Michael Yuhl, Prentice Hall

Press, 1993, $9.95. The best basic guide to the city, easy to read and easy to carry. Travelers on any budget will find the listings of places to eat, museums to visit, and instructions on how to get there extremely helpful. The book also discusses travel in the Chicago suburbs and even as far afield as Milwaukee. The book is packed with black-and-white photographs.

Michigan

Hunt's Highlights of Michigan. Mary and Don Hunt, Midwestern Guides, 1993, $12.95. Cleverly conceived and extremely well researched, this guide by Mary and Don Hunt tells you everything you wanted to know (and more) about big cities and tiny hamlets in the Great Lakes State. Specific stores, restaurants, and historic attractions are covered in brief but detailed descriptions.

Mackinac Connection: An Insider's Guide. Amy McVeigh, Mackinac Publishing, 1992, $8.95. Amy McVeigh has been summering on Mackinac Island since she was a kid. Insightful and literate, she gives first-timers the inside scoop on everything from where to find the cheapest bike rental to how not to look like a "fudgie."

Michigan's Town and Country Inns. Susan Newhof Pyle and Stephen Pyle, the University of Michigan Press, 1993, $14.95. She's a writer; he's a photographer. Together they provide an excellent look at 75 of the state's best-known lodgings. Detailed descriptions and well-lit interior and exterior photographs make this an invaluable resource for serious inn-hopping in Michigan. The book is currently in its third edition.

Minnesota

Walking Minnesota. Mary Jo and Jim Malach, Voyageur Press, 1991, $14.95. This is a clever guide for traveling on foot through Minnesota. Both indoor and outdoor walks are outlined here. You can tell that someone has traversed these paths personally, since directions are specific practically down to the inch. State parks and nature preserves are discussed, along with indoor walks in the St. Paul Skyway and even shopping malls.

Missouri

Shifra Stein's Kansas City Guide. Shifra Stein, Two Lane Press, 1991, $7.95. No lodgings are listed here, but travel writer Shifra Stein has included everything else, from museums to nightclubs. Brunches and cross-cultural cuisine just scrape the surface of the nearly 150 eateries listed here. Stein definitely knows her way around town, having lived in and written about Kansas City for the past 30 years. Her easy-to-read maps are especially helpful.

    A Complete Guide to Bed and Breakfasts, Guesthouses & Inns of Missouri. Harry Hagen, Missouri Publishing Company, 1991, $13.95. The inns here paid to be included, but also provided writer Harry Hagen with detailed descriptions of their rooms and amenities. Well-done line drawings represent the exteriors. Not really complete, but still an excellent roundup of lodgings in the state.

Ohio

Shifra Stein's Day Trips from Cincinnati. David Hunter. Globe Pequot, 1991, $10.95. The appeal here is probably limited to folks who live in the Cincinnati area, but it's still got lots of interesting stuff. Among the items listed are the Indianapolis Children's Museum, the Golden Lamb Inn, King's Island Park, and train rides in Kentucky.

Wisconsin

Guide to Wisconsin Outdoors. Jim Umhoefer, NorthWord Press, Inc. 1990, $19.95. This popular guide, first written in 1982, was updated in 1990. It still focuses on more than 70 state parks and national parks in Wisconsin. Plenty of helpful maps and black-and-white photographs pepper this guide, which is written with authority and a genuine love of the subject.

    Exploring Door County. Craig Charles, Northword Press, 212 pages, 1990, $16.95. The photographs here play up Door County's scenic beauty, but the information given is also helpful in planning a trip to this vacation hotspot.

Guidebook Series

Off the Beaten Path in . . . Various states, various authors, Globe Pequot Press, most updated in 1993, $9.95. The house that inspired Grant Wood to paint American Gothic; the Jesse James Museum; the World's Largest Sporting Goods Store; Al Capone's Vacation Retreat. Would a vacation in the Midwest be complete without visiting these marvels? Probably, but the joy of this popular guidebook series is its fun-loving approach to the unusual. Currently, Illinois, Indiana, Iowa, Kansas, Michigan, Minnesota, Missouri, Ohio, and Wisconsin all have their own well-researched editions.

Magazines

Midwest Living. Published bimonthly by Meredith Corporation, $2.50. This bible of midwestern travel keeps readers abreast of highlights in America's heartland. Aside from regular roundups of places to stay in various seasons, there is also a monthly column called Lodgings We Like, where quality inns get their chance to stand up and get noticed. A mention here means that an inn has arrived. A helpful calendar lists upcoming events.

Index

Best Places Report

Authors of the Best Places to Stay series travel extensively in their research to find the best places for all budgets, styles, and interests. However, if we've missed an establishment that you find worthy, please write to us with your suggestion. Detailed information about the service, food, setting, and nearby activities or sights is most important. Finally, let us know how you heard about the place and how long you've been going there.

Send suggestions to:

The Harvard Common Press
Best Places to Stay Suggestions
535 Albany Street
Boston, Massachusetts 02118

NAME OF HOTEL _____

TELEPHONE _____

ADDRESS _____

_____ ZIP _____

DESCRIPTION _____

_____

_____

_____

_____

_____

_____

YOUR NAME _____

TELEPHONE _____

ADDRESS _____

_____ ZIP _____

Best Places Report

Authors of the Best Places to Stay series travel extensively in their research to find the best places for all budgets, styles, and interests. However, if we've missed an establishment that you find worthy, please write to us with your suggestion. Detailed information about the service, food, setting, and nearby activities or sights is most important. Finally, let us know how you heard about the place and how long you've been going there.

Send suggestions to:

> The Harvard Common Press
> Best Places to Stay Suggestions
> 535 Albany Street
> Boston, Massachusetts 02118

NAME OF HOTEL _____

TELEPHONE _____

ADDRESS _____

_____ ZIP _____

DESCRIPTION _____

_____

_____

_____

_____

_____

_____

YOUR NAME _____

TELEPHONE _____

ADDRESS _____

_____ ZIP _____

Best Places Report

Authors of the Best Places to Stay series travel extensively in their research to find the best places for all budgets, styles, and interests. However, if we've missed an establishment that you find worthy, please write to us with your suggestion. Detailed information about the service, food, setting, and nearby activities or sights is most important. Finally, let us know how you heard about the place and how long you've been going there.

Send suggestions to:

The Harvard Common Press
Best Places to Stay Suggestions
535 Albany Street
Boston, Massachusetts 02118

NAME OF HOTEL _____

TELEPHONE _____

ADDRESS _____

_____ ZIP _____

DESCRIPTION _____

_____

_____

_____

_____

_____

_____

_____

YOUR NAME _____

TELEPHONE _____

ADDRESS _____

_____ ZIP _____

Best Places Report

Authors of the Best Places to Stay series travel extensively in their research to find the best places for all budgets, styles, and interests. However, if we've missed an establishment that you find worthy, please write to us with your suggestion. Detailed information about the service, food, setting, and nearby activities or sights is most important. Finally, let us know how you heard about the place and how long you've been going there.

Send suggestions to:

> The Harvard Common Press
> Best Places to Stay Suggestions
> 535 Albany Street
> Boston, Massachusetts 02118

NAME OF HOTEL _____

TELEPHONE _____

ADDRESS _____

_____ ZIP _____

DESCRIPTION _____

_____

_____

_____

_____

_____

_____

YOUR NAME _____

TELEPHONE _____

ADDRESS _____

_____ ZIP _____

Best Places Report

Authors of the Best Places to Stay series travel extensively in their research to find the best places for all budgets, styles, and interests. However, if we've missed an establishment that you find worthy, please write to us with your suggestion. Detailed information about the service, food, setting, and nearby activities or sights is most important. Finally, let us know how you heard about the place and how long you've been going there.

Send suggestions to:

The Harvard Common Press
Best Places to Stay Suggestions
535 Albany Street
Boston, Massachusetts 02118

NAME OF HOTEL _____

TELEPHONE _____

ADDRESS _____

_____ ZIP _____

DESCRIPTION _____

_____

_____

_____

_____

_____

_____

YOUR NAME _____

TELEPHONE _____

ADDRESS _____

_____ ZIP _____

Best Places Report

Authors of the Best Places to Stay series travel extensively in their research to find the best places for all budgets, styles, and interests. However, if we've missed an establishment that you find worthy, please write to us with your suggestion. Detailed information about the service, food, setting, and nearby activities or sights is most important. Finally, let us know how you heard about the place and how long you've been going there.

Send suggestions to:

The Harvard Common Press
Best Places to Stay Suggestions
535 Albany Street
Boston, Massachusetts 02118

NAME OF HOTEL _____

TELEPHONE _____

ADDRESS _____

_____ ZIP _____

DESCRIPTION _____

_____

_____

_____

_____

_____

_____

YOUR NAME _____

TELEPHONE _____

ADDRESS _____

_____ ZIP _____